"I watch/read a lot of scary stories. But f**k, *The Demonologist*, the true life account of Ed & Lorraine Warren, is the scariest book I've read."

—JAMES WAN,
THE AWARD-WINNING DIRECTOR OF *THE CONJURING* FILMS

"Primarily my research relied heavily on the nonfiction book, *The Demonologist*. It is unlike any book I have ever read. It's a book about mystical theology. In it, one learns just how and why mystical phenomena occur. It scared the daylights out of me. Profoundly. The preface insists that it is not dangerous to read and that 'knowledge is power.' Whatever. I felt a sense of terror every time I cracked it open. I never read the book in the sanctity of my home. I could only read it in flight, funnily enough. Somehow I felt safeguarded in an airplane."

—VERA FARMIGA,
ACADEMY AWARD–NOMINATED ACTRESS, WHO STARS AS
LORRAINE WARREN IN *THE CONJURING* FILMS

THE DEMONOLOGIST

The Extraordinary Career of Ed and Lorraine Warren

 GRAYMALKIN
MEDIA

Gerald
Brittle

To M.M.

Published by Graymalkin Media

www.graymalkin.com

Originally published by Prentice Hall
This edition published in 2013 by Graymalkin Media

Book design by Timothy Shaner
Cover design by Georgia Morrisey

ISBN: 978-1-935169-22-2

Printed in the United States of America

5   7   9   10   8   6   4

Contents

THE DEMONOLOGIST

Author's Preface

It is not possible to prepare the reader, in a few short paragraphs, for what follows in the pages of this book. For what is contained here is material that goes beyond ghost stories, beyond the vagaries of so-called poltergeist activity, into a dimension further back: a dimension of terror and evil that is not only real, its workings are literally beyond imagining.

What can be said, however, is that all the information presented in this book is true. These are real cases that happened to real people, and with only a few minor exceptions, all the incidents took place during the middle or late 1970s. Great care has been taken, furthermore, to include only those cases in the Warrens' files that were witnessed by ordained clergymen and exorcists, or in certain lesser circumstances, where the principals were credible and reliable and their comments are plainly recorded on tape. It should also be stressed that there is no exaggeration or hyperbole in the presentation of the phenomena in this book. If anything, space simply does not allow for the inclusion of the overwhelming detail that goes to make up any one particular case.

Yet, ultimately, it is not the case studies, the mind-reeling phenomena, or even the transcripts of spirit voices that is of primary concern here. Other cases could have been used. Other, more horrific, phenomena could have been brought forth. Instead, what causes one's spirit to tremble is the significance of what Ed and Lorraine Warren have to say. And there are no more credible spokespersons on the subject of spirits and supernatural phenomena. The Warrens have selflessly dedicated their whole lives to the study, teaching, and investigation of spirit forces: their experiences have been proven and documented by priests, rabbis, doctors, mediums, police, and recognized experts in psychic research.

In this book Ed and Lorraine Warren speak candidly and forthrightly and reveal the incredible secret of what breaks the peace in haunted houses. They identify the category of spirit that inflicts possession on human beings; and they name the poltergeist for what it is. The mystical principles disclosed by the Warrens in the course of their explanations have been meticulously researched for verification, and according to authoritative theological and academic texts on demonology and exorcism, their statements are correct. When considered in totality, what the Warrens say cannot help but challenge our whole notion of life, death, and man's place on this planet.

Nevertheless, the reader should be reminded that only infrequently do outside forces directly or forcefully interfere in people's lives. Man is capable of creating his own triumphs and monstrosities and it is irresponsible to assign blame to unnatural forces when the real fault all too often lies within ourselves. Therefore, it should not be presumed that the dynamics and disturbances detailed in these pages happens on every street corner. The Warrens' explanations and analyses pertain only to those cases where the phenomenon has indeed manifested, and where the agent *is* identified as being truly preternatural in origin.

Because of the potential dangers in creating an exact replication of a specific case or circumstance, conversations in some chapters are necessarily reconstructions of dialogue as Ed and Lorraine Warren recall the event, supported by first-person testimony by witnesses, and/or tape recordings the Warrens made on the scene while phenomena were in progress. Names, addresses, locations, and similar identifying details have been altered, where necessary, to protect the identity of the individuals who were either witness or victim to the phenomena. To all those persons and families whose names or experiences are mentioned in this book, I extend my sincere gratitude, and it is hoped that their efforts and uncommon travail will be redressed in some small way by its exposition here.

Finally, the text of this book was read for accuracy by two Roman Catholic exorcists, to whom I now formally express my appreciation in writing for their knowledgeable guidance. And to my wife and parents, I thank them completely: their unwavering support has made all the difference in the world.

Gerald Brittle

Foreword

To meet pleasant people in the midst of trouble and confusion is always a special experience. To meet pleasant people deeply concerned for the hurts and wounds of others—whether psychic or spiritual—is to be in touch with rare gifts.

In our times of turmoil, distress, and instability, it is inspiring to meet people who communicate a spirit of peace and respect for their neighbor irrespective of race, creed, ethnic background, or religious persuasion. Such are the pleasant couple, Ed and Lorraine Warren, who speak to us through the pages of this book.

I met Ed and Lorraine when I visited their parish church in Connecticut. As the story of their lives unfolded, two main impressions came out very clearly. First, this was a compassionate, loving, devout, realistic couple with special gifts of mind, spirit, and soul. Second, they were committed to fight for the protection and/or release of people who have come under the sway of evil forces and negative influences. Their yearning for the release of such hostages of evil is a holy and worthy aspiration and a serious career that draws upon some thirty-five years of study, investigation, and careful recording with scientific precision and analysis. The Warrens' personal gifts of psychic and spiritual discernment and devout prayer lead them to frequent consultation with clergy for the ministry of the Church and its power of good over the forces of evil.

As a Catholic priest, I am especially touched by the sincerity, humility, and prudence that this couple communicates and the spirit of congeniality that seems to travel with them.

In the face of rebellious, evil influences, intent upon the destruction of, or the obstruction of God's plan for man's temporal and eternal welfare, humility is the key to that truth which conquers the deceptive forces of evil. In both the Old Testament and the New Testament God speaks of the deception of Satan and his demons. Thus God warns man against the lies of Satan: truth is the core of God's words to man.

To the person who believes in the God of the Bible, demonic worship is an evil, paganistic practice that chooses to oppose God. Sometimes God is simply ignored; many times God is mocked by patterns of ritual and incantation; other times, God is directly blasphemed. The practices and "games" that are parts of demonic worship are truly dangerous, as the Warrens' story demonstrates. The danger, though, is profound and real, not a mere chance-happening. Because many lives have been deeply troubled and some lives taken through murder and "accidents," it is extremely rash for people to dabble with powers they cannot control, much less understand.

The God of the Bible is the God of truth Who described Satan as the Father of Lies. To open ourselves to the truths of God and His promises is to be humble. To live His truths is to be safe from the frightening evil that leads to destruction.

I personally hope that all who read this report will be touched by the gracious congeniality of Ed and Lorraine Warren and open their hearts and lives to the saving Spirit of Our God of Love.

Rev. John C. Hughes, M.S.

Spirit: (spir.it), A supernatural, incorporeal, rational being or personality, usually regarded as imperceptible at ordinary times to the human senses, but capable of becoming visible at pleasure, and frequently conceived as troublesome, terrifying, or hostile to mankind.

– The Oxford English Dictionary

Beyond Amityville

Outside Ed Warren's office in Fairfield County, an old chapel clock ticked away the passing moments with quiet, mechanical precision. All else stood still. It was the middle of a cold, dark night in New England.

Inside the office, a brass lamp lit the desk where Ed Warren, a pensive, gray-haired man of fifty, sat working. Hundreds of books surrounded him, most bearing strange, arcane titles on the mysterious lore of demonology. Above the desk hung photographs of monks and grim-faced exorcists, standing with Ed Warren in abbey-like settings. For Ed, working in the still silence of night, it had been a wicked day—one that was not yet over.

Just before the hour, the clock movement came alive in a series of clicks and relays, finally churning up three somber, resonating bongs. At the third stroke, Ed looked up, listened into the darkness, then went back to writing. It was three o'clock in the morning, the true witching hour, the hour of the Antichrist. And now, unbeknownst to him, Ed Warren was on borrowed time.

Only hours before, Ed and Lorraine Warren had returned to their home in Connecticut after having been called in to investigate claims of a "haunted house" on Long Island's south shore, in a pleasant residential suburb of New York City. In December 1975, the house had been purchased by George and Kathleen Lutz, who moved into it around Christmas of that year with their three young children. A year before the Lutzes bought the house, the eldest son of the previous owner murdered the six sleeping members of his family at 3:15 in the morning of November 13, 1974, with a .35 caliber rifle.* On January 15, 1976, the Lutzes fled from the house, contending that they had been victimized by manifest supernatural forces. It was a case that later came to be known as *The Amityville Horror.*

By the end of January 1976, the press had become fully aware of the Lutz family's claim of a bizarre experience in the house, and promptly called experts into the case. The experts brought in were Ed and Lorraine Warren. The Warrens were consulted because, in professional circles, they are considered to be perhaps this country's leading authorities on the subject of spirits and supernatural phenomena. Over the course of some three decades, Ed and Lorraine Warren have investigated over three *thousand* paranormal and supernatural disturbances.

The question the news media had essentially wanted answered was whether there was a "ghost" in the house at the time.

The answer the Warrens gave at the end of their three-day investigation, however, was something no one had bargained for. Indeed, their answer literally strained credulity.

"Yes," the Warrens disclosed at the time, "in our judgment, there was a *spirit* that had plagued the Lutzes in the house. But," they also concluded, "*no* ghost was present."

What did this paradoxical statement mean? Did this imply there were *other* kinds of spirits than ghosts?

Incredibly, the answer the Warrens gave was "Yes!"

---

* *The New York Times,* November 15, 1974.

"There are two types of spirits that are encountered in true haunting situations," the Warrens explained on March 6, 1976. "One is human; the other, however, is *in*human. An inhuman spirit is something that has never walked the earth in human form."

The Warrens' sobering information was not merely well-intentioned speculation—because fully two weeks before, Ed and Lorraine Warren had been confronted by an inhuman spirit in their own home. The visitation happened to Ed first.

Ed Warren's office is located in a small, cottage-sized building attached to the main house by a long enclosed passageway. As Ed sat working on preliminary details of the Amityville case that fateful February morning, the latch at the end of the passageway snapped open, followed by the percussive boom of the heavy wooden door. Footsteps then started toward the office.

Ed leaned back in his chair, waiting for Lorraine to enter with a much-needed cup of coffee.

"In here," Ed Warren called out. Long moments passed, however, and she did not appear. "Lorraine?" Ed called out again, but there was no reply.

What he heard instead, building in the distance, was an eerie, howling wind. It was not the whistling of wind under the eaves, but rather the menacing roar of a distant cyclone. Goose flesh rose on his arms.

"Lorraine?" he asked forcefully. *"Are you there?"* But still there was no response.

As the ominous swirling sound built in power and intensity, Ed quickly thought back over the last few moments. It then occurred to him that he'd heard only *three* footsteps in the passageway—not the continuous tread of a person walking. Something was wrong!

Suddenly, the desk lamp dimmed to the strength of a candle flame. Then, abruptly, the temperature in the office plunged to that of a walk-in freezer. A rank, pungent smell of sulfur rose in the room.

Suspicious of the unnatural clamor, Ed Warren opened a desk drawer and withdrew a vial of holy water and a large wooden crucifix. He then got up and walked a few steps out of his office into the anteroom. As he did, there swirled out of the passageway a horrendous, conical whirlwind.

Pointed at the bottom, broad at the top, the thing was blacker than the natural blackness of night. Far larger than a man, the swirling black mass moved into the dimly lit room and drifted slowly to Ed's left side and came to a halt some ten feet away. As Ed watched, it appeared to grow even denser and blacker than it was before! Indeed, within the swirl, he could see that something was beginning to take shape. An entity was beginning to manifest in physical form!

As a demonologist, Ed Warren knew he had to act quickly, to take the initiative before this fearsome black mass transformed itself into something even more forbidding and dangerous.

Holding the cross toward what was now rapidly changing into a macabre hooded spectre, Ed Warren stepped forward. The moment he did, however, the entity moved defiantly *toward* him!

Ed stopped and stood his ground as the form slowly drifted forward. When the swirling black mass was no more than a few feet away, Ed methodically, and with absolute determination, showered the thing in the sign of the cross with the contents of the holy water vial. Then he spoke the ancient command: "In the name of Jesus Christ, I *command* you to leave!"

For eternal seconds the black mass stayed motionless, no more than a foot away from the cross. Then, slowly, it began to back off—though not before giving Ed a clear vision of himself and Lorraine involved in a potentially deadly automobile accident along a highway. With that, the entity withdrew into the passageway from whence it came.

An enormous sense of relief came over Ed Warren as he stood, sweating profusely, in the freezing cold room. Yet, as he attempted to collect his thoughts, the vicious snarl of fighting animals suddenly erupted outside the house. Immediately, Ed realized there were *no* animals fighting: the visitation was still in progress. The entity had simply moved upstairs to attack Lorraine!

Avoiding the passageway, Ed flung open the side door to the office and ran up the back steps of the house.

He would be too late.

Upstairs, Lorraine Warren sat in bed reading the biography of Padre Pio, a remarkable Capuchin monk whom many believe is destined for sainthood. No matter how exhausted, Lorraine nevertheless will not sleep when Ed must work alone late at night in the office. After a lifetime of work in the supernatural, both Ed and Lorraine Warren know they are never alone, ever.

As Lorraine sat quietly reading, a dreadful pall swept over the room. Then, setting the book down, she too realized that something was wrong. *Very* wrong!

"I was terror-stricken," Lorraine recalls, "but I didn't know what I was afraid of. I looked around the room, but nothing was there. I then looked down at our two dogs, asleep beside the bed. They were absolutely motionless. Except the hair on each dog, from head to tail, was standing straight up in the air! Then, out of nowhere, complete pandemonium started up."

The swirling black entity that Ed had repelled only a minute before had apparently moved back through the passageway and into the house. The horrendous invader announced its arrival by producing a thunderous, pounding noise that sounded to Lorraine "like someone beating on sheet metal with a hammer." The violent bashing sound jolted her—then, within seconds, the heat was totally drawn from the room, leaving Lorraine quaking in the cold. After that, the terrible pounding stopped, and she too heard the swirling sound of a whirlwind coming toward her. The menacing, ungodly noise came from the direction of the passageway one floor below. Terrified, she listened as the whirlwind came up the stairs, and swirled into the kitchen, then the dining room, the living room . . .

"Whatever was out there seemed to be *searching* for me," says Lorraine. "What was it? Why was it here? Then instantly a swirling black cyclone flew into the bedroom and confronted me.

"I could not begin to relate the sheer desperate terror I felt as that morbid black thing inside the whirlwind came closer and closer to me," Lorraine remembers. "I tried to move, but I *couldn't*. I tried to scream, but no words came out! I felt a sense of doom then that I have never felt before. As a psychic, I knew this was a spirit of death. But it seemed to want even more than death: it wanted *me*, my self, my being.

"Then it got worse," Lorraine continues. "I felt myself being drawn *into* that raging black thing. And there was nothing I could do to prevent it! Mechanically, I did the only thing I could think of: I called out in the name of God for protection. Then, somehow, I got the ability to make a cross—a great *big* cross—in the air between it and me. That stopped the thing. But it wouldn't go away! I didn't know what to do next. At that point, thank God, Ed came running into the house. As he did, this thing swirled into the next room, went right through the bricks and up the chimney. Then it was over. Nothing was broken; nothing was smashed afterwards. Nevertheless, this was not our *first* physical encounter with an inhuman spirit!"

What confronted Ed and Lorraine Warren in those early morning hours was not a ghost. (Nor was it something seen only by them. The same swirling black mass has been reported by others.) Rather, this was the appearance of something far more ominous than a ghost could ever be: the manifestation of a comparatively rare phenomenon known as an inhuman demonic spirit. A preternatural entity, the inhuman spirit is considered to be possessed of a negative, diabolical intelligence fixed in a perpetual rage against both man and God.

What this spirit is, what it can do, and what its existence ultimately portends is the work and concern of the demonologist.

Until recently, few except other professionals and the exorcist clergy knew much about Ed and Lorraine Warren. Their work, by necessity, was not public. Instead, the Warrens remained in the background, either working privately with individuals experiencing *true* spirit-related problems, or as investigators, performing on-site research where strange or unusual phenomena were in progress.

The Warrens began investigating spirit phenomena in the mid-1940s, but not until the 1970s did they really come into public view. Wherever bizarre or ominous activity took place, it seemed the Warrens were always there. In 1972, for example, the ghost of a nineteenth-century manservant became active a mansion at West Point—and began harassing guests. It was the Warrens, the New York papers later reported, whom the Army called in to confront this rogue spirit and put a stop to its antics.

Early in 1974, the Warrens were again in the public eye. This time they were briefly seen at the conclusion of a case where exorcism by a Roman Catholic priest had to be performed in a home that was being plundered by invisible vandals that were even attacking people! Later in the year, the Warrens were again in the news, this time on network television, when a home in southern New England was being rocked by some of the most incredible "poltergeist" activity on record. "The cause of the disturbances in both cases," Ed says knowingly, "was *demonic*."

But not until 1976, when they were brought in to investigate reports of yet another outbreak of "demoniacal activity" in Amityville, was national attention fully trained on Ed and Lorraine

Warren, and their extraordinary work in the field of supernatural phenomena.

Who are these two people seen in the background of news photographs, but hardly ever identified? What are they like? And why do they do the kind of work they do?

Although one would think that people who involve themselves in demonology must necessarily be caught up in the macabre, Ed and Lorraine Warren are not occultists or eccentrics, nor are they engaged in some kind of religious crusade. On the contrary, the Warrens' perception of life is anything but negative. Indeed, the Warrens are effective in their work only *because* they are such positive people.

Ed Warren was born in Connecticut in September 1926. Burly, barrel-chested, and good-natured, Ed looks more like the corner grocer than a demonologist. Distinctly unpretentious, Ed gives no clue to the mysterious knowledge—and power—he carries with him. Calm and easygoing, he exudes the air of competence one finds in people who have learned what they know the hard way.

Lorraine Warren, born a scant few miles from her future husband in January 1927, is slim and attractive, with an ever-ready smile. Judging from her appearance—that of a fashionable New England housewife—one would never assume that she is a penetrating clairvoyant and light-trance medium. Yet, Lorraine is endowed with the Biblical gift of discernment of spirits, which St. Paul spoke of in his First Epistle to the Corinthians.

Together, Ed and Lorraine Warren are a cordial, happy couple in their mid-fifties who have a unique friendship in marriage, and a distinctly positive outlook on life. What the Warrens have seen, however, and what they have learned over the course of their extraordinary combined career, has given them wisdom way beyond their years.

Today, not surprisingly, the question most frequently asked of Ed and Lorraine Warren is, "What *really* happened in the Amityville case?" Although no brief reply could answer that question, perhaps the most comprehensive explanation the Warrens have so far given was at a benefit lecture held in their hometown of Monroe, Connecticut, during the summer of 1978.

The lecture was held in the town's tidy brick municipal building on a pleasant, balmy evening in late August. Ten minutes before Ed and Lorraine are scheduled to speak, the seats in the new, well-appointed auditorium are already filled to capacity. Those who can't find seats wander down the aisle and sit cross-legged in front. There is great bustle and chatter in the crowd. Words like *ghost, spirit,* and *exorcism* pop up in conversations all around. It seems like everybody, at least this night, has a ghost story to tell his neighbor.

On stage are two lecture platforms, a slender chrome microphone attached to each. At eight o'clock the house lights dim, a hush sweeps over the audience, and a moment later the Warrens walk out on stage. Lorraine is dressed in a long tartan skirt, ruffled blouse, and black velvet waistcoat. Ed wears a blue blazer and matching tartan tie.

"This evening, ladies and gentlemen, Ed and I would like to share with you some of our experiences inside a number of haunted houses that have recently been in the newspapers. We'd like to show you what we discovered in those houses, as well as discuss some of the information that came through in cases where communication with the haunting spirits was possible."

Ed nods to the projectionist who switches off the stage lights. A swell of anxious voices rise in the room. "Oh, no, they're going to show pictures!" exclaims a young girl who promptly slides down in her seat.

"Here we have a *real* haunted house," Ed declares, once the first slide comes up. "I say the house is haunted because that kindly-looking lady you see there standing by the window on the ground floor is a ghost."

And so it begins. . . . This is why the Warrens lecture: not to tell ghost stories, but to present valid case histories showing that supernatural phenomena exist, in order to explain how and why it occurs.

As Ed explains it, "The existence of spirits is not a matter of belief; it's a matter of evidence. In fact, the question is not so much a matter of *whether* the phenomena is there, but *why* is it there. And why is it so incredibly meddlesome in human affairs?"

The reason why the Warrens present public lectures goes back a decade or so, to the late 1960s. Then, amidst experimentation with alternate lifestyles, a sudden renewed interest in the occult sprang up. Closed for almost a century, the door to the "underworld" was suddenly thrown open, followed by a drastic upswing in reported incidents of negative spirit phenomena. Almost immediately, the Warrens were inundated with what proved to be genuine cases of negative spirit oppression and possession.

Most of those affected at the time were persons of college age. Concerned about this grave development, the Warrens embarked on a program of campus lectures, wherein they warned students around the country about the dangers of the occult. Supporting their statements with documentary evidence—slides, photographs, tape recordings, and physical artifacts—Ed and Lorraine Warren made an indelible impression on those to whom they spoke. The general public soon became fascinated with their firsthand experiences and ongoing research.

Although nowadays they lecture primarily to college audiences, the Warrens also speak to community groups and appear on radio and television when time allows. It is their honesty and experience that have made them popular. Their relaxed, informative, matter-of-fact style has changed many a skeptic into a believer. Yet although Ed and Lorraine offer an articulate explanation of spirit phenomena, they are aware of the gravity of their statements. Thus, the Warrens say nothing they cannot substantiate with credible evidence and documented case histories.

During the slide lecture, the Connecticut audience sits silently as Ed and Lorraine detail case after case of spirit phenomena, illustrating their comments with slides of ghosts, psychic lights, levitations, and materialized objects. (Dan Greenburg says in his book, *Something's There,* that if the Warrens said they saw a ghost, they saw a ghost!) When the auditorium lights come back on, dozens of hands immediately shoot up in the air.

An integral part of the Warrens' public lectures is the question-and-answer session that follows their talk. Here, people can sort out the whole strange topic of spirits for themselves, because it is possible to ask the Warrens a question and get a straight answer in reply. For Ed and Lorraine, this is neighbor talking to neighbor now.

"Now that you're all ready to move into a haunted house," Ed kids the audience, "let's take the first question!" An older man with gold-rimmed glasses stands up.

"I'm old enough to be your father, Ed Warren, but in my whole life I've never seen any of this sort of *phenomena*, as you call it. Have you seen a ghost yourself? Have you ever seen these objects levitate?" He sits back down.

"In my lifetime, I have seen many, many materialized ghosts," Ed tells him over the microphone. "The ghosts you saw on these slides tonight were photographed by me, or by psychic-photographers working with me on investigations. Later this year, in fact, we're going to England to try to get a photograph of the Brown Lady of Raynham Hall—Lady Dorothy Walpole, one of the most famous ghosts there is. Not far from there is Borley, the most haunted area in England. Both Lorraine and I have seen the Borley Nun walking along the road, and this time we'll try to photograph her too."

Taking a sip from a glass of ice water, Ed continues. "As for levitations—yes, I have seen levitations of all kinds. This case I showed you tonight was demoniacal activity, not ghosts. During the progress of the case, I witnessed a four-hundred pound refrigerator lift off the floor. In another case, I watched a console television set rise slowly in the air, then come down with a deafening, explosive crash. Yet, not one tube was broken! Those are just two instances that come to mind, although levitations occur in many cases where spirits—both human and inhuman—are behind the disturbance. So to answer your question, sir: yes, I *have* seen a ghost; yes, I *have* seen levitations occur."

Ed points to a tall blonde-haired lady who stands up to speak.

"In *The Amityville Horror,* the author cites an old belief that evil spirits can't cross over water," she says. "Is that true?"

"No, that's just an old superstition," Ed tells her. "Spirits are not affected by physical boundaries—or by distance, for that matter. Simply by *thinking* about a particular spirit is enough to draw that spirit to your side."

Lorraine calls on a teenage boy who'd been sitting up front by the stage. "What do you mean by *supernatural*?" he wants to know.

"If you looked the work up in a dictionary, you'd find that 'supernatural' means activity caused by God or His angels," Lorraine tells him. "But most people don't relate to the term that way. So, instead, we use the word in the way it's most commonly understood: that is, activity caused by any force or agent that is not part of our physical, earthly realm. Technically, the phenomena caused by *in*human spirits are called preternatural activity. To put it another way, the phenomena caused by inhuman spirits could be considered negative miracles."

Next, Ed points to a woman in the middle of the crowd. "If *I* were to die tomorrow," she asks, "would *I* become a ghost?"

"It's possible," Ed replies, "but not probable. Still, if you died suddenly and unexpectedly—say in an accident—and you refused to accept the fact that you're physically dead, then quite likely you'd remain earthbound until such time as you realized that you were out of the game; that you were dead. In the meantime, while you're trying to sort this problem out as a spirit, you'd probably remain earthbound in familiar surroundings—like your home. Nothing would seem different to you: you'd be able to see and hear other members of your family just like before, but they wouldn't be able to see or hear you. 'What's the matter?' you might ask, 'why don't they pay attention to me?' So, frustrated, you find a way—through mind over matter—to start causing objects to move, or you slam doors in order to get attention. Of course, all you'll really succeed in doing will be to scare the wits out of your family. At that time, your folks might get hold of Lorraine and me, who would then come to the house and have a little discussion with you as a spirit—so you'd be able to pass over correctly."

"How did you two originally become involved in the Amityville case?" a tanned gentleman in a rugby shirt asks the Warrens. "Also, what did you *do* during your investigation that the others didn't?" The questions enliven the audience; it's apparent they want to hear the answer too.

"Your long question, sir, requires a long answer," Lorraine warns him graciously.

"That's okay," he calls out.

"All right then," Lorraine begins, "our involvement started the last week of February 1976, when we received a telephone call at our home from a young woman, a television producer in New York City. She wanted to know if we had time to look into a so-called haunted house on Long Island? I told her *maybe*—but said first I'd have to know more details. She then explained about the 1974 DeFeo murders and the Lutzes' experience in the house. After that, the young woman told me that her TV station was covering the work of parapsychologists and psychic researchers who entered the home right after the Lutz family fled. However, after a month's time, these investigators hadn't come up with any concrete answers. So, she wanted to know, could we hold a séance in the house and tell them if spirits were behind the problem?

"Yes, I told her, we could investigate the house, however, holding a séance would be quite another matter. She understood. While I was on the phone I consulted with Ed, who agreed it would be all right to investigate the case.

"When we went to Long Island, we then met George and Kathy Lutz for the first time. The Lutzes had been staying at Kathy's mother's house. George and Kathy said they didn't want to even come near the house they owned: we had to go *to* them to get the house keys. In order not to prejudice our inquiry, we didn't interview the Lutzes at that time. We did, however, ask them a few pointed questions to test their sincerity. They were sincere all right: they were scared to death! For his part, George asked only one thing of us. If we were going to enter the house, would we please get the deed and bring it to him? We agreed to do this, and then left for the site.

"The house was quite beautiful," Lorraine continues, flipping the tartan sash back over her velvet waistcoat. "Ed parked the car in the driveway and we walked once around the house to get a drift of the place. After that, we unlocked the front door and went in.

"Once inside, the first thing Ed and I did was to walk through the house together, one floor at a time. What we found was a home that looked like it had been hastily evacuated. On the dining room table there was a gingerbread house all set for Christmas. Newspapers from mid-January '76 were laying about on tables, or on the floor. The kitchen cupboards were stocked with food, as was the refrigerator. In the basement, a stand-up freezer was loaded with a couple of hundred dollars' worth of provisions; laundry was folded on the dryer and ready to be put away. The bar was stocked with sealed bottles of liquor; the closets were full of clothes—suits, dresses, shoes, everything. Jewelry sat on the Lutzes' bedroom bureau; heirlooms, even the family photograph albums were left behind, out in full view for the taking. In short, the house looked just the way your own house probably looked tonight when you came down here to see us. Had these people concocted the story, they certainly wouldn't have left the deed to the house behind, along with a wealth of personal valuables.

"Our investigation involved going ahead with the séance," says Lorraine. "Therefore, we returned to the Amityville house at a later date to conduct a night séance before television cameras and recording equipment, as we'd been requested to do. All in all, I believe there were seventeen people present.

"Three psychic mediums, including myself, participated in the sitting," Lorraine relates. "The other two psychics were Mrs. Alberta Riley and Mrs. Mary Pascarella. Both Mary and Alberta are exceptionally fine trance mediums; both professionals, of course; both dear friends of ours as well. Before the séance was held, Ed used religious provocation. We knew that if an inhuman spirit was present, it would be provoked to react by exposure to holy objects: however, we did not know *how* it would react"

"Well, we got a response all right," Ed nods. "Phenomena let go— not in terms of terrifying external activity—but rather as a physical assault on at least half of us present, especially those who had a pivotal job to do during the séance. I began to suffer involuntary physical reactions, such as heart flutterings. These 'palpitations,' as I call them, affected me personally for some three weeks after we were in the house.

"At least half those present during the séance experienced or reported phenomena in the house that they considered to be out of the ordinary. So, although the séance was essentially a fiasco, that fiasco occurred as a result of some external agent."

Near the aisle, a dark-haired woman stands up. "I was told that the priest in the Amityville book never existed."

"Madam," Lorraine answers, "the priest in that case is a friend of ours. We know him very well. Not only did the things happen to him that were reported in the book, more things have happened to him since that were never reported. Father has suffered many times over for his involvement in that case."

With that reply, the Warrens thank their audience and bring the lecture to an end. As usual, though, it is not the end of the questions. Half the people file out, but the other half come to the front of the stage and surround the Warrens.

"How do you know these demonic spirits you talk about aren't really something human—just *mean* ghosts?" a man asks.

"Sir," Lorraine answers him, "sometimes in the beginning of a case you can't tell the difference between a negative human spirit and a negative *in*human spirit. Both can be extremely malicious, and sometimes they even work together. Only the demonic, however, has the *power* to bring about such incredible negative phenomena as fires, explosions, dematerialization, teleportation, and levitation of large objects. More than that, in cases of possession, the spirit comes through very clearly. It *says* what it is. Sometimes it calls itself by name. If you listened to a tape recording of the possessed, you would have no trouble recognizing the difference between a human and an inhuman spirit."

"Why don't you play them here?" a woman puts in.

"We used to play tape recordings for our audiences," Lorraine replies, "but in a large group of people, there are just too many receptive psychologies. Exposure to the real thing is bound to have negative effects on some."

It proves to be another hour before the Warrens are actually able to leave the municipal building.

Later that evening, after the talk is over, Ed and Lorraine relax at home with friends. Why do they take so many questions from the audience at the lectures?

"The questions are part of the program," Lorraine answers. "When we finish speaking, we always throw open the proceedings for questions. Although sometimes," she jokes, "I wake up in the middle of the night hearing the distant cry of 'One more question, *please.*' As far as our lectures go, we see them as being a two-way street. People come to hear us talk because they're interested in what we have to say. In return, we provide a good two-hour briefing, I guess you might call it, on the subject of spirit phenomena. When we're done speaking, we interact with the audience through questions. We see our role as being an educational one. This is why we try to answer everybody's question."

Why so much interest these days in spirits and supernatural phenomena?

"People have always been interested in the occult," Lorraine answers. "But in the last ten years, the public has been exposed to *so much* information on the subject of spirits and the supernatural that they're trying to come to grips with it. Wherever we go, people have read *The Exorcist.* They've read about our involvement in the Amityville case. They want to know more. They want to learn how and why these terrifying phenomena occur, and what's behind them. The argument that spirits are an illusion, or a psychological quirk, doesn't hold water any more. People want to know the truth, even if the answer is downright unpleasant."

The Warrens speak matter-of-factly about the existence of spirits. How do they reply to the assertion that there is no such thing?

"There has never been a person, past or present, who could *dis*prove the existence of the supernatural," Ed asserts. "But, given the same considerations any individual would have in a court of law, I could—if called upon for a proper reason—prove that ghosts exist; that apparitions exist; that haunted houses exist; that supernatural phenomena exist; and that the inhuman demonic spirit exists."

Ed displays a picture, taken in a demonically-infested house, of what looks like the ghost of a boy.

"That was no ghost," Ed says, shaking his head. "The spirit that had been commanding the environment at that time assumed many different guises. But, ultimately, they were all the same: they were *one*. As for the picture, the boy had no eyes. That is a trademark of the demonic. Whenever it manifests, there is always a flaw—there's always something unnatural about its appearance. Sometimes the flaw is so obvious you miss it at first, but the flaw is always there."

If there is one message that Ed and Lorraine Warren try to get across, it's that the occult is basically an accident waiting to happen. "In the last decade," says Ed, "there has been a hundred-fold increase in negative occult practices. Why? Because for the most part, people *don't know* that real, negative forces exist in the world. Instead, the occult is made to seem like a game, a diversion, a cure-all for what ails you. Just look at the way the occult is treated in newspapers and magazines these days—as a harmless novelty. Well it isn't harmless, it can be dangerous! When Lorraine and I lecture, we give what we feel is a needed counterargument to all this trumped-up interest in the occult. We show the negative occult, for what if really is: a fool's paradise. For those simply interested in the material, who want to learn how to avoid spirit problems, knowledge of the subject isn't just power, but a weapon of *protection*. Forewarned, in other words, is forearmed."

After thirty-four years in the work, they've seen it *all*: the shock, the terror, the incredible phenomena. For Ed and Lorraine, the phenomena make sense; they know *why* it happens. After a lifetime of investigation into the unknown, the Warrens now share this knowledge of the supernatural and how it functions. But beware! "The demonic comes in many forms," Ed intones, "some far worse than what we talked about tonight!"

"We work with any clergy of any religion that teaches love of God and love of your fellow man. We work with all people of all faiths." - Ed Warren

Ed and Lorraine Warren founded the New England Society for Psychic Research, the oldest ghost hunting group in New England.

It was through their paintings that the Warrens were first able to meet the homeowners of haunted houses and get to talk with them one-on-one.

2.

Art and Appraritions

Incredible as it may seem, demonology and exorcism are still practiced in this modern day and age. Indeed, there are seven recognized demonologists in North America alone. Six are ordained clergymen, members of various major religions—the seventh is Ed Warren. Each is unique; all have experienced horrors beyond imagining. And each man lives in constant mortal danger.

How did Ed Warren get involved in demonology? Was it a calling, he was asked?

"No, I think of a calling as being something lofty and majestic," Ed admits. "But I firmly believe the work I do today is something that was definitely meant to be. I say this because a number of strong factors affected me even as a very young child.

"I was five," he recalls, "when I first realized that something unusual was going on in this world. Where we lived, we had an old spinster landlady who didn't like dogs—or kids. She'd sit by the window and actually wait for you to do something wrong. When you did, she'd come flying out of the house, screaming like a madwoman.

"Well, about a year after she died, I was upstairs in the same house, taking off my play shoes. The sun was going down, and the room was getting dark. As I sat there on the floor, the closet door opened all by itself. Inside the dark closet I saw a dot of light, about the size of a firefly. In a few seconds, the light grew to human length, and then, incredibly, the apparition of the landlady stood before me, semitransparent, wearing what looked like some sort of shroud. She was frowning as usual, just like she looked in life. Then she vanished.

"Because I was only five, I didn't know if this kind of thing was natural, but I sensed it wasn't because it scared me. When I told my father, who was a Connecticut state trooper, he told me to forget what I saw and never tell anyone. Well, I never told anyone, but I also never forgot what I saw."

As Ed grew older, the search for answers about such strange goings-on became an intellectual quest that formed the basis for his later career. Being a perceptive child, he wanted to know why these strange things went on around him, and whether other people had experiences similar to his own.

"At the same time I spent my childhood in a haunted house, I attended Catholic school. I was hardly the most religious kid in class, in fact I didn't even like to go to church because I had to dress-up," Ed continues. "Still, when the good priests and nuns in school spoke about spirits and the devil I—more than others in my class—had reason to listen. Even at an early age, I was trying to figure out the weird incidents of psychic phenomena I saw go on in my own home. My early education, therefore, supplied me with a general metaphysical overview of the world. I didn't know whether that information was true or false, of course, but I remembered it nonetheless.

"At the same time, other things happened to me as a child. My father was a very devout man who never missed going to Mass a day in his life—perhaps it was because he saw the uglier side of life every day as a policeman. I do know, however, that my grandfather had a strong influence on my father. My grandfather was a very pious, very devout man; when he died, he bequeathed his life savings to the church we attended to buy a stained-glass window with the figure of St. Michael in the center. As a child, I used to go into the church and look at that big, beautiful window with the sun streaming through it and wonder who St. Michael was. Today, of course, I know it was St. Michael the Archangel who drove Satan from heaven and is the patron saint of the exorcist.

"One of the most perplexing things to happen to me as a child," Ed resumes, "was that I would have dreams of a nun coming to speak to me. It got to the point I told my father about this woman, and described her in detail. 'That woman,' my father said one night, dumbfounded, 'was your aunt.' I'd never met my aunt; she died before I was born. I was told she had been a nun who had gone through incredible physical sufferings. My father often called her a saint, for want of a better term. During one of my dreams, she told me something that took on meaning only when I grew up: 'Edward,' she said, 'you will tell many priests the right road to go down, but you yourself will never be a priest.' Well, I am not a priest today, but I do work closely with them, and tutor those who have been assigned to work in the area of demonology and exorcism. So, in all honesty, my work is not a calling. Instead, I'd say I'm simply living out my destiny."

Meanwhile, barely three blocks away from her future husband, Lorraine Moran was growing up as an intelligent, precocious young daughter in a dignified Irish family. Yet, she was a girl with a true sense of the beyond, for Lorraine was born with the gift of clairvoyance—the ability to see beyond physical time and place.

"I didn't know I had an additional sense ability," Lorraine recalls. "I simply thought everyone had the same God-given senses—you know," she jokes, "all *six* of them. Well, I found out differently when I was about twelve. I was attending a private all-girls school then. It was Arbor Day, and we were all on the front lawn, standing in a circle around a shovel-hole in the ground. Well, just as soon as they put the sapling in the ground, I saw it as a fully-grown tree. I looked up into its massive branches, filled with leaves blowing in the wind, with no idea I was experiencing second-sight. The nun standing beside me prodded my arm and said in her usual stern way, 'Miss Moran, why are you looking up at the sky?' I told her I was just looking up into the tree.... 'Are you seeing into the future?' she asked me, just as sternly. 'Yes,' I admitted, 'I guess I am.'

"Well, that did it—I was immediately sent off to a retreat home for the weekend. I couldn't talk or play or do anything, just sit there all day long in church and pray. That taught me. After that, when it came to things involving clairvoyance, I kept my mouth shut."

In retrospect, Lorraine's experience that Arbor Day served to channel her abilities toward the good, toward becoming a tool that would eventually help many thousands of others. Although Ed, like most people, possessed no overt psychic abilities, the continuous input of psychic data during the late 1940s and early 1950s (garnered during the Warrens' "ghost-hunting" period) caused Lorraine's clairvoyance to develop significantly. Later, in the 1970s, Lorraine was tested at UCLA, where her clairvoyance was judged as being "far above average."

One might be inclined to call it fate how the Warrens came together. Ed and Lorraine did not originally set out to make the supernatural their vocation. Instead, as Lorraine explains, it was a vocation that found *them*.

"Ed and I got married—both at the age of eighteen—while he was in the Navy. In fact, our only child, Judy, was six months old before Ed came back from the Pacific Theater and saw her for the first time. Once World War II was over, we had to find a livelihood like everyone else. Each of us had skills as landscape artists, and we each harbored a desire to paint. Ed had already attended art school in New Haven before the war, so we began our marriage under the assumption we were going to be artists."

The art, however, turned out to be a steppingstone to psychic research. "You see," Lorraine continues, "we needed a subject to paint—a good subject, something people could relate to. Well, haunted houses proved to be that subject. Ed would find a haunted house written up in the newspaper, or get a lead on one from the locals in town. Then we'd drive to the site in our old Chevy. Ed would do up a complete sketch of the house and grounds. All the while, of course, the owner of the place would be peeking out the window wondering what the heck was going on. We were just kids then, so one of us would knock on the door, show them the sketch of the house, then offer it in exchange for information about the haunting. If the story was engrossing enough, we'd paint up the house for our collection, then sell it later at an art show.

"All in all, we spent five years traveling around the country painting and investigating haunted houses—and not exactly by coincidence, I might add. Before we were married, Ed had already devoured all the available books on the supernatural, although I didn't know it at the time. So in addition to painting he was fully engaged in field research, all the while making notes on where the books were wrong."

In a very real way, the Warrens used the world for their university, acquiring a wealth of information in the process. Often they were the first, and sometimes the only researchers to investigate the site of a haunting. Although as a child, Ed had seen phenomena go on around him that would make other people's hair stand on end, Lorraine had no experience at all with ghosts and hauntings. As an adult, therefore, she remained naturally skeptical.

"In the beginning," Lorraine remembers, "I was more than a bit wary of the people with whom we spoke. I thought they were kind of suffering from overactive imaginations or were just making things up to get attention. In fact, some of the things people told us sounded completely outlandish—back then. Over the course of time, though, I began to become convinced. We would be in vastly different places, one week in Iowa and the next in Texas, but there was often a similarity, sometimes even an exactness, to the stories these people would tell. And there Ed and I would be, paint all over our hands and arms, offering consolation to folks who were often twice our age, telling them what we knew about the workings of the spirit realm."

What *did* the Warrens learn about ghosts during that period? *Is* the phenomenon real? And if so, they were asked to answer, how does the spirit manifest?

"Most people seem to think ghosts lurk around in the upstairs of old homes in a misty, vaporous state," says Ed in reply. "This is not so: in order to be seen with the physical eye, the ghost or apparition needs physical energy to manifest. We learned there are two basic processes a human spirit can go through to bring about its own materialization. One way requires a human presence; the other does not.

"When an earthbound spirit needs a human presence to manifest, then it engages in a complex process of energy transference to give itself substance," explains Ed. "And the Adam's rib of most ghostly manifestations is nothing other than the human aura. Surrounding the body of every living being is a bioluminescent glow caused by a natural discharge of energy from the body. Clairvoyants like Lorraine can see and 'read' the human aura, which appears in three layers, reflecting the physical, emotional, and spiritual status of the person. Spirits read auras too," he notes, "and an individual's aura may either repel or attract a particular spirit presence. Nevertheless, from this bioluminescent glow or aura, the ghost draws small amounts of energy which collect as an orb, or else as small pinpoints of light. This light energy, combined with heat and electromagnetic energy in the room, is what the human spirit uses to manifest."

Asked for a simpler explanation, Lorraine says, "Imagine you are staying overnight in your friend's home. The place is so nice and cheerful that the thought of a ghost would never enter your mind. That night, you're shown to the guest room, and in a little while you're sound asleep. Sometime in the middle of the night you wake up. Perhaps the spirit has psychically projected the sound of breaking glass, or the slamming of a door to get your attention. Sitting up in bed, you have an eerie feeling—you *know* something's not right. Glancing around the dark room, you see two bluish orbs of light, roughly the size of golf balls, floating near each other about five feet off the floor. As you watch, you might also see streaks of light flash away from your body—this is electromagnetic energy being drawn from your aura. In no time at all, these two balls of light come together and merge into one larger ball, about the size of a grapefruit. The ball will then elongate into a tall cigar-shape of human size.

"Instead of the orbs of light, other people report seeing hundreds of tiny pinpoints of light in a cluster that—like the orbs—blend into a larger cylindrical glow. In either case, within this tall, bioluminescent glow, the definable features of a person will begin to emerge until the spirit has manifested as much as it possibly can. To be accurate, by the way, it's called a *ghost* if the features are not recognizable to the viewer; if the features are recognizable to the viewer, it's an *apparition*. Either way, though, you've got a visitor."

"The other way a ghost will come up," Ed explains, "is essentially different—and a bit theatrical. On very humid days with a lot of rain or fog, or on stormy nights when there is electrical energy in the air from lightning discharges, a ghost is able to build itself from the energy in the atmosphere. When a ghost or apparition manifests in this way, there tends to be an intense smell of ozone in the room, and the resulting materialization comes across with a bluish glow— quite a spectacle, I assure you. All in all, though, the spirit is liable to manifest before you are aware of its presence, or as you watch. The important point is that in one case the spirit requires a human presence to materialize, while in the other, only Mother Nature is needed. But a ghost certainly does not have to manifest in order to be there, because it is not intrinsically a material entity. The ghost will *already* be there; it manifests simply to verify its presence to those in the physical realm."

How a ghost manifests is one thing—but how it looks to the individual is something else again. Why are some ghosts headless, or disfigured?

"The spirit's appearance," Ed states, "depends entirely on how that particular spirit determines to project itself, or how it sees itself in its own mind. This is why encounters with earthbound spirits are not always easygoing, passive affairs. Tragedy comes in many forms, often accompanied by violence, and an individual's last thoughts tend to dominate the mind of his spirit after physical death. Thus the ghost will often manifest as a grotesque spectacle, representative of the manner in which it died. Furthermore, a person who meets a tragic end often carries a negative attitude into the afterlife, many times blaming God for his troubles. Consequently, some spirits *are* mean, and—contrary to what people may think—a spiteful ghost can bring about physical and psychological effects that can lead to illness, injury, or even death. Psychologically, oppression by human spirits can result in unshakeable depression, unpleasant habits like drinking or insomnia, even impulses toward suicide. Physical effects can range from lingering illnesses to jabs of acute pain that have no medical origin in the body."

At least half the people who call on Ed and Lorraine Warren each year have never had anything to do with spirits or the occult. Rather, they tend to be normal, everyday people who inadvertently walk into situations where spirits were active before they arrived. This happened in Amityville, where the Lutz family lost a good deal of money and suffered emotional catastrophe as well. Some buy haunted cars, and then find themselves being oppressed to re-create tragic accidents. Still others find themselves being uncontrollably possessed by a spirit of someone or something that is distinctly *not them*. And often the most unsuspecting of people will fall prey to spirit phenomena. This is precisely what happened at West Point.

It was October 1972. An officer at the United States Military Academy telephoned the Warrens a day before they were scheduled to present a general lecture to the cadets there. Though the officer's comments were deliberately vague, he nonetheless told the Warrens that a curious security problem had arisen, and he wanted to know if they'd be willing to help—in a professional capacity—before they lectured the next day at the Point. Without probing, the Warrens agreed to lend assistance. "Good," the relieved officer said, "I'll send a car for you tomorrow at three P.M."

The following afternoon a shiny black limousine bearing government plates pulled up outside the Warrens' front door. Ed and Lorraine, dressed in evening clothes for the lecture, slid into the roomy back seat. The chauffeur, an Army staff sergeant, told them the drive would take about one hour, but volunteered no other information.

Moving north along the Taconic Parkway through occasional snow showers, the limousine nevertheless kept up a steady pace of sixty miles per hour. Travelers along the highway peered into the car while the Warrens wondered what kind of "security matter" had led the government to call them in.

A little past four P.M., they entered the gates of the United States Military Academy. The sergeant pulled the car up to the entrance of the headquarters offices, swung open the rear door, and escorted the Warrens to a head officer of West Point.

Major Donald Wilson, an orderly, good-natured man, offered Ed and Lorraine a seat in his office. He then briefed them on an already prepared schedule: dinner with the officers of the faculty at six, followed by a general lecture to all classes at eight.

"One more thing . . . " For the next few minutes, Major Wilson went on to explain how an unaccountable breach of security was occurring in the home of one of West Point's officers. Naturally, the military police had already been over the problem, but to no avail, he conceded. Matters had only gotten worse. Therefore, it had been decided to get an outside opinion on a problem that appeared to have no natural explanation. "So if there's no objection, the officer would like to speak with you before dinner."

"We'll be glad to help," Ed replied. "Do you know the nature of the problem?"

"Between us . . . " the major almost broke into a grin, "there's a ghost in the officer's quarters."

Switching off the lights, the officer took his cap, escorted the Warrens out the office door and introduced them to an Army photographer who sat waiting in the hallway. Strict limits had been placed on the collection of information that day—all documentary records would be the property of the U.S. government.

Outside, the call of cadences broke the silence as cadets marched through the gray stillness of the afternoon. The group took a leisurely stroll to the officer's quarters, an impressive brick structure.

An officer's staff aide answered the front door to the mansion and showed the group inside. Within moments, the commanding general and his wife entered the foyer and the officer introduced them to the Warrens. The officer impressed Lorraine as being a kind, compassionate man of great wisdom and intelligence.

The officer's wife directed everyone into a sitting room that was beautifully furnished with period antiques by previous generals over the course of two centuries.

"Nothing macabre has happened here," the officer said, sitting in what appeared to be his favorite chair. "Nevertheless, a number of incidents have gone on in this house that, so far, no one has been able to explain to my satisfaction. Some background: in the basement there is a private study; that room is kept locked and secure. But no matter how many times the bunk in there is made up, it's always found ripped apart later. Upstairs, ghosts have been seen flitting about the house. These I haven't seen, but they've been reported for years, and apparently they go with the billet. Now, I wouldn't mention any of this except that we have an unusual, persistent problem: personal belongings and other important articles are regularly found missing. Not *stolen*," he emphasized, "but missing temporarily."

The officer stopped for a moment to put on his glasses. "I grant you, none of this is terribly important unless put into perspective. One of the responsibilities of the commanding officer here is social protocol. In this house, we receive our fair share of government leaders and Army brass. Recently, on special occasions, some potentially serious events have occurred. Wallets have been stolen, pockets have been picked, money and personal mementos have been taken from eminent dignitaries and their wives. Later, all the stolen items are found upstairs, neatly laid out on the dresser in our master bedroom." The Warrens sat mum, taking in the unique nature of the problem.

"This foolishness *cannot continue*," the officer said forcefully. "Yet we know that no person has committed these actions. So my question to you (Mr. Warren, Mrs. Warren) is the following: if this is a ghost—and I stress, *if* it is—then you tell me: can a ghost manipulate physical objects?"

"Yes," Ed answered, "it can. Providing the objects are of no significant weight, such as the ones you describe."

"All right then," the officer said, "does this sound like a ghost to you?"

"Based on what you say, yes," Ed answered. "In fact, it is quite probable that a human spirit is at work here because the items did not disappear *completely*."

Taken aback by the reply, the officer looked at Ed for a moment. "Would you be able to tell if there is a ghost in this house that steals wallets?"

Lorraine saw this as her opportunity to reply: "Sir, I am a clairvoyant. The best thing would be for us to walk the house. This would allow me to determine if in fact a spirit is causing the disturbance. It's the best test."

The officer and his wife agreed, and the group rose to their feet. Ed and Major Wilson headed for the basement with the key to the downstairs study. As usual, the bunk was torn apart, as though someone had been sleeping in it. Yet nothing else was disturbed. They closed up the room and headed back upstairs. In the first-floor kitchen, Major Wilson showed Ed a cutting board with a wet spot on it. "It almost dries," he told him, "but every afternoon, it gets wet again!"

Elsewhere accompanied by the officer and his wife, Lorraine stood with her eyes closed in the center of the downstairs rooms, beginning with the sitting room, trying to perceive any invisible presence.

Nothing was apparent on the first floor, although Lorraine found herself somewhat transfixed in one of the mansion's back bedrooms. "This room," she said, "this room right here is where John Kennedy stayed whenever he visited the Point. The vibrations in here are truly beautiful."

A bit amazed, the officer's wife told Lorraine that she was right: "This *was* the President's bedroom: he couldn't climb the stairs because of his back."

After leaving the first floor, the officer's wife led the way up a banistered staircase to the second floor. In each room, Lorraine picked up impressions of the powerful individuals who had spent time in the house, but hardly any sense of a mischievous spirit.

In one upstairs bedroom, Lorraine again paused for long moments. "An elderly woman spent a long time in this room," she mused. "The woman would often stand by that open veranda and look out to a field."

Lorraine walked to the window. In the distance, she saw the cadets standing in formation on the parade ground; then she turned back into the room. "This was a very wise woman who shared a burden with a man in her life. She counseled him . . . but the man was not her husband."

"The man is Douglas MacArthur," said the officer. "The old woman is his mother. This was Mrs. MacArthur's bedroom when her son was Superintendent here."

The upstairs group then walked back down to the sitting room, where everyone met once again. "After walking the whole house," Lorraine admitted, "I did not feel the presence of anyone who would be responsible for causing the phenomena that you described. On the other hand, it is possible that a spirit has deliberately avoided us."

"Is there any way of finding that out?" asked the major.

"Yes," answered Lorraine, "this could be determined in the trance state."

A concerned expression crossed the major's face. "Does this mean we have to hold a séance?"

"No," she laughed, "I'd just have to sit down sometime this evening, once the hubbub and vibrations of the day have died down."

With Lorraine's consent, it was decided to hold a gathering in the mansion after the evening lecture. If the problem could perhaps be solved once and for all, it was at least worth a try.

At a cordial dinner held at six o'clock that evening, the Warrens were introduced to officers of the West Point faculty who, with their wives, proved extremely curious about the whole subject of the supernatural. At eight, Ed and Lorraine presented a general lecture on spirits to a wide-eyed Army audience. The Warrens illustrated their talk as usual with slides of ghosts, apparitions, and other unusual phenomena, which brought the customary response of "Ooo"s and "Wow"s. Although the lecture was received with enthusiasm, none of the cadets thought for a moment that such things could go on at the Point.

During the question session at the end of the lecture, a young lady in her thirties stood up and told the Warrens that she felt it was a good time to say something she'd been carrying around all her life. She wanted everyone to know that what the Warrens were talking about was true. These unusual things do go on. Her father was the flight leader of that squadron of fighters lost over the Bermuda Triangle in 1945 and he never returned home. He and the other men were really lost at sea. And though people might like to think it's some sort of hoax, it isn't.

When she sat down, the entire audience spontaneously erupted into cheers and applause. Seeing this as the perfect opportunity to end the lecture, Ed saluted the cadets and bid everyone good night.

Five minutes later, the Warrens were on their way back with the officer, plus a private group of other officers and their wives whom the Warrens had met at dinner. Lorraine explained to the major that she felt Mrs. MacArthur's bedroom was the most favorable place to attempt communication.

The major in turn told Lorraine that the officer and his wife had to depart for New York by helicopter at ten. Though elsewhere on campus, they would stop by the mansion before leaving.

"Fair enough," she replied.

Upon being met at the front door by a staff aide, the group made its way upstairs to the MacArthur bedroom, where the officers and their wives found seats on the floor. Lorraine sat on the bed. ("A bed," notes Lorraine, "where people spend a third of their life sleeping, is an excellent source of vibrations.") All lights were turned off but one, and Lorraine closed her eyes.

"I see a black man approaching," she soon said, speaking out loud like a newscaster. "He's wearing a dark uniform with no braid or decoration. This man is with us now."

Eyes darted around the room, but no such figure was visible.

"This man is overtaken with a sense of fear, guilt, and lack of acceptance. He feels very sorry for something." Lorraine stopped, her body tense, her arms straight out beside her. "He's speaking to me now. He tells me that he has been accused of murder. His cell is in the basement. But the Army has ex— exonerated him of that murder. He is very, very sorry and he cannot hold his sorrow any longer. This is why he has been taking wallets . . . he wants the Army to know his sorrow."

Everyone in the room sat silent, waiting to hear more.

"What is your name, young man?" Lorraine asked. "Tell me your name. . . . He tells me his name is Greer. He spells it G-R-E-E-R. What is the date?. . . It is the early eighteenth—no, it is the early eighteen-hundreds. He doesn't know the date anymore. He says he just wants his sorrow to be understood. He wants to know who I am."

Lorraine, deep in trance, began to bend forward. Ed told her to lean back.

"Mr. Greer," she said, "I have been sent by the Army to find out your problem. . . . No, Mr. Greer, you are *not* held in dishonor," she said in an apparent reply. "Your exoneration was for a purpose. It is on the records that the death you caused was not a murder. Your exoneration stands.

"Listen to me, Mr. Greer. Your sorrow is understood by the Army. But it is only proper that your sorrow be over. There is nothing we can do for you. *You* are holding yourself back; *you* must exonerate yourself. Enough time has passed. It is now the twentieth century—this is the nineteen-seventies. You do not understand the present day.

Each time you take belongings from an important person, you put the Army in a very dangerous position.... He tells me he has no more need to do this. He feels confused. He wants to come back to life...."

Lorraine's arms slackened, then she began to drift away from the trance.

"Lorraine," Ed said forcefully, "stay with him. Try to send him on."

Lorraine sat silent for long moments, and then again spoke. "To live again, Mr. Greer, you must go to the light. It is time for you to surrender yourself and begin again. Everyone must do this. Focus on the light and step toward it. Go to your friends and family. Go home to the light, Mr. Greer. Focus on the light and be drawn toward it...."

Lorraine suddenly snapped awake, her eyes wide open. "He's gone. I lost him," she declared.

The lights were switched back on as the officers and their wives rose to their feet, speaking in anxious hushed tones. Lorraine, standing in the center of the group, gave a complete description of the man and said at the end, Greer had simply vanished.

Shortly thereafter, the entourage made its way downstairs and left, while the Warrens and the major waited in the sitting room. A few minutes later the officer and his wife arrived. Lorraine briefly reviewed the communication she'd had, noting in conclusion: "I didn't get the impression that Greer really wanted to be here. In a way, I think he was just waiting to be dismissed. After this, I seriously doubt that any more pockets will be picked. But if it does happen again, please let me know—there *are* things I can do at a distance."

"That's very nice of you," said the officer. "However, there's one small item. No black man has ever served at the Point until this century. But I promise you, the major will have this matter checked out completely in the next few weeks."

As they spoke in the foyer, a helicopter could be heard descending outside. It was time to go. After an exchange of gratitude and farewell on the front steps, the officer and his wife crossed the lawn and boarded a large service helicopter bound for New York. The Warrens slipped into the back seat of the waiting limousine, wondering if Greer had indeed ended his travail of over a century.

A few weeks later, while lecturing at Boston University, Ed and Lorraine were called from the stage to take a telephone call from West Point. The Army wanted them to know that a complete and thorough search of the records had been made. It was discovered that a black man, a porter by the name of Greer, *had* served at the Point. Assigned to the Thayer Mansion in the early nineteenth century, he'd been accused of a murder, but the Army exonerated him of it. His records had been out of order, and he would now be filed as "Deceased." "And by the way, the next time you lecture at the Point, could you please do something about the ghost of a Civil War cavalryman who refuses to leave one of the dormitory rooms? We need the space."

Of course, the Army is not the only large organization that has recently had to contend with a ghost. After the crash of one of its L-1011 jetliners in the Everglades, Eastern Airlines experienced recurring spirit phenomena on its planes, as was reported in *The Ghost of Flight 401*. In the year following the disaster, many hundreds of people reportedly witnessed the spirits of the deceased crew members in full physical form aboard other Tristar jets. On one occasion, the voice of the spirit of Don Repo, the flight engineer killed in the crash, was allegedly captured on the flight recorder when he materialized in the cockpit and spoke with crew members. Sometimes it is possible to deny or ignore that such unusual events occur. However, on such occasions as at West Point, when phenomena simply will not go away, the most direct route is to acknowledge that something *is* there—if only to stop it from happening.

"Actually," as Ed points out, "it's a credit to the Army that they considered the supernatural as a valid option. In my travels, I've often found that people who *don't* believe in ghosts, many times *won't* believe in them. They see the supernatural as something threatening, so they blot out the information. Fortunately, these Army officers didn't adjust an unpleasant reality to suit their purposes. Instead, they analyzed the data, logically weighed the evidence, and came to a rational conclusion that led to the solution of the problem."

When one brings up the subject of ghosts, the mind almost automatically conjures up images of haunted castles and manor houses in England. In the Warrens' experience, are there more ghosts in England or in America?

"I was asked the same question in London by the BBC not long ago," Ed responds. "There are places in the world that are *really* haunted, and many of those places are in England. Borley Rectory, for example, is a virtual doorway to the supernatural, as it has been for hundreds of years. One need only read the late Harry Price's books, such as *Poltergeist Over England,* to find that out. But by far, there are more ghosts in America than in England. The reason is a matter of numbers. Although the day-to-day level of spirit activity is about the same the world over, there are simply more people in America. In other words, where there's a very large population, there is also a greater probability that some of them will get caught up in the ghost syndrome when they die."

Where in America would a person be most likely to encounter a ghost?

"In terms of *physical* places," Ed replies, "we've found that one is most likely to confront a ghost in old, isolated buildings. Farmhouses or older brick homes built near the sea during the colonization of America have the greatest *potential* for being haunted because of the generations of people who have lived and died there. But ghosts don't appear only in haunted houses. For example, recently a number of people around here, including our assistant Judy, commented on seeing an adult man in a trench coat pacing out in the road at night in front of our house—though he disappeared whenever anyone got close! It turned out that a few days before, a young man brought us some jagged parts from Flight 401, that jetliner that went down in the Everglades. The very moment he handed the first part to Lorraine, the young man standing next to her saw the apparition of Don Repo—the flight engineer on the jet. It was the same man who had been seen on the road. He was pacing and waiting because, as coincidence would have it, we were meeting with relatives of his family later that week, at which time Lorraine saw him and another apparition present during the entire length of our discussions. By the way, I should also mention that the name *Steward* or *Stewart* came through to Lorraine the minute she began psychometrizing the 401 parts."

The answer opened the door to even deeper questions: why does the phenomenon occur in the first place? Is there some reason why one person will become a ghost and another won't? These are the sort of questions Ed and Lorraine are able to answer in intricate detail. As young artists, they came to learn that earthbound human spirits are no more than individuals whose bodies have been deducted from the total entity. Caught up in a confused state of mind, such unfortunates possess life but no body. Yet, body or no, these human spirits are stuck in a temporary limbo between this realm and the next. Factors have somehow conspired to prevent the spirit from making any onward progress.

"The ghost syndrome," Ed explains, "is caused by a tragedy in the life of an individual, where death occurs suddenly or under very traumatic circumstances. Less often, the spirit will linger because of an unusually strong attachment to things of this world. But in either case, the earthbound spirit identifies with *this* realm rather than the next. Now, it's a general rule that people who can contemplate an afterlife will pass over correctly. However, the mind of the earthbound spirit tends to be rigidified in a particular state of emotion. Deep down the spirit seeks resolve, of course, but it is *so* caught up in its own trauma and misery that nothing makes sense to it except the contemplation of its own emotional state. Many times the ghost isn't even aware that death has taken place. This is because the individual as a ghost no longer has the same awareness it had as a flesh-and-blood person. When communication takes place, you often have to tell them—in fact, you've got to *convince* them—they're dead, that they've been dissociated from their physical body. The mind, you see, is unaffected by the advent of death. So if death comes suddenly or in the midst of emotional trauma, the spirit gets caught up in a state of unresolve. This is why spirits linger, sometimes for ages. Time is not a factor with spirits; they live in a sort of perpetual present. It is wisdom and realization that allows the human spirit to progress successfully.

"Essentially, when a ghost is responsible for haunting phenomena," continues Ed, "there has either been an emotional situation in the home that triggers the disturbance, or a spirit present is trying to communicate its problem to the physical realm. Take emotional situations first. People often wonder why two, three, a dozen families will live in a house, but only one person or family will experience spirit phenomena. The answer is that an emotional interlink has usually taken place.

"For example, you have an old house in which someone committed suicide a hundred years ago. In the meantime, a half-dozen families may live there and never once experience anything strange. Then one day, in moves someone who's also bent on self-destruction. Immediately activity starts up. An emotional interaction has occurred. It's like putting batteries in a flashlight: a connection is made between compatible emotions.

"Take another example. Up until maybe fifty years ago, women gave birth at home, and sometimes these women would die in childbirth. Now, a woman who very much wanted to bear a child and be a good mother would hardly want to die at the point of delivery. So she might remain earthbound in the home—emotionally fixated to the place. A hundred years later, a family with a newborn baby moves in. All of a sudden, the ghost of a Victorian woman is seen in the nursery. The presence of the child has triggered an emotional response. This kind of haunting phenomenon is very common and has happened more times than I can count.

"Another reason a ghost will manifest is based on a need to communicate. In these cases, the earthbound spirit is so caught up in its own tragedy or unresolved state that it will manifest to anyone in order to try and communicate its plight. That's why lights will be switched on and off, or you'll hear knockings, or small objects will move in your presence. The spirit is *trying* to gain attention. This happened at West Point. Sometimes, though, the ghost doesn't know he's there. I've got a picture of one of them. He's a monk in England and I inadvertently photographed him in Borley church while he was leafing through a great big book.

"A better example of this," Ed goes on, "is a case that happened a few years ago here in America. A family of seven grown children and their recently widowed father had a ghost in their home, all right, but it was a little more than that—the spirit was the apparition of the mother. About two months before the family called on us, the woman had been driving her own 65-year-old mother back from Christmas shopping when it began to snow quite heavily. Anxious to get home before the storm took hold, this lady hit a bad spot on the road. The car slammed into a tree, killing both women instantly. Though the grandmother passed on immediately, the mother did not.

"Why did she stay behind in spirit form? Because the final thing on her mind was to get home: and that's where she went, but as a *spirit.* Soon after the accident, unusual movements began to occur in the house. After a few months, it became apparent that the source of the activity was the mother's spirit. I say *apparent* because the more sensitive of the children saw her in a semi-materialized state, watering plants, straightening the beds, closing cupboard doors; in the middle of the night when it was cold, she'd shut the windows—things like that. In her new state of awareness, this woman was totally *un*aware that she was now discarnate."

How could a person be oblivious to being a ghost?

"Well, it's a lot like an amputation. A person may think his amputated leg is there when it's not. For the ghost it's the same thing, only in the spirit's case, the *whole* body is amputated away.

"Nevertheless, in that case, I had to use a deep-trance medium to communicate with this woman," Ed concludes. "It was a long, emotional sitting. At first, I got the 'Not-me-*I'm*-no-ghost' routine, because she naturally refused to accept the fact that she was dead. Eventually, though, that afternoon we *were* able to get the woman to transition correctly as a spirit. The phenomena in the house stopped immediately, of course. To some, it might seem cruel to send this woman on, but the human spirit is no pet. Therefore, it was imperative for this woman to know her condition. Otherwise, in the future, when the family moved away or also died, she'd still be fixed in her earthbound state. Once again, tragedy and unresolve are the watchwords of the ghost syndrome."

Communication with a ghostly entity ordinarily takes place by means of mental telepathy. This is the process Lorraine used at West Point. It was not necessary for Greer to display himself in order to communicate; telepathy was perfectly sufficient to get the job done.

Telepathy, a latent ability in everyone, is a form of thought transference. Instead of an idea being projected vocally, it is projected directly *by the brain.* Just like the eyes and ears, the brain—the most complex organ of the body—is also an organ of perception. Put another way, the brain can handle sense data the other five senses cannot. Spirits find this "sixth" sense the easiest to use as a channel of communication; however, what is not commonly understood is that thought transference is a *physical* phenomenon.

"Thought has substance," Ed explains, "and the substance of thought is vibrations. *All* sense data, regardless of type, come to us by means of vibrations. Our body is like one great big antenna with specialized receivers to collect these specialized vibrations. Like radio waves, these vibrations can't be seen, although they are all around us. Not only thoughts, but everything in the world has its own unique vibration, its own special frequency. Because each frequency is different, the brain is able to physically sort one thing out from another.

"The one hitch is that it's impossible for the human brain to distinguish between a real physical sound and the psychically-created *impression* of that sound. The frequency is identical. So when a ghost communicates by telepathy, it is no more or less than the transfer of vibrations from one mind to another. The result is communication. Of course, it follows that there would be no communication from the other side unless there was an intelligence, a mind, generating telepathic vibrations to the physical realm."

As young artists, Ed and Lorraine discovered that much of the phenomena in haunted houses could be attributed to the workings of earthbound spirits. They learned in time that these discarnate entities—though sometimes responsible for frightening phenomena—did not really exist for a sinister purpose. Furthermore, despite the strange activity these earthbound human spirits were able to bring about, they did not have truly mysterious powers.

In some rare cases, however, it was evident to the Warrens there was another category of phenomena altogether. Forces active in these homes had powers that *were* truly mysterious. "Many times," says Lorraine, "we would arrive at the site while the disturbance was still occurring. We would see the activity *ourselves*, firsthand. But most of all, I'd have to say the deportment of the people told the real story. We'd go into a home, and the family would be frightened senseless from what they'd seen or experienced. In those days, too, there were few if any institutes or agencies for people to call on, so many times these families would have to weather these incredible assaults by malicious spirits alone. By the time we arrived, they'd often be worn out, spent by the unrelenting phenomena going on around them. And though many of these folks were being harassed half out of their minds, a lot of times they didn't realize that spirits— not to mention *demonic* spirits—were often responsible. There was nothing debatable about what was happening to these people: they were under siege. Ultimately, what Ed and I got out of these early experiences was an understanding that there was a spirit behind the phenomena, *but* that spirit was far worse, far more threatening than a mere ghost."

"A ghost is essentially a passive entity with limited powers and abilities. Usually, it will manifest at random, attempt to communicate, and then dissipate from view. It works out to a cycle: manifestation, communication, dissipation," states Ed. "And other than make itself known, the ghost only rarely *does* anything. We came to find the ordinary earthbound human spirit to be a loner, caught up in a personal problem, seeking resolve to its primary nature. The ghost behaved in predictable ways, either wanting to communicate its plight or be left alone to contemplate its own misfortune. However, these other cases bore no markings whatsoever of the earthbound spirit. The enormous upheaval, the negative phenomena, the shock and terror indicated that something *else* was at work."

In the worst cases, the Warrens walked into situations where things would be running completely amuck. Whereas a relatively docile human spirit might levitate a pencil or break a cherished teacup, here the whole house would be ruined in a deliberate, orderly way. Not infrequently, people in the home would be attacked, mentally *and* physically. At first the Warrens attributed these disturbances to gangs of spirits, perhaps marauding after death as they once had on earth. But this hopeful explanation never bore out, for this was a phenomenon with a purpose—something that *was* possessed of a mysterious intelligence—something that bespoke an absolutely wicked wisdom.

While a ghost would manifest at any time, day or night, this species of phenomenon occurred most frequently in the absence of natural light. Disturbances tended to begin after sunset and end before sunrise. And unlike the ghost, which requires light energy to manifest, this thing was black when visible to the human eye, and desisted in the presence of light. It came in a large, formless mass, typically described by witnesses as "blacker than natural black."

Moreover, everything associated with the spirit was terrifying and negative. Quite distinct from a ghost, which would vanish if fear was aroused, this spirit only *intensified* in an atmosphere of fear. Its arrival was accompanied by a sense of utter terror and foreboding; an undeniable sense of evil and wild animosity would fill the room. Often a foul, revolting stench—of sulfur, excrement, or rotting flesh—would fill the area where it materialized; many times it would leave behind a residue of blood and other bodily fluids. And like a beacon, it projected an unmitigating sense of hate and destructive jealousy; its every action was cruel, violent, and wrong. Furthermore, the Warrens noted, when these bizarre entities were present they played dirty, used foul language, and caused injury.

In case after case, the phenomena the Warrens came across bore the same foul, terrifying imprint. What *was* this depraved force of hate and violence? Eventually, however, they no longer needed to guess, for to make itself known, this spirit often left deliberate, forthright clues: upside-down crosses, piles of excrement, pools of

urine. Indeed, it often boldly wrote what it was, usually on mirrors—
backwards, from right to left:

DEMONIC

Or more straightforwardly:

DEATHTOGOD

"When it didn't scrawl blasphemies," says Ed, "then it would
scribble debasing, vulgar obscenities. The first time I saw these filthy
markings, I thought someone in the house had a *really* sick mind.
Naively, I tried to wipe these graffiti off the walls and mirrors so that
Lorraine wouldn't be exposed to them. But no sooner did I wipe
them clean than they'd appear again in front of my eyes. It soon
became apparent to me this wasn't the work of human beings—*or*
human spirits.

"At first," Ed admits, "the whole concept of demoniacal phenomena was incomprehensible to me, as I'm sure it would have been
for anyone caught up in the same situation. Yet it was also apparent to me that these disturbances were totally unlike those brought
on by earthbound human spirits. Not only did these entities write
on walls, in rare cases they even *spoke*—with a physicalized voice.
Still, neither Lorraine nor I could accept it. These consistently negative powers were so powerful and menacing that we did our best to
avoid them in our work. Just to be in the vicinity of the phenomenon was emotionally abysmal. Although I knew we were making
real progress categorizing the behavior of the earthbound human
spirit, this was something we never planned on."

For Ed Warren, discovery of the demonic realm was not some
end point in an overblown religious quest. He had not gone out in
the world and found "demons" to suit his fancy. "We came across
this activity inadvertently, in the process of our investigations. *It*

was there when we walked in. But unlike human spirits, these things were nothing to mess with. We kept our distance and studied their workings as much as we could, while helping the person or family involved. Only later did we find out how viciously these inhuman entities attacked any religious emblem—and then, how grave a problem the demonic really is to the pious clergy." Could the Warrens' religious beliefs possibly affect what they see? It rather seems that a person would be more prone to perceive supernatural activity if he or she believed in it first.

"That sounds reasonable," Ed agrees, "but what we've seen in our work couldn't have been influenced by what we believe. We have no reason to put our thumb on the scale: we're not Bible thumpers; we don't charge money for our services; and we're both physically and mentally fit. You have to understand that we're called in by other people who are *already* experiencing troublesome activity. Their children have suddenly begun acting peculiar, or things are flying around the house and they don't know why it's happening or how to stop it; so eventually these people call on us for help. When Lorraine and I get involved, it's *after* the disturbance has erupted, not before—at which time we do our best to identify the source of the disturbance, and act accordingly to stop it, or bring in someone who can.

"These days," says Ed, "people who aren't familiar with the problem like to philosophize about the demonic as being a purely psychological event, or say it's not even there at all. But these people have never witnessed the phenomena themselves, or they would not make such empty statements. Just *once*, they need the experience of walking into a home where these inhuman spirits have manifested.

"Outside, neighbors will be milling around on the sidewalk. They instinctively know something is wrong. When you go inside, the family is liable to be sobbing or huddled together in terror, totally petrified from some horror they've been through. Their clothes could be half torn off. In the air, there may be a powerful stench of sulfur, ozone, or excrement. If there is possession, that individual is liable to come at you like a hulking monster. Objects will be levitating. The inside of the house may be completely vandalized by unseen forces; everything, big and small, turned over and broken. Very often there will be incredible poundings coming from the walls. And *on* the walls themselves, there are liable to be obscene or antireligious statements written by unseen hands in any of a dozen languages. Things will materialize and dematerialize right in front of your eyes. Religious objects will be desecrated or hung conspicuously upside down. Little fires may be flickering on the corners of chairs; the curtains may already have gone up in flames. Sheer havoc! And over it all there'll be an atmosphere of evil so thick you could cut it with a knife. Ungodly screams, deep baleful moaning, or maniacal laughter will rise up, enough to make your blood run cold. Then, somewhere along the line—if you're unlucky—the spirit itself may come through the doorway, or the wall, or manifest behind you and suddenly it all becomes quite clear this is not some explainable twist of fantasy. This is a real physical attack on humankind that occurs in a purposeful, directed way."

Curiously, the Warrens came to find that the phenomena brought about by inhuman spirits occurred in stages. In the beginning, the activity was relatively mild as the spirit took hold, cautious not to cause alarm. However, not everyone was subject to the phenomena. Often specific individuals were singled out for encroachment or attack. And there was a reason *why* they would be a target—as two young nurses recently found out.

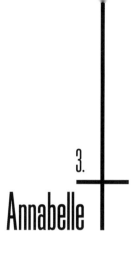

3.
Annabelle

When the telephone rings at the Warrens' house, and a somber-toned clergyman on the other end of the line asks for Ed Warren, there's a better than even chance that something serious has happened. Such was the case with "Annabelle."

The referral this time came from an Episcopal priest. Calling from the Church's administrative offices in Connecticut, the clergyman was relaying a message he'd received from a minister elsewhere in the state. Though the information the priest had was sketchy, he none-theless told Ed Warren that two young nurses had "communicated" with what they took to be a human spirit. The priest doubted that was the case, however, because the plea for help included the fact that one of the girls' friends had been attacked—physically. Though the wounds were not serious, activity was still in progress, and one of the girls seemed to think there was something alien inside her apartment "Would you," he asked, "investigate the case further, and as a demo-nologist, recommend if any formal church action should be taken?"

Agreeing with the clergyman's assessment that something of a negative spirit nature might conceivably be at work, Ed Warren accepted the referral. With that, the priest gave Ed the phone number and names of the two young women. After speaking with the priest,

Ed immediately called the number he'd been given. Upon reaching one of the nurses, Ed verified the existence of the problem and told the young women that he and Lorraine were on their way. . . .

Though traffic was light on the Interstate that day, it took the Warrens well over an hour to reach the address of the modern, low-rise apartment complex. After parking the car, the Warrens walked up to the front door and Ed rang the bell. He carried with him a tape recorder, camera, and black attaché case. Footsteps soon approached from inside. Bolt locks were unsnapped, and the door was opened by Deirdre Bernard, an attractive but sober-faced young lady of twenty-five. Ed and Lorraine Warren introduced themselves, and were then ushered into the apartment

The young nurse led the Warrens through a spacious living room into the kitchen. There Cal Randell and his fiancée, Lara Clifton, sat at the table drinking coffee. Deirdre introduced the Warrens to them, but the young people said very little. The serious, drawn look on their faces said it all. The Warrens then took a seat with the others at the table. After loading a cassette into the recorder, Ed switched on the machine and entered the time, date, address, and full names of the principals.

"Okay," Ed began, "I'd like to hear the whole story, right from the beginning. Who here can tell me?"

"I can," said Deirdre.

"All right. Cal, Lara, please add any details she leaves out," Ed directed.

"There are two stories, really," Deirdre said. "One that began earlier in the week with Cal. The other one's about Annabelle. But I suppose they're both about Annabelle. I'm not sure."

"Who's Annabelle?" Ed promptly asked.

"She belongs to Deirdre," Lara replied.

"*Belongs?*" questioned Lorraine. "Is Annabelle a live, breathing being?"

"*Is* she alive?" Deirdre repeated quizzically. "She moves. She acts alive. But no, I don't think she's alive."

"Annabelle's in the living room," said Lara, pointing across the table. "She's sitting on the sofa."

Lorraine looked to her left, into the living room. "Are you talking about the *doll*?"

"That's right," Lara replied, "the big Raggedy Ann doll. That's Annabelle. She moves!"

Ed got up and walked into the living room to inspect the doll. It was big and heavy, the size of a four-year-old child, sitting with its legs stretched out on the sofa. The black pupil-less eyes stared back at him, while the painted-on smile gave the doll an expression of grim irony. Looking it over without touching the thing, Ed then returned to the kitchen.

"Where did the doll come from?" Ed asked Deirdre.

"It was a gift," Deirdre replied. "My mother gave it to me on my last birthday."

"Is there some reason why she bought you a doll?" Ed wanted to know.

"No. It was just something novel—a decoration," the young nurse answered.

"Okay," Ed went on, "when did you first start noticing activity occur?"

"About a year ago," said Deirdre. "The doll started to move around the apartment *by itself*. I don't mean it got up and walked around, or any such thing. I mean when we'd come home from work it would never be quite where we left it."

"Explain that part a little more," Ed requested.

"After I got the doll for my birthday," Deirdre explained, "I put it on my bed each morning after the bed was made. The arms would be off to its sides and its legs would be straight out—just like it's sitting there now. But when we'd come home at night, the arms and legs would be positioned in different gestures. For instance, its legs would be crossed at the ankles, or its arms would be folded in its lap. After a week or so, this made us suspicious. So, to test it, I purposely crossed its arms and legs in the morning to see if it really was moving. And sure enough, every night when we'd come back home, the arms and legs would be uncrossed and the thing would be sitting there in any of a dozen different postures."

"Yea, but it did *more* than that," Lara put in. "The doll also changed rooms by itself. We came home one night and the Annabelle doll was sitting in a chair by the front door. It was kneeling! The funny thing about it was, when *we* tried to make the doll kneel, it'd just fall over. It *couldn't* kneel. Other times we'd find it sitting on the sofa, although when we left the apartment in the morning, it'd be in Deirdre's room with the door closed!"

"Anything else?" Lorraine asked.

"Yes," said Deirdre. "It would leave us little notes and messages. The handwriting looked to be that of a small child."

"What'd the notes say?" questioned Ed.

"It would say things that meant nothing to us," Deirdre answered. "Things would be written like HELP US or HELP CAL, but Cal wasn't in any kind of jeopardy at the time. And who 'us' was—we didn't know. Still, the thing that was weird was that the notes would be written in pencil, but when we tried to find one, there was not one pencil in the apartment! And the paper it wrote on was *parchment*. I tore the apartment apart, looking for parchment paper, but again neither of us had any such thing."

"It sounds like someone had a key to your apartment and was playing a sick joke on you," Ed stated flatly.

"That's exactly what we thought," said Deirdre. "So we did little things like put marks on the windows and doors or arranged the rugs so that anyone who came in here would leave a trace that we could see. But never once did it turn out that there was a real outside intruder."

"While the doll was moving around, and we'd become suspicious of burglars, something else screwy happened," Lara added next. "The Annabelle doll was sitting on Deirdre's bed, as was usual. When we came home one night, there was blood on the back of its hand, and there were three drops of blood on its chest!"

"God, that really scared us," Deirdre said frankly.

"Did you notice any other kind of phenomena occur in the apartment?" Ed asked them.

"One time around Christmas we found a little chocolate boot on the stereo that none of us had bought. Presumably it came from Annabelle," said Lara.

"When did you come to determine there was a spirit associated with the doll?" questioned Lorraine.

"We knew something unusual was going on," Deirdre answered. "The doll *did* change rooms by itself. It *did* pose in different gestures: we all saw it. But we wanted to know why. Was there maybe some plausible reason why the doll was moving? So Lara and I got in touch with a woman who's a medium. That was about a month, or maybe six weeks after all this stuff started to happen."

"What did you find out?"

"We learned that a little girl died on this property," Deirdre told the Warrens. "She was seven years old and her name was Annabelle—Annabelle Higgins. The Annabelle spirit said she played in the fields long ago before these apartments were built. They were 'happy times' for her, she told us. Because everyone around here was grown-up, and only concerned with their jobs, there was no one she could relate to, except us. Annabelle felt that we would be able to understand her. That's why she began moving the rag doll. All Annabelle wanted was to be loved, and so she asked if she could stay with us and move into the doll. What could we do? So we said yes."

"Wait a minute here," Ed interjected. "What do you mean it wanted to *move into* the doll? Do you mean it proposed to possess it?"

"Right, that was the understanding," Deirdre replied. "It seemed harmless enough. We're nurses, you know, we see suffering every day. We had compassion. Anyway, we called the doll Annabelle from that time on."

"Did you do anything different with the doll after you learned it was supposedly possessed by a little girl spirit named Annabelle?" asked Lorraine.

"Not really," said Deirdre. "But of course it wasn't just a doll any more. *It was Annabelle.* We couldn't ignore that fact."

"All right, before you go any further, let's back up a minute," Ed requested. "First you got the doll for your birthday. After a while the doll began to move—or at least change places enough for you to notice it. This made you curious, so you decided to have a séance, and a spirit came across that called itself Annabelle Higgins. This supposed little girl spirit was seven years old and asked if it could come live with you by possessing the toy doll. You said yes, out of compassion. Then you renamed the doll Annabelle. Right?"

"Right," said Deirdre and Lara.

"Have you seen the ghost of a little girl at any time in this apartment?" Ed asked.

"No," both the girls answered.

"You said a chocolate item showed up here once," said Ed. "Has anything else strange ever happened that you couldn't explain?"

"One time a statue lifted up across the room," Deirdre recalled, "then it tumbled in the air and fell on the floor. None of us were near the statue—it was on the other side of the room. That incident frightened us totally."

"Let me ask you something else," Ed went on. "Didn't you think that maybe you shouldn't have given the doll so much recognition?"

"It wasn't a doll!" Deirdre corrected him. "It was the spirit of Annabelle we cared about!"

"That's right!" said Lara.

"I mean, *before* you knew anything about Annabelle?"

"How were we to know anything?" Deirdre asked. "But looking back on it now, maybe we shouldn't have given the doll so much credence. But really, we saw the thing as being no more than a harmless mascot. It never hurt anything . . . at least until the other day."

"Do you still think what's moving the doll is the spirit of a little girl?" Lorraine queried.

"What else could it be?" Lara said in reply.

"It's a damn voodoo doll, that's what it is," Cal blurted out. "I told them about that thing a long time ago. The doll was just taking advantage of them. . . ."

"Okay, Cal, I think it's time you told your side of things," Ed remarked to the young man.

"Let me put it this way: I didn't like the doll, and the doll didn't like me right back," he said. "The thing's got a mind, and dolls don't have minds, right? So, from the beginning, I didn't think this thing moving around their apartment was cute."

"Beyond that, tell me about what's happened to you," said Ed.

"Tell them about the dreams," coaxed Lara.

"Well," Cal picked up, "the thing gives me bad dreams. Recurrent ones. But yet what I'm going to tell you is not a dream as far as I'm concerned, because I somehow saw this happen to me. The last time it happened I fell asleep at home, a really deep sleep. While I was lying there, I saw myself wake up. Something seemed wrong to me. I looked around the room, but nothing was out of place. But then when I looked down toward my feet, I saw the rag doll, Annabelle. It was slowly gliding up my body. It moved over my chest and stopped. Then it put its two arms out. One arm touched one side of my neck, the other touched the other side like it was making an electrical connection. Then I saw myself being strangled. I was writhing and trying to push the doll off my chest, but I might as well have been pushing on a wall, because it *wouldn't* move. I was literally strangling to death, but I couldn't help myself, no matter how hard I tried."

"Yes, but the priest I spoke with said you'd been *physically* attacked. Is this what you consider to be a physical attack?" Ed pressed him.

"No," Cal asserted. "That happened here in this apartment when Lara and I were alone together. It was about ten or eleven o'clock at night, and we were reading over maps because I was going off on a trip the next day. Everything was quiet at the time. Suddenly, we both heard sounds in Deirdre's bedroom that made us think that someone had broken into the apartment. I quietly got up and tip-toed to the bedroom door, which was closed. I waited until the noises stopped, then I carefully opened the door and reached in and switched on the light. Nobody was in there! Except, the Annabelle doll was tossed on the floor in a corner. I went in alone and walked over to the thing to see if anything unusual had happened. But as I got close to the doll, I got the distinct impression that somebody was behind me. I swung around instantly and, well. . . "

"He won't talk about that part," Lara said. "When Cal turned around there wasn't anybody there, but he suddenly yelled and grabbed for his chest. He was doubled over, cut and bleeding when I got to him. Blood was all over his shirt. Cal was shaking and scared and we went back out into the living room. We then opened up his shirt and there on his chest was what looked to be a sort of claw mark!"

"Can I see the mark?" Ed asked.

"It's gone now," the young man told him.

"*I* saw the cuts on his chest too," Deirdre spoke up in support.

"How many were there?" Ed asked.

"Seven," said Lara. "Three were vertical; four were horizontal."

"Did the cuts have any sensation?"

"All the cuts were hot, like they were burns," Cal told him.

"Did you ever have cuts or wounds in the same area of your chest before this incident happened?" questioned Ed.

"No," the young man replied.

"Did you lose consciousness before or after the attack took place?"

"No," was his answer again.

"How long did it take the wounds to heal?" Lorraine then wanted to know.

"They healed up almost immediately," said Cal. "They were half-gone the next day, and fully gone the day after."

"Has anything else happened since that time?" asked Ed.

"No," came the joint reply.

"Who did you first contact after the incident occurred?"

"I contacted an Episcopal priest named Father Kevins," Deirdre told Ed and Lorraine.

"Why did you decide to call him instead of a doctor?" Lorraine asked.

"Do you think someone off the street would have believed where that claw mark on Cal's chest came from?" Deirdre asked rhetorically. "Besides, we agreed the cuts weren't half as important as *how* Cal got them. We wanted to know if this was going to happen *again*. Our problem was who to ask?"

"Was there some reason why you specifically called on Father Kevins?" Lorraine questioned.

"Yes. We trust him," said Deirdre. "He teaches nearby here, at a junior college, plus Lara and I both know him."

"What did you tell the priest?" asked Ed.

"The whole story—about Annabelle and how it moved on its own, and especially about Cal's cuts," Deirdre replied. "At first we were afraid he might not believe us, but that was no problem—he believed us all right. Although," she finished, "he said he'd never heard of such a thing happening these days. At the time we were all scared out of our wits, and I asked him what he thought had happened to us?"

"What'd he tell you?" Ed asked her.

"He said he didn't want to speculate," replied Deirdre. "But he did seem to feel it was a spiritual matter, possibly an important one, and said he was going to contact someone higher up in the Church—a Father Everett."

"That's what he did," Ed told her.

Lara then asked the Warrens concernedly, "What do *you* think did that to Cal's chest?"

"Let's discuss that in a minute," Ed answered. "First, to finish up, let me just ask you a few questions. Has this kind of thing ever happened to you before—to any of you?"

"No," they told the Warrens.

"Did the name Annabelle, or Annabelle Higgins mean anything to you in real life before this incident occurred?"

"No," they again answered.

"Although you never saw anything spiritwise in here, Cal said he felt a presence in the room before he got hurt . . . "

"There *is* something in here," Lara stated firmly. "In fact, I can't even stand to be here. We decided to get a new apartment. We're moving out!"

"I'm afraid that's not going to help you very much," Ed said dryly.

"What do you mean?" Deirdre asked, astonished.

"To put it in a nutshell, folks, you inadvertently brought a spirit into this apartment—and into your lives. You're not going to be able to walk away from it that easily."

Ed's statement was understandably troubling. Prudently, he and Lorraine remained silent and allowed the three young people to collect their thoughts.

After a long minute, Ed spoke again. "We're going to be able to help you, beginning right now. Today. The first thing I'd like to do is to call Father Everett and have him come over here. Then you're going to have to understand what has happened and why Cal got that ugly claw mark on his chest. May I use the phone?"

Ed had no trouble getting hold of the Episcopal priest who had been waiting for him to telephone. Lorraine, in the meantime, walked into the living room to discern the spirit presence that was in the apartment. After the phone call, the Warrens both returned to the kitchen with the others.

"All right," Ed said matter of factly, "when Father Everett comes here, he's going to have to perform a sort of blessing, an . . . exorcism of the premises."

"I knew it!" Cal proclaimed. "I knew it would lead to this."

"Yes, I think you did," Ed told him. "But I'm not sure any of you know the reason why. To begin with, *there is no Annabelle!* There never was. You were duped. However, we *are* dealing with a spirit here. The teleportation of the doll while you were out of the apartment; the appearance of notes written on parchment; the manifestation of three symbolic drops of blood; plus the gestures the doll made are all meaningful. They tell me there was *intent*, which means there was an intelligence behind the activity. But ghosts—human spirits—plain and simply can't bring on phenomena of this nature and intensity. They don't have the power. Instead, what's taken over here is something *in*human."

"Inhuman?" Cal asked, perplexed.

"*Demonic,*" Ed told him immediately. "Ordinarily, people are never bothered by inhuman demonic spirits, unless they do something to bring the force into their lives. And, I regret to say, you girls did something to bring the demonic into your lives."

"Like what?" Deirdre urgently wanted to know.

"Well, for the most part, you made honest mistakes, but in this case, you made the *wrong* mistakes," replied Ed. "Your first mistake was to have given the doll so much recognition. You see, the reason why the spirit moved the doll in the first place was to draw attention to itself. Once it had your attention, it exploited you. Rather than reciprocating your care and concern, it simply brought you fear and even injury. This is the nature of the inhuman spirit: it's negative, it enjoys inflicting pain. Right at the very beginning you should have been intolerant of the unnatural activity. However, instead of cutting the thing off at the start, it aroused your curiosity, and that fact got noticed—supernaturally.

"Your next mistake was in calling a medium," Ed went on. "Whoever functioned as the medium was unwittingly used as an instrument of communication by the entity. During the sitting, this inhuman spirit fed you false information. The demonic is a liar. It's even been called the Father of Lies. Well, you were lied to—by a spirit of deception—and unknowingly you believed the lie. Your worst mistake, though, was in giving the spirit the *permission* it needed to 'move into the doll.' That's what it wanted and it preyed off your ignorance of its existence to do so."

"Why?" asked Lara.

"Because to really interfere in your life, the demonic has somehow got to get your permission to do so. And unfortunately, through your own free will, you gave it that permission. It was like handing a maniac a loaded gun."

"Then the doll is possessed?" questioned Deirdre.

"No, the doll is not possessed. Spirits don't possess things: spirits possess *people*," Ed informed her. "Instead, the spirit simply moved the doll around and gave it the illusion of being alive. But because you girls believed this was the spirit of a little girl, Annabelle, the appearance and reality were the same to you. In short, you left yourselves wide open, and a deceptive, negative spirit took advantage of you—with your permission, of course. This is how the phenomenon was brought on."

Ed paused to see if there were any further questions, but none were asked.

"Now, what happened to Cal earlier this week," Ed proceeded, "was bound to occur sooner or later. In fact, you all stood in jeopardy of coming under possession by this spirit; this is what the thing was really after. But Cal here didn't believe in the charade, so he was an ongoing threat to the entity. One way or another, there was bound to be a showdown. And what happened? For starters it tried to strangle Cal to death. When that failed, it cut him with a symbolic claw mark. We've seen this claw mark in other cases: it's a telltale sign of an inhuman presence. You got off easy this time. Had this spirit been given another week or two, you might all have been killed."

"Is this—this . . . demonic spirit in the apartment now?" Lara asked, petrified.

"Yes, I'm afraid so," Lorraine answered her. "There is only one entity involved, but its behavior is completely unpredictable."

The Warrens' words seemed to hit home. "You're for real, aren't you?" Deirdre said incredulously.

The front doorbell rang. Father Everett had arrived. The interview session ended in the kitchen as Deirdre got up and answered the door. With the sun about to go down in an hour, Ed was eager to have the house blessed, remove the doll, and return home.

As the Warrens packed up their gear, Father Everett—whom Ed and Lorraine had never met in person—came into the kitchen. A tall, middle-aged man, the Episcopal priest was clearly uncomfortable in his role as exorcist. Once the preliminary greetings were out of the way, Ed then told the priest that in his judgment the spirit that was responsible for the malicious activity was inhuman, that it was still in the apartment, and the only way it could be made to leave was through the power of the words written in the exorcism-blessing.

"I'm not totally familiar with demonology," admitted Father Everett. "How do you know such a spirit is behind the disturbance?"

"Well, in this case, it wasn't all that difficult to determine," Ed said frankly. "These spirits work in characteristic ways. What's going on here is essentially the infestation stage of the phenomenon. A spirit, in this case an inhuman demonic spirit, began moving the doll around the apartment through teleportation and other means. Once it aroused the girls' curiosity—which was the spirit's purpose in moving the doll—they made the predictable mistake of bringing a medium in here, who took matters a step further. She told them, in the trance state, that a little girl spirit named Annabelle was moving the doll. Communicating through the medium, the entity preyed on the girls' emotional vulnerabilities, and during the séance managed to extract permission from them to go about its business. Insofar as the demonic is a negative spirit, it then set about causing patently negative phenomena to occur: it aroused *fear* through the weird movements of the doll; it brought about the *materialization* of disturbing handwritten notes; it left a residue of *blood* on the doll; and ultimately it even *struck* the young man, Cal, on the chest with a bloody claw mark.

"Beyond the activity, Lorraine has also discerned that this inhuman spirit is with us now. Lorraine's an excellent clairvoyant, and she's never been wrong about the nature of a spirit that's present. However, if you want to go a step further, we can challenge the entity right now with religious provocation. You'll be able to see for yourself. . . ."

"No, I don't think so," replied Father Everett. "Why don't I just do what has to be done?"

In this case, the recitation of the exorcism-blessing took the priest about five minutes to perform in each room of the apartment. The Episcopal blessing of a home is a wordy, seven-page document that is distinctly positive in nature. Rather than specifically expelling evil entities from the dwelling, the emphasis is instead directed toward filling the home with the power of the positive—the power of God.

There was no trouble or mishap during the procedure. When

he was finished, the priest then blessed the individuals who were present, and after doing so, declared all was well. Lorraine also confirmed that the apartment and the people were free from the infesting spirit entity.

Ed and Lorraine's work done, they then took their leave and started for home. At Deirdre's request, and as a further precaution against the phenomena ever occurring in the apartment again, the Warrens took the big rag doll along with them. Placing Annabelle in the back seat of the car, Ed decided it was safer to avoid traveling on the Interstate, in case the entity had not been separated from the rag doll. His hunch was correct.

In no time at all, Ed and Lorraine Warren felt themselves the object of a vicious hatred. Then, at each dangerous curve in the road, their new car began to stall, causing the power steering and brakes to fail. Repeatedly, the car verged on collision. Of course, it would have been easy to stop and throw the doll into the woods. But if the profane item didn't simply "teleport" back to the girls' apartment, at the least, it would place anyone who found it in jeopardy.

The third time the car stalled along the road, Ed reached into his black bag, took out a vial, and threw a sprinkling of holy water on the rag doll, making the sign of the cross over it. The disturbance in the car stopped immediately, allowing the Warrens to reach home safely.

For the next few days, Ed sat the doll in a chair next to his desk. The doll levitated a number of times in the beginning, then it seemed to fall inert.

During the ensuing weeks, however, it began showing up in various rooms of the house. When the Warrens were away and had the doll locked up in the outer office building, they would often return to find it sitting comfortably upstairs in Ed's easy chair when they opened the main front door.

It also turned out that Annabelle came with a "friend," a black cat, that would occasionally materialize beside the doll. The cat would stalk once around the floor, taking particular notice of books and other objects in Ed's office; then return to the doll's side, and dematerialize from the head down.

It also became apparent that Annabelle hated clergymen. During the follow-up process on the case, it was necessary for the Warrens to consult the Episcopal priests associated with the incident in the young nurses' apartment. Returning home alone one evening, Lorraine was terrified by loud, rolling growls that reverberated throughout the house. Later, when she was listening to the playback on the telephone answering machine, there were back-to-back calls from Father Kevins. Between his two calls was recorded the incredible growling noises she'd heard earlier in the house.

One day Father Daniel Mills, a Catholic exorcist, had been working with Ed and asked about the new addition to the office—Annabelle.

Ed told Father Daniel about the case and gave him the paperwork for his review. After hearing Ed's account of what had happened, the priest picked up the rag doll and off-handedly said: "You're just a rag doll, Annabelle. You can't hurt anything." The priest then tossed the stuffed figure back on the chair.

"That's one thing you'd better not say again," Ed warned him with a laugh. Yet, when Father Daniel stopped to say good-bye to Lorraine, upon leaving an hour later, she pleaded that he be especially careful driving, and insisted that he call her just as soon as he arrived at the rectory. "I discerned tragedy for that young priest," says Lorraine, "but he had to go his way."

A few hours later the telephone rang. "Lorraine," said Father Daniel, "why did you tell me to be careful driving?"

"Because," she told him, "your car would go out of control: you would have an accident"

"Well, you were right," he stated flatly. "The brake system failed: I was almost killed in a traffic accident. My car is a wreck."

Later in the year, at a large social gathering at the Warrens' home, Lorraine and Father Daniel went into the den to chat for a few moments. By a strange coincidence, Annabelle had moved into that room the day before. While speaking with Lorraine, the priest saw an ornamental wall decoration make a quick movement Suddenly, the twenty-four inch long Boar's tooth necklace above them exploded with percussive force. Hearing this stunning noise, other guests immediately converged on the room, at which time someone in the crowd had the foresight to snap a photograph. When developed, the print was otherwise normal—except above the doll were two beacons of bright light, both pointing in the direction of Father Daniel Mills.

"On another occasion," Ed recounts, "I was in my office, working with a police detective on a case that concerned a witchcraft-related murder in the area. As a cop he's seen every kind of crime; he's definitely not the sort of man who gets 'scared.'

"While we were talking, Lorraine called me upstairs to take a long distance call. I told the detective he was free to look around in my office, but to be careful and not touch any of the objects, because they'd come from cases where the demonic had been invoked.

"Well, I wasn't away any more than five minutes when upstairs came this detective stark white. When I asked him what had happened, he refused to tell me," Ed remembers, breaking into a grin. "He just kept mumbling 'The doll, the rag doll is *real*. . . . ' He was talking about Annabelle, of course. That little doll made a believer out of him! In fact, as I think back on it, any meetings I've had with the detective from that day on have always been in *his* office."

"Just last week, a similar incident occurred here," Lorraine adds. "While Ed was away in Scotland, we had a carpenter over to build additional bookshelves in his office. The carpenter came upstairs and asked me if I'd move the Raggedy Ann doll to another place so he could continue working. In all honesty, the doll scares me. But Ed wasn't around, so I had to move it

"Profane objects like the Annabelle doll have their own aura. When you touch them, your human aura mingles with theirs. This change immediately attracts spirits; it's almost like setting off a fire alarm. Therefore, for protection, I blessed myself with holy water then 'blessed' the rag doll with holy water in the sign of the cross. When I asked the carpenter if he wanted to bless himself too, he gave me a kind of accommodating smile, saying he didn't believe in spirits or religion, and told me he'd pass on the holy business.

"Now, our tabby cat, Marcie, had been lying around in Ed's office as she always does. Just as soon as I picked up Annabelle to move her across the room, Marcie's hair raised up and she began screeching in pained terror. She edged over to the outside door and began making a strange-sounding call I've never heard a cat make before. Marcie wouldn't stop until I opened the office door and let her out in the sunlight. The carpenter watched all this in amazement. Then, without saying a word, he reached over, took the holy water bottle from my hand," she says, smiling openly, "and promptly blessed himself with it. Like I say when we're doing field work—I've never met an atheist in a haunted house."

"It's difficult for people to accept the existence of something they've been conditioned *not* to believe in," Ed asserts. "Still, *lack* of knowledge allowed this negative spirit to wrangle its way into the lives of three unwary young people. Had they known such sinister spirits exist, then it's quite likely that today a young man would not have been physically struck with the mark of the beast."

Many, nevertheless, contend that the notion of spirits is irrational or unfounded. They say the phenomenon is an illusion, or a hallucination, or that it doesn't exist at all. At best, the activity can be explained away by science. Or can it? Recently, the Warrens broached this very subject on nationwide television.

The real Annabelle doll locked away in her cabinet.

4.

Unnatural Phenomena

An hour and a half after leaving Connecticut, Ed and Lorraine Warren sit in an off-stage lounge waiting to tape The David Susskind Show in New York City,

The show's theme that night is "The Occult," and during the opening segment three folks tell what it's like to live in a haunted house. The Warrens will be featured on the remainder of the program in a panel discussion with Father Alphonsus Trabold, Dr. Alex Tanous, and two psychic researchers they've just met. Father Trabold, a long-time friend of Ed and Lorraine, is a Franciscan friar and professor of theology. He is also an expert on demonology and paranormal phenomena. Dr. Tanous is a respected psychic and theologian who teaches at the University of Southern Maine. To this group watching on the monitor, it quickly becomes apparent that the real theme of the show is not so much the occult in general, but spirit phenomena in particular.

When the opening segment is through, these experts and authors move from the green room to their place on the set. Following the commercial break, David Susskind guides the discussion right to the point: "Is this phenomenon real—or is it just some quirk of man's mind?"

Providing parapsychological explanations, Dr. Tanous and other guests supply the judgment that much of the phenomena is caused by psychokinesis—the power of mind over matter. Father Trabold and the Warrens agree with their explanations, but also warn that some of the activity *is* caused by an external agency. They also add that it is foolish, if not dangerous, to underestimate unusual happenings in a home, especially those which might actually be demoniacal in origin. The Warrens further explain that the Amityville case was not a hoax, and the preposterous, often fantastic phenomena reported by the principals in the case were *indicative* of the strategy of the demonic. "Nevertheless," Father Trabold points out, "one should not be too eager to believe that all strange occurrences are supernatural in origin."

The show went well. Yet, it never explored the deeper significances of spirit phenomena, and what's really behind them. Still, when the program was over, David, as soft spoken off camera as he is on, thanked everyone for making it a very interesting evening. All were glad to oblige. For the viewer, though, who was now being treated to light entertainment on the same channel, there were many lingering questions. What is the role of science in the study of the supernatural? What is parapsychology? What are the limits of the scientific approach to spirit phenomena? Where do the parapsychologist and demonologist part ways?

Certainly, Ed and Lorraine Warren will be the first to explain that all strange movements and activity are not the work of spirits, let alone the demonic. "Very often," says Ed, "there are natural explanations for odd goings-on in a house, as scientists have been able to prove beyond doubt. But it is wrong to believe that the legitimacy of spirit phenomena ultimately depends on the verdict of the scientific establishment. The supernatural is not a scientific subject, *per se*; its validity cannot be determined by scientific analysis alone. True, spirit activity has been captured on film and other recording devices, but there is far more to the subject than observable phenomena."

Still, as Ed notes, evidence is not lacking: "Those of us who deal with the supernatural day in and day out *know* the phenomena are there—there's no doubt about it. Therefore, when people tell me they don't believe in ghosts and spirit forces, what they're really saying to me is that they're not familiar with the data on the subject. Yet, the data is there—should one care to look. In fact, much of it has been collected under such rigid conditions as to make a lot of other scientific research look pale in comparison. For example, take a case Lorraine and I began investigating this past summer [1978] in Enfield, England, where inhuman spirit phenomena were in progress. Now, you couldn't record the dangerous, threatening atmosphere inside that little house. But you *could* film the levitations, teleportations, and dematerializations of people and objects that were happening there—not to mention the many hundreds of hours of tape recordings made of these spirit voices speaking out loud in the rooms. [In a Transatlantic linkup to Enfield, these voices were broadcast on WVAM radio (Pennsylvania) on June 16, 1978.] I won't repeat the vile language the voices used when I entered the room with them, but while we were there, the British Society for Psychical Research had already videotaped 1,300 hours of this phenomena going on. The BBC was there separately filming the case, apparently for a television documentary.

"The phenomena are there, really there! That's why I say, either you know *or* you don't know spirit phenomena exist. If you don't know, go investigate the findings yourself, but don't tell me you don't believe in spirits. Because I'll *prove* them to you: in fact, I'll show you things that go on in this world that you wouldn't believe could happen!"

Despite the vast amount of data scientists and other investigators have been able to collect, the scientific approach nevertheless remains somewhat of a double-edged sword. Although the scientist may be able to confirm unusual phenomena, he is really in no position to judge whether that activity is being *caused* by spirit agents. For this reason, the most appropriate role for science in the study of the supernatural is to show where strange events are *not* the work of spirits. Because, more often than not, natural explanations can be found for the occurrence of unusual activities in a home.

"Misinterpretation, misidentification, delusion, and hallucination account for a great deal of reported 'supernatural' activity," Ed points out. "A string of coincidences may lead a family to jump to the conclusion that they've got a ghost. Other people may hear 'spirit voices' when actually their hi-fi speaker is picking up radio waves on its own. Faulty house wiring will cause lights to flicker or appliances to fail when the circuits are overloaded. And, people with paranoid tendencies will seize on any unusual activity to satisfy their fantasies.

"Many times people will read a horror story or watch a scary movie and spook themselves. In a few weeks, these people come to believe they have a ghost in the basement or a vampire in the attic, and you can't convince them otherwise. So they hire so-called experts to come in and get rid of their 'ghost.' These experts will come into the house, parade around in wizard robes, set off smoke charges from a magic shop, recite a bunch of mumbo-jumbo, and generally put on a performance! Then they'll charge thousands of dollars for occult services rendered. This will go on until they've wrung every last cent out of these poor people. I know of one instance where these kinds of fakers bilked two women out of fifty thousand dollars!"

Perhaps the primary *legitimate* explanation for peculiar goings-on in a house is *psychokinesis*, the power of the mind to levitate or teleport small objects through space. PK, as it's abbreviated, is caused by the transfer of psychic energy to objects. Typically, the individual giving off this energy is under a great deal of stress. Frustrated or angry children are quite often the source of PK activity. Though unusual psychokinesis may be similar to phenomena brought about by spirits," Ed indicates, "PK levitations rarely involve weights of over one pound. No experiment has yet shown the human mind able to move weights of over two pounds. Demonic spirits, by contrast, regularly move furniture or appliances that would require two strong men to lift.

"Sometimes there are everyday physical reasons for strange movements," he continues, "such as magnetic or geological disturbances in the area where strange movements are reported. Now and then, electricity creates forces that bring about a suspension of gravity or other unusual effects near walls. Electrical baseboard heating can generate static electricity that may attract or levitate lightweight plastic or paper items. Inside the walls, steel pipes and other metal objects have been known to become magnetized, thus giving them the power to attract small nails or paper clips. Although such activity may *look* mysterious, what's really happening is perfectly normal. On those occasions when there is neither a human nor a physical explanation for strange events, then spirits do in fact tend to be the cause of the disturbance. And when spirits *are* at fault, then over half the time the activity can be attributed to *in*human spirit agencies."

Yet, unusual phenomena, in and of itself, are not the demonologist's primary concern. That tends to be the work of the parapsychologist, who studies unusual phenomena from the scientific point of view. In the past, parapsychology received a lot of bad press because those who called themselves parapsychologists were often self-ordained experts waving mail-order degrees as credentials. Nowadays, though, the subject is a legitimate area of inquiry, being studied by accredited professionals in major universities and research organizations.

"In general," Ed asserts, "the parapsychologist is looking for one thing and one thing only: a link between unusual phenomena and the latent abilities of man's mind. However, when the parapsychologist comes up against inhuman spirit phenomena, he tends to refer to it as 'poltergeist' activity. *Poltergeist* is an old German word meaning 'noisy or mischievous ghost.' The term is poor bookkeeping though, because it doesn't specify or come to grips with the *true* cause of the disturbance.

"Yet parapsychology, because it is allied to science, can offer only explanations falling within the range of approved scientific concepts and testing techniques. As a result, the parapsychologist is often put in the contradictory position of analyzing the supernatural realm with principles that apply only to the natural realm. Unfortunately, given this limitation, the parapsychologist frequently concludes that what he can't test is not there at all. Hence, he uses a noncommittal word like 'poltergeist' when more specific language is called for."

As Ed notes, "Much spirit phenomena is invisible and unmeasurable; the outward manifestations represent only part of a much bigger picture that can't be measured with testing instruments. Though parapsychology has given us much data on unusual phenomena and its link to man, it has still never approached an understanding of the true principles of metaphysics governing most of spirit phenomena. In fact, as a rule, the parapsychologist does not believe in the existence of spirits—sometimes even to the point of being ridiculous. Just recently, for example, I was in a home where I knew a spirit was causing the trouble. I casually mentioned this to the head researcher on the project. 'There's no such thing as spirits,' he told me. Well, no sooner did he say that, than a tissue box lifted up in the air, flew across the room, and hit him squarely in the head. 'I think I stand corrected this time,' he said, astonished."

The Warrens do not consider themselves parapsychologists, since there is a fundamental difference between parapsychology and demonology. Parapsychology gives no credence to the supernatural; whereas demonology is concerned *only* with supernatural events. Although both the parapsychologist and demonologist may investigate the same case, each tends to look at the same phenomena from entirely different perspectives.

"My work," says Ed, "is to make sure people aren't hurt— physically or mentally—and to put a stop to the phenomena, or get hold of someone who can. When the demonic is involved, that 'someone' is ultimately the clergy. The parapsychologist, in my experience, seems only concerned with his log book. He's usually at an investigation because he's been sent there, or he's working on some sort of grant. He looks at *people* as being the source of the problem, and his job is to list and record as much phenomena as he can. And he jolly well better not go back to his superiors with an explanation that a ghost was behind the disturbance!

"I don't have these problems. I go into a case as a psychic investigator first," Ed continues. "I go in *not* expecting to find spirit activity. If I satisfy myself that no spirit is involved, I leave. As a demonologist, I am only interested in *supernatural* phenomena: if it's natural, it's not my thing. Natural activity will go on aimlessly and eventually resolve itself. But supernatural disturbances take place for a *reason*. The scientist may have spent months at a haunting site and nothing testable happens. Then I come on the scene one afternoon with religious objects, *provoke* what's there, and suddenly, right in front of witnesses, all hell breaks loose. These are unnatural phenomena: you've got to go beyond the science book to find the answers here."

"In our work," Lorraine picks up, "we're not just interested in the phenomena, as the strict scientist tends to be. The basis of our work is with people because most of the time, spirit activity is directed *at* people. We'll come in on a case where the family has been under siege for some time. Often the police, psychologists, parapsychologists will have told these individuals that they're imagining things, or aren't telling the truth. They say this because they don't understand—or don't *want* to understand—spirit phenomena.

"Given our experiences, we see things differently; we see otherwise normal people in the grips of true terror. We don't summarily dismiss them as being off balance, or tell them they're overreacting. We ask them *why* their feelings are so intense. You know, sometimes people in a case will stay out all day long, then come home late at night just to avoid their home because they know it's haunted. Other times, people will be oppressed to become prisoners in their house and never go outside. This is not normal behavior."

"To put it another way," says Ed, "when I had to get the keys from George Lutz to go into the Amityville house, George wouldn't come any closer than four blocks to his own home! This is a big, burly man with a red belt in karate, an ex-Marine. He doesn't respect what's not there. Before moving into that Amityville house, George's attitude was that the dead are dead and can't hurt anything. That night when he handed me the keys, I asked him what he saw inside the house. He looked me right straight in the eye and said, 'Mr. Warren, *you know what I saw.*'

"That's the people aspect," Ed points out. "But the phenomena are also important. As a demonologist, I look for certain types of activity, because it's my job—and that of the specialist clergy—to determine if there is an external agent; if, in fact, there is an intelligence behind the activity—an intelligence that is supernatural in origin."

But how can the Warrens know if an intelligence is truly behind the disturbance, when that external agent is invisible?

Lorraine explains it this way: "Although this intelligence often chooses to remain invisible, there is no mistaking what's behind the phenomena, especially if it is an inhuman demonic spirit. Activity will occur in circles, in reverse, counterclockwise, or in distinct violation of the laws of physics. Stones, for instance, or nuts and bolts will fall out of the blue sky onto a home under demonic attack. These stones will come down with such force that they may actually penetrate the roof. We have seen the same downpour of stones happen *inside* a house as well. And so that it will be understood that these events are *not* of natural origin, the objects will fall in a zigzag manner, in defiance of the laws of gravity so there is no question as to what's really behind them. This falling of stones or even small animals like frogs or fish isn't rare, by the way—it happens somewhere in this country about once a week.

"And it won't just be objects falling: a dozen other unnatural things will be happening inside the home at the very same time. And all the while this outward show of phenomena is going on, a similar, subjective assault will be launched against the people themselves. Terrifying things, like innocent children becoming debased monsters with superhuman strength. Or adults suddenly aging overnight, or taking on features of the dead. And many times, these effects are not totally reversible. Yes, these things happen! This is very real, very serious business. When the demonic is responsible for a disturbance, lives are often ruined."

When the Warrens are called in to investigate a possible demoniacal presence, what procedure do they use to determine the nature of the spirit present?

"When a case is referred to us," Ed answers, "it's usually through church authorities. Once we learn about the problem, we immediately contact the principals involved. Naturally, time is of the essence. We are dealing with something quite capable of causing injury, even death.

"Once we arrive at the scene, I sit the family down and interrogate them completely. I tape-record these interviews. I've got thousands of cases on tape. Generally I say very little so that the people have to tell *me* what they've experienced. I listen for certain clues and characteristics that distinguish the performance of the demonic spirit from other types of phenomena.

"I'll want to know, for instance, *when* the family experiences the activity. Most spirit problems occur during the night, after the sun goes down. Has the family noticed odd smells in the house or quick fluctuations of temperature? Often a spirit projects odors to signal its presence, or draws energy from the room, leaving it freezing cold. Have they heard noises that resemble the sound of a stranger in the house? Doors that slam by themselves, muted talking, heavy breathing, lights being switched on and off are strong indications of a spirit presence. Is the family awakened at specific hours of the night? Many times a spirit will re-create its own tragedy at the same time every day, usually at the moment its physical life was ended. Is the family afraid to enter some particular room or area of the house? A human spirit will tend to remain in a room that was familiar to it in life; an inhuman spirit will dwell in an area of the house that it finds the most psychically hospitable.

"If I get yeses to a number of these questions then I go further and ask have they used a Ouija board. This is the most common way negative spirits are brought in. Have they conducted a séance? Those who encourage invisible entities to enter their home often draw in spirits of a kind they never knew existed. Have they performed satanic or black witchcraft rituals? People may laugh about selling their soul to the devil, but the sorry fact is, it can be done—and quite easily, at that. Has anyone in the family been inside a haunted house? A person who shows enough interest to go into a truly haunted house is apt to bring a desperate spirit home with him. Have they been having realistic dreams or threatening nightmares that later come true? Many times, sudden knowledge of future events is a sign of a spirit presence. Spirits often communicate to people through the dream state when the unconscious is open and receptive. Have they killed anyone, by accident or otherwise? The grave is not the end, and a ghost seeking revenge for an untimely death is sometimes capable of exacting its own form of justice. Has a member of the family been in contact with someone who is possessed or who routinely performs occult rituals? More often than not, individuals who are possessed or engage in the black arts are surrounded by a multitude of spirits. A vulnerable person who comes in contact with the possessed—or even with a dabbler in the occult—risks coming under the influence of spirits himself, whether the influence is wanted or not. Does anyone in the family know if he has been cursed? This sounds like superstition, but I've personally dealt with dozens of cases where people were cursed or damned by others in a methodical way. One of the worst cases of possession ever recorded by the Roman Catholic Church in America occurred in the 1920s when a father cursed his own daughter to the devil.

"Once I get certain questions answered," Ed continues, "then I have them explain the phenomena that have occurred. Have they seen objects move or levitate? If they tell me a refrigerator has levitated, I know this is beyond the power of human PK. Have they seen things disappear? Have they seen objects move through walls? Have substances, objects, or animals manifested mysteriously? After an hour of such questioning, I'll know whether or not the people are on the level; if the activity is by chance or design; if there is an intelligence behind the phenomena, and if that intelligence is apt to be human or demonic in origin."

When called in to investigate a typical case where bizarre events are happening, do the Warrens work alone or are others present to witness the disturbance?

"First," says Lorraine, "there is no such thing as a 'typical case': every case is different and has its own peculiar dynamics. As for witnesses, most of the time other people see the activity besides Ed, myself, and the principals involved. Sometimes Ed and I do happen to be the first outsiders to arrive on the scene, but once arrangements are made for us to begin an investigation, we'll work with a number of very capable assistants. For example, Ed's chief assistant is a knowledgeable young man named Paul Bartz, who's been with us now for many years and has frequently been exposed to demoniacal activity. Also, we'll usually arrive with a photographer who'll be there to photograph the activity as it occurs, as well as any spirit forms that can be captured on film. In rare cases where communication with the entity is called for, a deep-trance medium may also come along. If inhuman spirits seem to be behind the disturbance, then Ed will often bring along a priest or acolyte who wants firsthand experience with demoniacal phenomena. Later on, if the activity *is* being caused by inhuman powers, a local clergyman and an exorcist will be present as witnesses.

"However, you should also remember that before we arrive, friends, neighbors, relatives, police, parapsychologists, psychologists, and psychic researchers may all have witnessed the activity in an attempt to help determine what's behind the problem. Since spirits are usually the last thing people think of, Ed and I are therefore the *last* ones to be called in."

Is there some special way these cases initially start—the bad ones, that is?

"That's a very general question," Lorraine replies, "but let me answer it this way. Emotions in a home will tend to trigger off phenomena. A happy home is therefore your best protection against invisible intruders. Ghosts don't tend to be happy, as a rule; they'll usually manifest to someone they can relate to emotionally. The same holds true for inhuman spirits—except in those instances, emotions would have to be *very* intense to draw in a negative demonic entity. But in a great many cases we have investigated, the phenomena were *invited* in. People who thought the supernatural was harmless or didn't believe it was there at all, brought the activity into their lives *through their own free will!*"

A particularly striking aspect to demoniacal phenomena is that the demonic spirit is actually moved to violence when exposed to religious articles, the recitation of prayers, or reference to God or Jesus Christ. As Ed explains, this is why the study of the demonic is a religious, not a scientific subject.

"The subject is not religious because *I* say it's religious, or because *I* want to believe it's true," declares Ed. "I say the phenomenon is religious because that's the power that *it*—the demonic spirit—responds to. People might not believe in God, but these spirits do."

Is there any other way to understand the inhuman demonic spirit except in a religious context?

"Ultimately, the answer is no. Don't you think I've gone through the same course of reasoning?" Ed asks. "You can *call* this phenomenon a poltergeist, as the scientist does, but once the spirit goes into its irreligious act, that label fizzles out pretty quickly. There is simply no secular—that is, no non-religious—explanation for these spirits' existence."

Ed and Lorraine Warren have been speaking to the public—and professional groups concerned with spirit phenomena—for a little over a decade. In 1968 when the Warrens delivered their very first public lecture, Ed and Lorraine had already spent twenty-two years researching and studying supernatural phenomena. Yet, they had no idea everyday people were interested in hearing about their experiences. For mass audiences, Ed and Lorraine rationalized, the subject matter was too frightening. Besides, only those who had experienced the phenomena would be interested in the subject. Better leave well enough alone.

"Not so," contended the head of a local scholarship committee. "Why not bring a dozen of your paintings of haunted houses to the town hall, and then lecture on the day of the Silver Tea Art Show? The admission money would be a real boost to the scholarship drive."

As a community gesture, the Warrens agreed. On the appointed day, their paintings were lined up on easels across the stage. Nervously, Ed Warren, pointer in hand, unraveled the bizarre details of each case before a packed house. The talk went on for well over an hour. In the end, the Warrens generated enough money for the town to support not one, but two scholarships that seventh day of September 1968: Ed Warren's birthday.

Although people were interested in hearing ghost stories, Ed and Lorraine Warren eventually found that they could not speak openly on *demoniacal* phenomena. The subject was unpopular: it smacked of paradox and superstition—and offended the sensibilities of the time. Not everyone was ready to accept what the Warrens had to say. Then, for some strange reason, all that suddenly changed.

"In 1970," Ed explains, "when we first went out to speak in colleges, I became disgruntled, even disgusted with the lectures. Lorraine and I honestly assumed that educated people wanted to know the *whole* story on the subject of spirit phenomena. But back then everyone was searching for 'the truth,' except it had to be a certain *kind* of truth that conformed to the prejudices of the day.

"As long as we talked about haunted houses and ghosts, people were delighted. When we had to mention demonic spirits, demonology, the devil—or worse, if we brought up Christ, or priests, or religion—a swell of animosity rose up from the audience, as though someone had thrown a switch. The hostility was sometimes so overwhelming we could hardly go on. Although many were following what we were saying, others got up and walked out on us. Professors became instant experts and challenged us with half-baked arguments on how spirits didn't exist. Some went so far as to tell us that everything we'd experienced since the 1940s never even happened at all! It got to the point I considered going back to my studio and living a nice quiet life as an artist, while working with people who really needed help in spirit matters.

"One day in the car, I said to Lorraine, 'That's it. I'm not even going to mention the subject of demonology anymore. If people want to think it stops with ghosts and haunted houses, that'll have to be it. I'm not going to put our work up for ridicule so some reporter with a grudge can get a story published, and I'm not going to let people make a farce out of the serious work the specialist clergy does in this field.' Lorraine agreed with me.

"As I was talking, we happened to drive past a big, domed mission headquarters that's located along the Hudson River. I'd always wanted to go into the place, so I turned the car around and parked. We walked through the front door and into a quiet, tasteful lobby. An old, stooped-over priest with a cane was looking into a showcase at vases and other ornate Chinese objects. I walked across the lobby to where he was standing. 'Gee, Father,' I said, 'these things certainly did come a long way.' He had a very serene, beautiful face. He looked up at me and said, 'I spent many years of my life serving in China as a missionary.' With that we got to talking. I explained my work to him, and he kept nodding in a knowing manner.

"'I performed many, many exorcisms in China,' he said, 'but I do not tell some of the priests here what I have done. They don't know. They don't believe.' Then he looked up in my eyes and said, 'I would like you to go and see the Japanese nun in the library upstairs.'

"'Why, Father?' I asked him.

"'Because she has something to tell you. Something you should know.'

"Lorraine and I went upstairs to the library and came across the nun. She was a very intelligent-looking woman, over fifty, dressed in black robes. We introduced ourselves and I then told her about my conversation with the old priest downstairs. She smiled and nodded in the same way he had.

"'You are very discouraged by things that have been happening to you lately, Mr. Warren,' she said, just like that. 'Do not feel discouraged any longer. The work you are doing has a purpose. Things are going to change for you very soon. Sooner than you think!'

"She then went on and told us about her work as a nun, and her experiences with exorcisms all around the world. After she finished speaking, she gave me a very learned book on religious demonology and exorcism. That book became important to me later. But do you know, *from that day on,* when we went out to lecture and came to tell people about the existence of the demonic, there was no longer any ridicule. It was as though a great weight had been lifted off me. All of a sudden, people became interested in what we were saying and began asking serious questions. It was a major turnaround; and now, today, there is tremendous interest in the subject."

5.

A Conjuring Book for Christmas

By the middle of May 1978 the daffodils were up, but spring hadn't yet arrived in Connecticut. Lorraine had planned to spend Saturday the thirteenth planting coleus in her backyard garden, but gale-force winds blew across the state, followed by five days of heavy rain. The weather was a fitting end to a week in which nothing had gone right. In fact, tensions had been building for Lorraine since the beginning of the month, and she knew something would soon have to give.

With torrential rain beating on the house, the Warrens spent that wet Saturday afternoon planning the itinerary for their upcoming trip to England. Because their work often takes them to the United Kingdom, they've developed an additional expertise in British haunting sites, and were therefore booked to lecture on board the *Queen Elizabeth II* in June. Upon arriving in England, they would spend two days in London, honoring interview commitments with the BBC, then travel to Yorkshire, Edinburgh, the Scottish highlands near Loch Ness, and Stonehenge before returning to Southampton in July to lecture on the return passage.

Having made a dent into their U.K. plans that afternoon, the Warrens went out to dinner in the evening. Arriving home just after midnight, Lorraine reviewed the calls left on the answering machine: there was a message from a friend in Los Angeles; then a call from their daughter Judy, on vacation in Virginia; after that a young man's request for an appointment with Ed; then a bizarre series of clicks and odd whirring sounds, followed by the distraught voice of an unfamiliar woman:

"I hope you can hear me. My name is Foster, Mrs. Sandy Foster I don't exactly know what has happened here," she said in a barely controlled voice, "but my children have been hit and . . . and . . . and chased by something. . . ." Hesitation, "And there is somebody or something *in* the house, upstairs, in one of the children's bedrooms. Please call me back just as soon as you possibly can."

Both Ed and Lorraine listened silently as the distressed woman gave her address and telephone number. Although it was 12:40 A.M., Lorraine immediately tried to return the woman's call. "When a case is referred to us," Ed explains, "we immediately contact the individual or family in trouble. If it seems necessary for us to enter the case, then we'll offer to help. We tell the family that we don't charge money for our time, but we must be reimbursed for basic expenses [such as airfare, hotel rooms, and so on]. When that's understood, we set up an appointment as soon as possible. Usually, we're on our way within an hour or two."

Mrs. Foster's phone rang continuously, then the connection was broken. Lorraine hung up and dialed again. This time it sounded as though someone had picked up the receiver, but the phone still kept ringing. The third time she tried the telephone number, Lorraine got the same frustrating response.

At a loss, Lorraine dialed the operator, who then dialed the number and met with the very same problem. In turn, the operator summoned her supervisor, who listened to Lorraine's explanation that she was trying to return a distress call. Understanding and helpful, the supervisor ran the call through a number of electronic test procedures, but to no avail. She admitted being puzzled:

"There is nothing wrong with the telephone on the receiving end; your call *should* make a connection." Nonetheless, the Warrens were unable to get through that night.

As Ed and Lorraine know very well, what happened with the Fosters' phone was not unusual. In fact, such electronic tricks are commonplace when a malevolent spirit is at work. Interference, obstruction, confusion—tactics which cause delay—are routine for a determined spirit with the ability to manipulate both physical and metaphysical variables.

The next morning, Sunday the fourteenth, the Warrens drove to church. On the way, a powerful, rank smell of excrement filled their car. Then, midway through the church service, the same foul psychically-projected odor assaulted the Warrens' senses. Once again, as they were returning home in the car, they were nauseated by a disgusting stench. Ed and Lorraine, however, did not associate it with the demonic case they were about to investigate that afternoon.

When the Warrens returned from church, Lorraine immediately telephoned the Foster family. Mrs. Foster answered the phone on the second ring. Lorraine told her the difficulty that she had reaching them the night before. "The phone was in working order," the woman replied, "but it didn't ring after midnight. I know, because I was waiting for you to call." The problem with the telephone upset the woman even further, and so Lorraine made an appointment to visit the family that afternoon.

By two P.M., the Warrens had arrived at the Foster home. The Foster home was a typical Cape Cod house on a wooded plot where, Ed and Lorraine later discovered, the family had lived for the past thirteen years.

All members of the family were present that afternoon. Al Foster, a phone company lineman, was a youthful looking thirty-five. His wife, Sandy, with whom Lorraine had spoken on the phone, was her husband's age, but she looked drawn and upset. They had not witnessed the phenomena, however. It had been experienced by their three children: Meg, fifteen; Joel, fourteen; and Erin, eleven.

Ed arranged his recording gear on a nearby table while Lorraine asked their permission to walk the house. When the Warrens are working together, Lorraine will usually investigate the premises clairvoyantly, while Ed interviews the family. She'll begin in the basement and work her way up to the topmost floors, stopping in each room of the house. Because clairvoyance is a sense ability like the other five, it is not possible for her to deny psychic input anymore than she can refuse to see or hear. Therefore, if there is a spirit presence in a home, chances are excellent that Lorraine will become aware of it.

As she left the room, Ed began an extensive interview.

Both Mr. and Mrs. Foster made it clear that they had not experienced any of the phenomena their children talked about. "But I would imagine," Mrs. Foster said, "that this is probably my fault, at least from what little I know about the subject. Meg has always been interested in the occult—witchcraft, spells, that sort of thing. She has a small library, but none of the books were on conjuring. So last Christmas, I bought her one on conjuring demons as a present. I honestly didn't think anything like this was going to happen."

"Okay," Ed said, turning to Meg. "Where is this book?"

"Upstairs," the girl answered. "It's a paperback. It explains how to conjure something like seventy-five different demons. It tells the correct ritual and explains the debt you pay if the ritual works."

"And did you perform any of the rituals?"

"Yes."

"What demons did you try to conjure?"

"Which ones?" she repeated. "I don't know. I only did a few of the easy rituals, the ones I could understand and had the equipment for. When I did them, though, nothing happened. So I didn't bother anymore."

"Sometimes the response will come days, weeks, months, even years later," Ed informed her. "Tell me about what happened to you this week. You had trouble, I believe?"

"Twice," said Meg.

"Who was here when it happened?"

"Joel, Erin, and me," she answered, "The first time was this past Thursday. Dad and Mom went out to their friend's house. We stayed home because we had school the next day. Erin and Joel were already in bed. I'd just taken a shower. I went downstairs to make sure the doors were locked. I also turned off the radio and downstairs lights before I went back upstairs.

"When I got to my bedroom, I heard the water running in the bathroom. I didn't think about it at first, but a few minutes later, I went down the hall and saw that all the faucets were turned on. I turned them off. Then I heard the radio on again downstairs. The lights were on too! I yelled, 'Who's there?' But nobody answered me. Before I went downstairs again, I looked into Erin's room. She was asleep in her bed. I looked in Joel's room too, but he wasn't asleep yet. I asked if he turned the radio on downstairs. He said he hadn't. So I then went down and turned off the lights and radio *a second time*.

"When I came back upstairs, the water in the bathroom was running again! This got me mad because I was sure Joel was doing it. But when I came out of the bathroom, the radio was on real loud and all the lights were on downstairs! I went into Joel's room and said, 'There's someone in the house.'"

"Joel, did you hear the radio?" asked Ed.

"Yeah, I heard it, but I didn't think anything about it," he answered.

"Did you turn on the water?" Ed asked quickly, hoping to catch him off guard.

"No way!" the boy replied. "I never even got out of bed."

"Okay, Meg," Ed said, "please go on."

"From upstairs I could hear the radio changing stations, so I went right back down again, thinking my parents might be home. When I got down there this time, the radio dial was moving back and forth *all by itself.* I stood there and watched it, and that's when I started to get scared. I turned off the radio and the lights again, but when I got halfway up the stairs, I felt an icy-cold hand touch me on the shoulder, just for a second in the dark. I almost screamed, but I didn't. I just went right to my bedroom, shut the door and turned off the light. Before I got to my bed, though, I heard the sound of footsteps, like someone was walking out of my room into the hall. But the door never opened!"

"Didn't you think any of this was strange?" Ed wanted to know.

"Sure I did," said Meg. "I was scared out of my mind!"

"Erin, did you hear the radio?" Ed asked her.

"No, I was asleep," answered the little girl.

"Now, Meg, did anything else happen after you heard the footsteps leave the room?"

"Yeah, plenty! When I got in bed I lay down and closed my eyes. Suddenly, I heard a door downstairs slam *real* hard. After that I heard furniture being pushed around and crashing, like it was being thrown by somebody who was very mad. I really thought there was someone in the house, but I was too scared to do anything so I just kept my eyes closed. But even though my eyes were closed, I could see my whole room *through* my eyelids! I opened my eyes, but nothing was different. So I closed my eyes again. Then—through my eyelids—I saw a silver light come out of the woods and glide into my bedroom. It was there when I opened my eyes too. The next thing I knew, something—some hand—yanked my hair three times. Each time it pulled harder, until the third time it made my eyes water. Then I screamed and ran into Joel's room."

"Joel," asked Ed, "did you hear all the noise downstairs?"

"Yeah," he replied.

"Why didn't you do anything?"

"I was too scared," he admitted.

"Good answer," said Ed. "Erin, did you hear anything?"

"I heard the furniture being thrown around, and when Meg screamed I went into Joel's room too."

"About what time did all this happen?" Ed questioned.

"That's the funny thing," Meg told him. "It was about ten-thirty when I got out of the shower, but my bedroom clock was three hours *ahead*. And when I went into Joel's room, his clock was three hours *behind*."

"All right, once you were in Joel's room, did the noises stop?"

"Everything got even louder," Meg said.

"Did you hear any other sounds in the house at the time? Poundings on the walls? Voices? Knocking?"

"No, just doors slamming, footsteps, and furniture being thrown around," Joel said.

"What did you hear, Erin?"

"The same thing Joel heard."

"I heard what sounded to me like loud whispering, too," Meg offered.

"Could you make anything out?" Ed asked her.

"No."

"What about the footsteps?" Ed went on. "Did they lead anywhere?"

"They went around in *circles*," said Joel. Meg nodded agreement.

"After you all went into Joel's bedroom, and you kept on hearing these sounds downstairs," Ed repeated, "what did you do then?"

"We had an argument," Joel answered. "Meg wanted to call the police, and I wouldn't let her because I knew there wasn't anybody down there! If the police came, I figured they might have thought we were playing a joke on them."

"Finally we called my parents at their friend's house," Meg spoke up. "But by the time they came home, everything had stopped. All they did was tell us we were 'hearing things' because we were tired. They didn't believe us!"

"Mrs. Foster," Ed questioned, "have you ever seen or heard anything unusual in this house?"

"No, like I said before, I've never seen anything. The only thing unusual I've heard is the songbird." She paused. "For years we had a large pine tree outside our bedroom window. A few months ago, we cut the tree down. But every night now, for the past three weeks, Al and I hear a songbird singing outside our window where that tree used to be."

"Al, did you hear the bird too?" asked Ed.

"Yeah, every night," he replied. "I never gave it any thought, but birds don't sing at night, do they?"

"No," said Ed. "Not ordinarily."

"Well, it turns out you've all experienced something here," Ed summarized. "Do you think this house is haunted?"

"*I* think so," said Meg.

"I think so too," Joel replied. Erin and her mother also tended to agree.

"Mr. Foster?" Ed asked.

"Well, I don't know. I've never been around when any of this kind of thing has happened."

Just then Lorraine came back downstairs. She nodded discreetly to Ed, indicating, there *was* a spirit presence in the home, and then took a seat at the dining room table. Rather than alter the mood of the conversation, Ed held off asking Lorraine for her impressions until he had the family's statements on tape.

"You said these phenomena happened to you *twice*," Ed reminded the children. "What happened the second time?"

"The second time was last night," Joel replied. "Only Meg

and I were here. Almost exactly the same thing happened as on Thursday. This time Meg was in her bedroom, and I'd taken the shower. When I came out of the bathroom, I heard the radio on downstairs. The stations were being changed slowly, and I yelled down, 'Leave that one on.' But when I walked down the stairs, no one was there except the dog. He was snarling viciously at something in the room. That was really strange, because he couldn't have heard anything. Our dog's deaf! Then I remembered the other night and I ran upstairs and went to bed. About five minutes later, the footsteps started downstairs, making the whole house vibrate. And the furniture started being thrown around again. I was scared the first time, but this time I was *really* scared."

"Did you hear it too, Meg?" asked Ed.

"Yeah, just like he did. I even yelled out to Joel, 'Do you hear it?' But he hollered at me, saying 'Shut up!'"

"I guess I didn't want to admit it was really happening again," admitted Joel.

"When you were in your room, did you see or feel anything unusual?" Ed asked him.

"No, nothing."

"How about you Meg?"

"Well, the more scared I felt, the louder everything became downstairs. The second time, I also saw a dark, purplish cloud in my bedroom. I could never look at it directly—only out of the corner of my eye. When that purple ball was in my room, I kept my eyes closed so I couldn't see it. As I lay there, my hands were closed up in tight fists. All of a sudden I felt *another hand* try to force mine open! It was a really strong hand, like a grown man's. It couldn't get my fist open, so it yanked at my arm and tried to pull me out of bed. It pulled me almost halfway out of bed before I screamed for help. Then it let go, and I ran into Joel's room."

Ed looked to Joel. "What happened next?"

"Meg and I wanted to call the police or my parents or somebody," the boy replied, "but we didn't want to go out of the room. Meg told me about the hand, and we both felt something else was going to happen."

"Like what?"

"We didn't know," the boy answered. "But we felt a really strong sense of *evil* all around us. I don't know how to say it. Anyway, we wanted to get out of the house, but we didn't want to go through the downstairs. Meg said we ought to jump out the window, but I thought that was nuts. I told her we were gonna *run* out. Meg got dressed in clothes from my closet because she wouldn't go back into her room. Then I opened the bedroom door. We could see the lights were on downstairs, and we could hear the footsteps stomping around. But we didn't care, we just wanted out: so we decided to make a break for it."

"We went into the hall and nothing happened," Meg said, "except the whole upstairs was sweating hot. So we ran down the stairs as fast as we could and got out the front door."

"Did you see furniture tossed over in the room downstairs?"

"No, I don't think so. The furniture was out of place, but I don't remember if I saw any of it knocked over."

"Did you, Meg?"

"I didn't even look," she admitted.

"All I remember about the inside of the house," Joel went on, "was that the radio wasn't playing—it was buzzing, like it was picking up static. Anyway, we got out of the house and decided to run up to the university campus to call somebody. I'll never forget that. There were dogs outside, and when they saw us running, they started to run with us too. But when they got close, they ran *backwards!* And the birds—as we ran along, the whole woods were full of screeching birds!"

"About what time was this, Joel?"

"Between eleven and eleven-thirty that night."

"Beside the fact that birds aren't active at night, was there anything unusual about the incident? Did you notice if the screeching came from only one side, maybe from the left?"

"Yeah, *only on the left side*," the boy said emphatically. "How did you know that?"

"It doesn't matter right now," Ed told him. "Just continue with what happened out on the road."

"We were running up the road, but something was chasing us from behind," the boy went on. "Whatever was in the house had *followed us*. We were running toward the street light, because we felt we'd be safe if we made it there. But it didn't seem like we could make it to the light. We couldn't make any progress. It was like running in place. We were being held back by some sort of force field."

"If that force caught up with you, Meg, what do you think would have happened?" Ed asked.

"It *did* catch up to us!" she said. "It was heavy and it tried to force us down on the road. If we didn't get to the light, it would have killed us."

"Why do you say that?"

"Because there was no air to breathe," she responded

"Somehow," Joel recalled, "we did get to the street light. From there, we could see the house. We weren't that far away. The screeching birds died down a lot. Under the light, we felt safer; at least we didn't feel the pressure pushing down on us anymore. But the light seemed to be getting dim, so we decided to run all the way to the campus without stopping. As soon as we got away from the light, though, the screeching got louder than before. It scared us really bad. But we ran, and kept running as hard as we could until we got to the intersection where the cars were. That's the first time we felt safe. Then we walked along the road until we came to a store that was still open. I had a dollar bill and we got change in there. Then we walked up to the campus and found a phone. Meg's feet were all covered with blisters from wearing my shoes. So she sat in a doorway while I called my parents."

"Did you have any trouble with the phone call?" Lorraine interjected.

"No, ma'am," Joel replied. "I got hold of Mom and Dad at their friend's house. I told them what happened, but they said we were dreaming and better go back to bed," the boy answered somewhat angrily. "I told them we weren't home—that we were on campus, and we weren't going home! While I was talking I saw a campus cop pull up and start talking to Meg. Mom told me to get him to bring us home, and told me they'd meet us there. After that, nothing else happened—at least nothing so far today."

The rest of the family sat quietly, each one absorbing the strange, incredible tale the children had related.

Ed then questioned Lorraine. "Downstairs," she reported, "I felt only an overlay of negative vibrations. But there does seem to be something upstairs, in one of the children's bedrooms. I'm not sure which one. When I was in Joel's bedroom, I felt an extreme sense of confusion come over me, as if I'd been gassed."

"We felt that too!" Meg said, amazed.

"This feeling made me lose all sense of where I was," Lorraine went on. "When I extricated myself from that room, I went to the door of what I supposed was Meg's bedroom. Standing by the door, I felt pressure on my head and shoulders that began forcing me backwards, down the stairs. I decided not to go into *that* bedroom. It was an inhuman presence, and to the best of my ability, I consider it to be located in Meg's bedroom. Do you happen to have black conjuring candles in your room?" Lorraine asked.

"Yes," Meg replied, astonished by the question.

Ed looked around the table. The family looked frightened and helpless. Mr. Foster seemed to feel himself diminished in his family's eyes for not being able to cope with a problem—albeit invisible—going on in his own home.

"If things haven't gone too far," Ed told them, "I'll try to take care of the matter. Why don't you all go out and take a Sunday drive? Stay away for about an hour," he recommended. "And while you're out, please don't discuss, or even think about, the events of the past few days. When you return, then we can talk."

They were glad to hear that something could be done. Mr. Foster brusquely marshaled his family out the front door, and in less than a minute they were in the car and on their way.

Ed and Lorraine remained inside. They knew the children could not have made up their story; it contained too many specific details that could have been learned only through experience. Indeed, nothing the children had said was new to Ed and Lorraine. All the details the children had related squared with demoniacal activity they'd encountered in the past. Now, however, their task was to discern the true nature of the spirit presence—in order to dispel it.

The Warrens cannot always determine the precise nature of a spirit simply by interviewing the people involved. "The demonic spirit attempts to remain anonymous," Ed explains, "but in the long run, it really can't. It leaves telltale signs of preternatural power. For example, these spirits usually disregard the physical environment. A few years ago we were in a home where a television cameraman was being hit with marbles being thrown at him—right through a wall! Other times, the demonic makes things out of nothing. If solid, these materializations are warm to the touch, indicating some process of energy manipulation. Sometimes the materializations *de*materialize just as quickly; other times, they'll remain. I have a collection of these apports, as they're called."

Have these "apports" or teleported substances ever been scientifically analyzed?

"Absolutely," Ed replies. "This physical evidence is necessary to document the need for an exorcism. Whenever these substances manifest in a case, I take a sample and send it out to a laboratory for a compositional breakdown. The apports most frequently produced are urine, bile, vomit, blood, or excrement. These substances appear because they've either been teleported into a home, or they've been synthetically assembled by the spirits holding sway. Such apports usually contain all the minerals, trace elements, and amino acids found in nature. There's nothing especially new or mysterious about them usually, other than *how* they got there. Demonic spirits may be able to do strange things, but they *are* limited to manipulating the physical environment. Contrary to what our friends the Satanists may think, a devil is not a god," Ed says wryly. "It has no true powers of creation: it can only rearrange what's already here."

Why is it necessary to send the family out of the house?

"If the data I get during the interview is ambiguous, or if there is no visible phenomena going on," Ed answers, "then to determine if the spirit presence is human or inhuman, I have to resort to *religious provocation:* it's a dangerous, but also a revealing tactic. Almost anything can happen in this kind of situation, so if I have to provoke, I'll send everyone out to lunch and stay in the house by myself. In some cases Lorraine will stay with me, but her role goes no further than discernment. There is nothing a clairvoyant can *do* against a malicious demonic spirit, although there are a number of ways a negative entity can seriously harm a 'sensitive' individual. When I go it alone, I use provocation because I'm *not* a psychic—I've got to cause activity that I can perceive it with my five senses like anyone else. I always carry a relic of Padre Pio along with me for protection; the more religious power I add, the more likely *it* is to be provoked to respond. Knowing what I'm up against, many times I'd feel more comfortable carrying a tire iron and a shotgun. But you can't kill something that's existed since the beginning of time.

"Nevertheless, when I'm there alone, the house is still and quiet. Nothing seems wrong. If there's a place where the disturbance is localized, then I'll go to that area first. If the family has told me there's no specific locale, then I'll just go from room to room until something happens. If a ghost is responsible for the problem, then it'll usually show itself to me, as I'm going through the house. It knows the joke's over, and a ghost really wants no quarrel with God. But if it's a demonic spirit, sworn to hate God and repulsed by the religious objects, then sooner or later, things will let go. The temperature in the house will drop until it's freezing cold, or rise to oven-hot levels. Up will rise the stink of rotting flesh or some other foul odor. I may hear something explode. A threatening voice, sounding like no human being you ever heard, will order me to leave. I may hear footsteps—telepathically projected—running up stairs. This is a ploy to get me to follow so that I could possibly be cornered in some room. Unseen hands may scrawl an obscenity on the walls in front of me. Other times, none of this will happen. And then when I least expect it, the spirit will betray itself and begin to manifest in black. And why does this religious provocation process work? *Is it me?* No. It works because the demonic spirit hates, I mean *hates*, any mention of the name of God or the use of religious objects. This entity is so full of guilt, hate, and jealousy that religious provocation is actually painful to the inhuman spirit."

In the Foster house, the Warrens worked together. For provocation purposes, Ed used a crucifix and holy water—items both anathema to the demonic. Finding their way to the basement, Ed scattered holy water at all four points of the cellar floor. Then he said aloud, "In the name of Jesus Christ, I command all spirits—whether human or diabolical—to leave this dwelling and never return." The Warrens waited for a response, but there was none.

Why is Ed allowed to use holy water when he isn't a priest?

"It isn't a matter of being *allowed*," Ed says. "People are allowed to use holy water in their homes. The difference is that the water I use in my work has been blessed by certain special priests who are exorcists. The water carries a very real positive power to it. It's not the water itself that's of importance, but the piety it represents. I only *use* the water, I don't bless it."

On the first floor, Ed repeated the same procedure in each of the rooms. The process, known to the exorcist as *binding*, requires the infesting spirit to either show itself (if present) or move on. Having "bound" the cellar and all downstairs rooms without incident, the Warrens were ready to approach the second floor where they knew difficulty was lurking. But as they prepared to act, a dread terror swept over them. For the Warrens, this telepathically-projected emotion, experienced simultaneously by both, was a distinct indication of an inhuman demonic presence. "The demonic," says Ed, "projects terror the way a rattlesnake uses its rattler—as a warning."

A dank smell of mildew rose in the room. Suddenly a flash of movement was seen at the top of the stairs. Then a door slammed— the sound practically jolting them off their feet. The Warrens thought twice about going any further. They knew that any error in judgment on their part could result in a backlash of terror that might last for years.

As is usually the case, though, the Warrens decided to press on. They began climbing the staircase to the second floor. Yet, as hard as they tried, neither Ed nor Lorraine could get any more than halfway up; pushing against them was an impenetrable, unyielding force. Says Lorraine, "It felt like we were walking shoulder-deep against a powerful, fast-moving river." As much as they resisted, the power being exerted against them was impossible to overcome. Slowly, the Warrens backed down the stairs, so as not to be knocked over backwards.

At the bottom of the stairs, for a brief second, diabolical laughter rang out. Annoyed, Ed threw more holy water on the stairs, which caused the pressure to diminish enough to let them reach the top. The second floor was partitioned into bedrooms; a long hallway ran the width of the house.

Ed sprinkled Erin's room with holy water and then recited the expulsion command, without incident. That room bound, the Warrens moved to Joel's room next. The lightweight door, which had stood open before, was now closed. Ed turned the knob and pushed the door open with his fingertips. To their relief, the room was vacant. Again Ed went through the binding procedure without trouble. Meg's room was the last stop.

The door to the older girl's room was also closed. What awaited them on the other side the Warrens did not know. Ed twisted the doorknob, cracked the door ajar, and then swung it wide open. They both stepped back involuntarily. There was something in the room. Though invisible, it projected a horrible sense of misery; it was an absolutely heart-breaking emotion projected by an entity that is damned to perish. Yet the Warrens knew better than to react to this emotional ploy. It was but a ruse, an appeal for sympathy. Instead, with a steely composure, Ed walked into the room, cross in hand.

Though no physical presence was there to be seen, the bedroom was freezing cold. One last time, Ed threw holy water in all four corners of the room. Then, commanding, he stated, "In the name of God, show yourself now—or leave." . . . A dead silence lingered. "Give us some sign of departure," Ed said aloud in the empty room, "or exorcism will be conducted here *this very day.*" Almost instantly the morbid sense of misery began to drain away from them. Then the temperature in the room gradually returned to normal. The spell was broken.

Looking around the bedroom, the Warrens saw why the spirit had taken up this room as its abode. Meg's bedroom contained black conjuring candles, occult vestments, and books containing the rites for profane rituals of all sorts. Ed placed the items in the girl's trash basket, set them out in the hallway, and then "sealed" the room by reading a prescribed prayer of sanctification.

Their job done, the Warrens walked back downstairs. For them, the long, tense Sunday afternoon needn't have been spent in such a ghastly manner. Looking through the living room window, Lorraine noticed the Foster family sitting in their car in the driveway. She opened the door and waved them inside.

"Everything depends on your future actions," Ed explained once they came in. "Any improvements you may have thought about making in your lives ought to begin right now. Certainly," he told Meg, "there should be no more rituals of any sort! All the occult books and conjuring paraphernalia that were up in your bedroom belong in the garbage.

"Beyond that, I strongly recommend that you folks have the house blessed by a clergyman in the area. What happened, you see, is that your daughter's meddling with supernatural rituals actually drew a negative spirit into your house. The blessing needs to be done as a precaution against that spirit's return. However, it will be effective only if you folks keep up an emotional atmosphere that does not attract such entities to your home again. My advice is to arrange for this blessing to be done today, not tomorrow.

"Most of all," Ed stressed, "your best protection in the coming weeks and months is to develop positive interests as a shield against the negative. If you're religious-minded people, consider going to church as a family once a week as a show of sincerity. This gesture would be a good start toward counteracting the spirit force that was drawn in here. In short, your daughter has done something negative that now has to be balanced out by something positive. As matters stand, you're all vulnerable for a replay of these events—unless you develop a desire for this not to happen again. Lorraine and I have done all we can. The rest is up to you."

At the front door, Ed made a final comment: "By the way, the spirit in this home is dormant," he warned, "but it hasn't vanished."

With that, Lorraine's eyeglasses suddenly rose from her hand in full view of everyone, looped once in the air, and then smashed to the floor, breaking the left lens. The Fosters watched in amazement, though they barely understood what happened in their home. They were simply victims who had seen the supernatural as a plaything, when in reality, they had been its toy.

6.
Of Unworldly Origin

Of all the common and familiar objects of conversation that
are entered upon in company, of things remote from nature
and cut off from the senses, there is none so ready to hand,
none so unusual, as that of spirits; and whether what is said
of them is true. It is a topic people most readily discuss and
on which they linger the longest because of the abundance
of examples, the subject being fine and pleasing, and the
discussion being the least tedious that can be found.
—Pierre Le Loyer, 1586

Some of the first books ever printed in the English language were on the subject of spirits and demonology. Spirits were no less a fact of life in the sixteenth century than they are today: the same ruin and terror went on, the same violent scenario applied.

During Biblical times, Jesus spoke knowingly about ghosts, spirits, demons, and possession. "In fact," Ed notes, "Christ himself appeared at least a dozen times as an apparition to his followers before the Resurrection."

Receding even further back into history, it seems the question of spirit has preoccupied man right from the very beginning of civilization. Writers, as far back as the ancient Greeks, saw all this malicious activity as something more ominous than the occasional manifestation of a black specter in the middle of the night. Even then, the ancients saw it as a spirit, one with a *negative* purpose and assigned it the name "daemon," meaning evil or unclean spirit.

Today, documentation on the existence of earthbound spirit phenomena is available in most any large city or university library, thanks to work done over the past century by reputable psychic research organizations. However, proper information about the *demonic* spirit remains as difficult to come by as always. The subject is shrouded in secrecy. Most books on the occult give passing reference to "demons," but such information is usually intermingled with the disclaimer that the phenomenon is simply medieval superstition. Scientists rule out the existence of "spirits" entirely; the medical establishment tends to see the subject as either illusion or psychosis; and, academics conceive of demons as fantasy. Only the religious establishment gives credence to the notion of the demonic in high theology, and then the subject suddenly becomes quite real. It is given a name: the *Mysterium Iniquitatis*—the Mystery of the Iniquity. And the devil is given a symbol: XPISTOS—the *Anti*christ.

The best way to get a handle on the subject would be to ask the experts, but one does not simply walk into a church or synagogue and ask to speak with a demonologist. There are not that many of them; their names are confidential, and they are obliged to report their experiences only to their superiors. Even Ed Warren will not tell all about these horrendous black spirits that come in the night bearing messages and proclamations of blasphemy. When pressed on the matter, in fact, Ed's reply is: "There are things known to priests and myself that are best left *unsaid*."

Upon what, then, does Ed Warren base his opinions? Is there proper evidence or corroboration to substantiate his claims?

"People who aren't familiar with the phenomenon sometimes ask me if I'm not involved in a sort of ultrarealistic hallucination, like Don Quixote jousting with windmills. Well, hallucinations are visionary experiences. This, on the other hand, is a phenomenon that hits back. My knowledge of the subject is no different than that of learned clergymen, and they'll tell you as plainly as I will that this isn't something to be easily checked off as a bad dream.

"I can support everything I say with bona fide evidence," Ed goes on, "and testimony by credible witnesses and blue-ribbon professionals. There is no conjecture involved here. My statements about the nature of the demonic spirit are based on my own firsthand experiences over thirty years in this work, backed up by the experiences of other recognized demonologists, plus the experiences of the exorcist clergy, plus the testimony of hundreds of witnesses who've been these spirits' victims, plus the full weight of hard physical evidence. Theological dogma about the demonic simply proves consistent with my own findings about these spirits in real life. But let me be more specific.

"The inhuman spirit often identifies itself as the devil and then—through physical or psychological means—proves itself to be just that. Again speaking from my own personal experiences, I have been burned by these invisible forces of pandemonium. I have been slashed and cut; these spirits have gouged marks and symbols on my body. I've been thrown around the room like a toy. My arms have been twisted up behind me until they've ached for a week. I've incurred sudden illnesses to knock me out of an investigation. Physicalized monstrosities have manifested before me, threatening death, ruin of my family, and afterlife torment. But whatever I've witnessed has been suffered far worse by the clergy who must challenge the demonic.

"I'm talking about activity that's going on *right now*. Tomorrow, for example, I'll be submitting proof papers to the Catholic Church to justify the exorcism of a young woman who is under possession now, *as I speak.*

"As for evidence," Ed continues, "I have many thousands of hours of tape-recorded interviews with people and families all around America and Britain, which fully document the reality of demoniacal phenomena. I could fill a good-sized auditorium with witnesses to back up what I say. I have a collection of objects and substances— the apports I spoke about—that have been synthetically created by the demonic. I have documented photographs of demoniacal phenomena *in progress,* showing levitations, materializations, and spirit forms. I have evidence on audio tape of these spirits speaking. Many times they go so far as to even identify themselves by their diabolical names. Furthermore," Ed discloses, "these entities have confronted me personally by speaking through the possessed; and by taking manifest physical form, just as solid as you and me. And they tell me—just as clearly as I'm speaking now—who they are, why they're here, and what they're going to do!"

When asked to provide an example of the last point, Ed goes into his office and returns with a reel-to-reel tape. "This came from a session in 1972," he says, threading the tape through the recorder. "At the time, we were trying to determine who, or what, had been oppressing and sometimes possessing a woman named Mary since she was eight years old. When the recording was made, Mary was in her mid-fifties. Also present on that day were Lorraine, myself, a Catholic priest, and a deep trance medium. Just before this segment, the spirit had been speaking through the medium—lying, switching into foreign languages to keep us from understanding it, and talking in a falsetto voice, claiming to be an 'angel.' To get to the truth, we placed a crucifix on a table behind the medium—who was in a trance, her eyes tightly closed. We then commanded the spirit to speak, at which point something *very* different came through." Ed switched on the tape recorder:

Voice: I do not choose to be here!

Ed: Why did you come then?

V: I am under the Power!

Ed: Whose power?

V: A white light!

Ed: Describe yourself to me.

V: No. *(The crucifix is then set in place, followed by agonized screaming by the possessing spirit.)*

Ed: Describe yourself to me!

V: I must in truth tell you what I look like. I am wicked—and ugly looking. I *am* inhuman. I am vindictive. I have a horrible face. I have much gross hair on my body. My eyes are deep-sunk. I am black all over. I am burnt. I grow hair. My nails are long, my toes are clawed. I have a tail. I use a spear. What else do you want to know?

Ed: What do you call yourself?

V: *(Proclaiming)* I am Resisilobus! I am Resisilobus!!

"Though Ed and I don't pretend to be academic theologians," says Lorraine, "we have found nothing in our work to indicate the demonic spirit is anything but a fallen angel. The spirit's routine behavior, its metaphysical powers, and its violent reaction to holy objects certainly supports this conclusion. In fact, I'd go so far as to say transcripts of exorcisms would prove that the demonic spirit is the proverbial fallen angel."

One finds no justification for this spirit's existence other than what's suggested in the Scriptures. In both testaments of the Bible, angels and demons are mentioned some three thousand times.* No other reliable precedent exists for the demonic spirit, except in arcane religious texts that offer the same basic point of view.

---

* Father John Nicola, *Diabolical Possession and Exorcism*. Rockford, Ill.: TAN, 1974.

The exact quarrel between the demonic spirit and God is not known to man. As Pope Paul VI said in 1972, "we know very little about this whole unhappy drama before the world began." (Yet the same papal pronouncement also made it clear the Devil is a *real* entity—not a symbol or psychological metaphor. Even in his short reign of one month, Pope John Paul I reaffirmed his predecessors' convictions that the Devil exists as a real being.) Some of the best explanations about this truly haunting subject are contained in Nicolas Corte's *Who Is the Devil?* and in Billy Graham's *Angels*, but the definitive explanation remains to be found in St. Augustine's *City of God*. The classical story of the Fall of the Angels can be summarized as follows:

The first beings God created were angels. Of all the angels created, none was higher than Lucifer. God created Lucifer in such perfection that he was all *but* God. Not content with his own being, however, Lucifer sought through envy what was not his. Indeed, Lucifer sought to *be* God, to negate the existence of God and rule the heavens himself. Thus, the demonic spirit proves to be a negative spirit of possession.

Other angels in league with Lucifer participated in the same ruinous desire, "covetousness": that is, they were willing to forsake the gifts of their being in order to take what was not their own. God's supposed response to this cosmic treachery was to banish Lucifer and his legion from Heaven, whereupon these fallen angels swore perpetual disobedience to God.

Lucifer was renamed Satan—the slanderer, the accuser, the Father of Lies. Though fallen from grace, these angels were not depotentiated, but retained all the preternatural—beyond earth—powers given them at creation. These powers essentially consist of immortal existence; mystical knowledge of the universe; and the power to bypass the physical laws of nature, giving them the ability to bring about psychic phenomena and produce synthetic creations.

Yet despite their awesome powers, the demonic was restricted from overwhelming man. Instead, the covenant was that God would protect man, if man in turn respected the powers of God.

In the end, of course, no one knows the whole story. The demonic spirit's opposition to God does not, in itself, represent a proof for the existence of God. Only by inference do we see God as existing, through the hateful words and actions of these blasphemous, unworldly beings.

"However," as Ed notes, "apart from any one Scriptural interpretation, vile, inhuman spirits do roam the earth today. And when commanded to speak, the spirits' reply is a grave one: My name is Legion: We Are One. It is also true that these spirits possess overwhelming powers, and work with a ferocious rage, malice, and spite against mankind. Oddly, the only protection man can summon against these negative forces is mention of the name of God— though more particularly Jesus—and the presentation of blessed objects. Otherwise, nothing will stay these bizarre spirit entities."

Yet, if the activity is so overt, why haven't scientists come to similar conclusions about inhuman spirit phenomena?

"Scientists are people," Ed replies, "and some scientists and psychic investigators *have* seen what's happening, and now they understand. The most vocal skeptics, however, have never been witness to the phenomena themselves. Nevertheless, the movements and activity caused by these spirits is scientifically documented in a great many cases. Unfortunately, parapsychologists usually dismiss the activity as PK, or at the most, attribute the disturbance to earthbound human spirits. But even that isn't correct: by its own admission, the inhuman spirit has never been 'slave to God' in the form of man. It prides itself on that point. In fact, testimony and evidence given by principals and credible witnesses, tape-recorded sessions with the possessed, transcripts of exorcisms, two thousand years of church records all show them to be nothing more than what they've been known to be all along: inhuman diabolical spirits, possessed of hate and the evil wisdom to use it; spirits that have existed for all ages, harboring a violent hatred for God and vowing the ruin of man. Most of its hate is directed against God, however, and only rarely does man witness the full rage of its fury.

"As for the phenomenon itself," Ed goes on, "a dozen investigators can go through a demoniacally infested dwelling and come up with zero. Because, for the most part, the scientific investigator is fishing without a hook. The scientist, coming at the problem with his stopwatch and litmus paper, poses no threat to the infesting entity. Certainly the entity is not going to voluntarily tip its hand to its presence. But go in with a religious object, and an inhuman spirit will respond to the challenge.

"Let me be quick to say I absolutely do not recommend any investigator or psychic researcher to follow this procedure, however. Provocation is a distinctly *religious* procedure, not a scientific one. It requires special preparation before it is even attempted, or the results can be disastrous. I say this as fair warning to those who may try. No matter how dedicated the investigator, there is a point where he must stop, accept an impasse, and go home. There is no such thing as 'conquest' in this work. The end point is exorcism, the elimination of the negative force. No other attitude will succeed. The demonic is a very grave, serious problem and neither good intentions nor 'manly intolerance' will drive it away. It backs off only in the name of God. That's it."

Probably the most disturbing aspect to demoniacal phenomena is that behind all the terror and chaos, there stands a shrewd, calculating intelligence.

"Bear in mind, too, this is not something that is dead," Ed points out. "This is an active, negative intelligence that predates man in cosmic evolution. It is more knowledgeable than us because it's older than us. See it as a powerful negative intelligence completely lost in its hate for God. Once you do that, you'll start getting the picture of what the demonic spirit really is."

Perhaps no item more vividly illustrates the "wicked wisdom" of the demonic spirit than the five-foot antique conjuring mirror that hangs on the wall near Ed's office. One can't help but notice its ornate carved frame, but it is anything but a treasured *objet d'art*. Instead it's under the watchful eyes of Ed Warren because it is a profane object.

"These days," Ed explains, "people's only real familiarity with mirror magic comes from the rhyme in S*now White*: 'Mirror, mirror, on the wall; who's the fairest one of all?' Witches and sorcerers once used mirrors to foresee or manipulate future events through magic—not illusion, but *true* magic, the real manipulation of nature and events. That ornate mirror by my door came from the home of a vindictive fifty-five-year-old Pennsylvania man named Steven Zellner who used it to practice a little-known medieval ritual we call *speculum*, or mirror magic.

"Now magic, like witchcraft, can be used to produce either good or bad effects. This man used the mirror as an instrument of black magic. First, he performed a lengthy incantation ritual or conjuring formula, inviting the spirit world to assist him in manipulating the future. After the incantation, he then directed his gaze into the mirror, using it in much the same way one uses a crystal ball: as a point of concentration.

"When he first started out, Steven saw very little in the mirror other than the movement of blurred forms, or quick little incidents that meant nothing to him. But day by day, week by week, the more he concentrated his attention into the mirror—that is, the more he opened up his free will to the experience—the more control Steven gained, and consequently, the more he could see. Eventually, after performing this speculum ritual obsessively for many months, Mr. Zellner got to the point where all he had to do was state what he wanted to see, and the desired image would appear.

"In time, once he perfected the ritual, he could actually tune into the future whenever he liked. He could see—indeed predict—self-oriented events that would occur a day, a month, even a year later. But as the saying goes, 'Power makes slaves of us all,' and he soon decided to *use* this occult power. Going a step further, then, he projected people into the mirror. Invariably these were folks Mr. Zellner didn't like—whom he singled out for revenge or punishment. God help the butcher who shortchanged Steven Zellner!" Ed jokes.

"In order to wreak his own personal form of justice, Steven would select a victim whose image would come up in the mirror. The unwitting individual would be seen in some actual future situation. Then, with the victim literally in his sights, Steven would *will* some misfortune to befall that person. For example, he would see his victim standing at the top of a flight of stairs. At that point, if he wanted to make his victim fall down the stairs and break an arm, all he had to do was desire to see it happen. Working this kind of magic, the man would actually see his spiteful justice occur in the mirror just the way he planned it—kind of like watching an instant replay before the action takes place.

"Neat trick, right? Except there was a sticking point. These malicious acts wouldn't happen just on his mortal say-so; they'd be carried out by inhuman spirits that he commanded as part of the ritual process. In order to make a victim fall down the stairs, an inhuman spirit would either momentarily disorient the person, apport some grease on a step, or go so far as to even give the victim a psychokinetic push—and, whammo!

"*However*, somewhere along the line, Steven made a mistake, and his magic went awry. No doubt he neglected the part of the ritual where he had to give homage to Satan. As a result, the evil he proposed for others began to occur to him. But this was only a secondary grievance, because the spirits that he'd turned loose on his enemies had infested his own home instead, and were actively engaged in oppressing him. Disembodied footsteps and heavy breathing were heard in the otherwise empty house. Doors opened by themselves. Objects levitated or were flung around the room by unseen hands. Unearthly noises woke him up in the middle of the night. In short, an invisible presence roamed the house, and there was nothing he could do about it

"After about a week, this man was so absolutely terrified he called a prominent Catholic official here in the East, and literally begged him to send a demonologist to his house. Rather than send over a busy priest though, that church official contacted me in Connecticut and asked if I'd investigate and try to straighten things out. At the time, Lorraine and I were working a tight schedule, but with us, people come first. So I canceled the remainder of our appointments that day, along with an appearance on an important interview show that night, and drove off with Lorraine to Pennsylvania.

"When we arrived at the address, we met a man frightened out of his wits. Of course, he had every right to be. Doors were opening and closing by themselves. Objects were flying here, there, and everywhere. Every minute, something would crash and break, or bounce off a wall and hit the floor and smash—a real ruckus! At one point during the afternoon, my own car even got involved. About an hour after we got there, cars in the street started honking their horns. When I looked out the window, I saw our car parked in the middle of the road crossways blocking both lanes of traffic. When we arrived I had parked the car in Mr. Zellner's driveway, pulled the emergency brake, and locked the doors. Yet, someone on the street said they saw the car roll backwards out of the driveway all by itself. When I went out to get it, of course, the car's doors were still locked and the parking brake was still set.

"Anyway," Ed goes on, "it was apparent I was going to have to do something that very afternoon to stop the disturbance. In a situation like this, the best solution is to 'Stab the devil with his own pitchfork,' so to speak—therefore, what I had to do was *reverse* the ritual that Steven had performed. I did this, at considerable danger to myself, but it put an immediate stop to the action, and also nullified any future evil the man had projected—because it committed the demonic to perform the evil on itself, or else cease the oppression altogether.

"That afternoon, when our work was done, Mr. Zellner wanted to know if we would take the conjuring mirror with us when we left I said, 'Sure.' That way, at least I knew I wouldn't have to come back on the same case twice. So, I put the mirror in the trunk of our car, and Lorraine and I started back home, just before dark.

"When I was young and new to the dangers of this work," says Ed, "I sought the advice of very learned people who had long ago learned the deeper secrets of this world. At that time, a very wise man told me, 'Ed, I would never go into homes and confront the kind of entities you do for any reason—especially where the demonic is concerned. Once you cross the threshold into the world of darkness, you will forever live in danger, as will all those whom you love. Like it or not, you will be unique—and alone—among men. Never forget, the diabolical forces you challenge are clever, for unlike any mortal, they possess the wisdom and the knowledge of the Ages.'

"It was bitterly cold that evening. The roads had ice patches on them, so we took our time. I also knew that removing the mirror incensed certain malicious spirits and made me the object of their wrath, so I made it a point to be *extra* careful driving. Well, caution or not, about five miles from the man's house, I hit a small pothole. Under ordinary circumstances, it wouldn't have been of any consequence, but on this occasion it exploded a new, hundred dollar, radial tire—something that's almost impossible to do. This made our car veer into the oncoming lane of traffic. Cars screeched and swerved, missing us by an inch. It was a miracle we weren't killed right there.

"After I changed the tire, I got onto the parkway. A large tractor-trailer came up from behind our car, moved around the left side, and then inserted itself in the lane in front of us. I noticed there was something strange about the truck right off: it didn't have any lettering, plates, or markings on it. Suddenly, off this dry pavement, the truck began throwing up gallons of green, gelatinous sludge on our windshield, making it impossible for me to see out. The windshield wipers were barely able to move the slop away. When I was able to see again, the truck had vanished. Yet, no sooner did I clear off the windshield, than this *same* truck moved up from the left, got into the lane in front of us, and caused the same mess to occur again.

"By the third time this happened, it was evident that something sinister was going on, so I pulled off the road and let traffic go by while I cleaned the mess off the windshield. Five minutes later, after we got rolling again, the very *same* truck appeared, passed on the left, recklessly swung into the lane ahead of us, and immediately proceeded to throw up gallons of this thick, green slop. The stuff *only hit our car,* and when I managed to regain visibility, the truck was gone, just like before. Similar things have happened to us when we've been driving to or from other investigations. It's never been this green sludge before, but our car has been deluged with downfalls of urine and—on one occasion—beer. As usual, it's only our car that gets hit.

"Anyway, this business with the truck repeated itself at least a half-dozen times, and there was no way I could shake him—or *it.* The situation was *so* dangerous we fully expected to be killed. I finally managed to exit off the parkway at the first opportunity, and got onto a back road leading to Connecticut.

"Things went all right for about an hour after that," Ed continues. "There was almost no traffic on that back road, so we both felt pretty safe. But then suddenly, in my rear-view mirror, I noticed a car moving up from behind at tremendous speed. It was dark by now, yet this car had no headlights on at all! The only thing I could make out was a pair of dim parking lights. In no time at all, the car rushed up behind us, swerved into the passing lane, and raced on up the road. This was a jet-black car, and I swear the driver missed hitting us by no more than an inch. Lorraine, looking at the car as it went by, said it was as though the devil himself had just passed! 'It might as well be,' I told her, 'because the damn fool nearly killed us.' The guy was nuts, traveling that fast at night on an icy road with no headlights.

"I continued on my way as this guy went tearing down the road ahead of us. In the distance, I saw him travel over a one-lane suspension bridge, then begin climbing up a hill. All I could see of his black car were the rear parking lights, and I was glad to be rid of him. But when he got to the top of the hill, about a mile off, I saw him hit the brakes, turn his whole car around, and come racing back down the hill. An awful, sick feeling came over me then. All I could think was that we were going to have a terrible accident.

"Now, I had already started our car across that narrow suspension bridge, but by the time I'd driven no more than a third of the way across, this character had traveled full speed down the hill and was starting onto the bridge from the other side! 'What's this?' I remember saying to myself at the time. 'Is this guy on some kind of death trip?'

"With him bearing down on us at high speed, there was no chance to do anything like back up and let him pass. Just the opposite— *if he didn't stop immediately, we were going to crash head on!* But he just kept coming! The bridge arched, like a trestle, over a ravine. If I swerved to the left or right, we'd have plunged into the valley and been wiped out for sure. When my headlights picked up the chrome grill of his car, I yelled to Lorraine to get down on the floor. Because, sure enough, here comes this maniac right down the middle of the bridge, racing straight at us.

"He's doing ninety. I'm doing forty. At that point, even if we both tried to stop, the momentum would have still carried our cars into a collision. It was an impossible situation. Still, I had to do *something*. With five seconds to go, my life was reduced to one basic question: Should I swerve or go straight? At the last moment, something told me *keep going straight!*

"There was no time left. My last words to Lorraine were 'Call on Saint Michael!' With two seconds to go—and in these situations you think in terms of time, not distance—my arms are braced and I'm ready for the hit. One second before crashing, I draw my final breath. Then, right smack at the moment of impact . . . SWISH!!! He's a *phantom!* Lorraine was right."

Religious writers have often called the demonic spirit an "evil genius"—a veiled reference to the premeditated strategy that can be discerned when the demonic is responsible for disturbances in a home. During an investigation, therefore, it is this intelligence—a rational moving force behind the phenomena—that the demonologist primarily looks for.

Because of the extraordinary nature of Ed and Lorraine Warren's work, the strategy of the demonic often envelops them too. Indeed, it begins even before they are requested to enter an investigation, or follow up a call for help. Ed explains recent vandalism that occurred in his office:

"This happens a couple of times a year, usually after sunset. The last time, though, it happened in broad daylight. Lorraine and I were in the kitchen after lunch. First the phone rang. Lorraine picked up the receiver, but since there was no one on the line, she hung up. About a minute later, the phone rang again—but instead of the normal, intermittent rings, it rang continuously. When Lorraine picked up the receiver, a deep-throated, animal growl came across the line.

"She became upset and handed the phone to me, and I listened to the growling too. No sooner did we hang up than our German shepherd began barking savagely outside. At that point, what sounded like a violent brawl started up in my office. You could hear furniture being thrown around, with crashing and breaking sounds going on for a good ten minutes. Most people's inclination would have been to run down and find out what's happening, of course, except you *wouldn't* want to have seen what was going on down there!

"An hour later, we went into the office. It was a complete wreck. Pictures were torn off the walls, files were dumped over. Books, papers, chairs, lamps, tables all were thrown into a pile in the center of the room. We know from experience this was not the work of human beings. This is the demonic.

"Understand, these entities are spiritual hoodlums. They're always down there. You see them sometimes out of the corner of your eye, flitting from here to there. Other times, they'll be loitering between the physical and non-physical state: semi-materialized, formless, like a charcoal-gray cloud. We've got an understanding," Ed says ironically, but deadly serious. "They don't bother me, and I don't throw holy water on them."

Then why was the office torn up?

"Right now," Ed answers, "we don't know why this build-up is taking place, but most likely more strange things will go on— hopefully nothing serious. This kind of thing routinely occurs a week or two before we're called in to investigate a serious case where the demonic is involved. Right now, all we know is that somewhere, someone is being either oppressed or possessed by the demonic. The person or family under siege probably has no idea who Lorraine and I are, let alone how to get hold of us. But one way or another, they'll call for help. The spirits, however, know this too. That's part of the reason why the office was torn up: to try and intimidate us right now. As I say, there's a method and a strategy to *all* these phenomena."

The religious community has long been the target for demonia-cal attack, with the pious being the very select target. Compare Ed

Warren's statements with this passage from the biography of Padre Pio:

> Many times, entering his modest little cell, Pio found everything upside down, his cot, coverings, books, and ink splattered over the walls. These strange spirits appeared to him under the most diverse forms, often in the habit of monks. One evening he saw that his bed was surrounded by fearful monsters . . . they grasped him, shook him and threw him on the floor and against the walls as they had often done to the Curé of Ars. . . . To no one, outside his confessor, did he say anything about these visitations.
>
> One night he saw enter his cell a monk under the form and aspect of Padre Agostino, his old confessor. The feigned monk counseled him and exhorted him to give up his life of asceticism and privations, affirming that God could not approve of his way of living. Padre Pio, stupefied that Padre Agostino should speak in this manner, ordered him to cry out with him, *"Viva Gesu"* [Long Live Jesus].
>
> The strange personage disappeared immediately, leaving in the room a strange odor of stinking sulphur.*

Obviously, demonology arose in the religious community as a necessary protection against this incredible unworldly influence. And though the matter is usually kept confidential today, all major religions have specialist clergy assigned to demonology and exorcism; not as a remnant from the past (Padre Pio died in 1968) but as a real contemporary necessity. For Catholics, demonology is a subject important enough to be taught to clergy at the Pontifical universities in Rome. "The religious community would rather not

---

*Padre Pio: The Stigmatist, by Rev. Charles Carty, TAN Books. 1953 edition.

have to deal with the problem of demoniacal phenomena," says Ed. "They only do so because they have to."

As a discipline, demonology incorporates the study of philosophy, theology, psychology (both normal and abnormal), anthropology, chemistry, biology, physics, and metaphysics. Such a broad-based approach enables the clergyman-demonologist to determine, when other researchers cannot, whether unusual phenomena are ultimately supernatural in origin. Such judgments are serious; people's lives often hang in the balance.

Besides knowledge, the demonologist or exorcist must possess an unshakeable inner strength and be totally in command in situations of wild, unrestrained pandemonium. "A person who walks into a full-blown demonic situation without self-control," Ed notes, "would be haywire in five minutes. The phenomena come at you separately through all five senses; at the same time, it pounces on your personal psychology. If you even waver, you falter, and if you falter, you fall prey to a force that specializes in the innocent, the ignorant, and the fallen.

"What's worse,' Ed astonishingly adds, "these spirits know your whole life: past, present, and to some degree, the future. In fact, when I'm working with the possessed, the first thing the possessing entity usually says to me is, 'Ed Warren, I KNOW WHO YOU ARE!'"

Although Ed is not a clergyman, he nevertheless performs much of the work of the clergy in this field. "Traveling, long-term investigations, data analysis, discernment of spirit forces, counseling, follow-ups—things the clergy have no time to do—this is my work, and more," says Ed. "Being a demonologist is something you don't broadcast, you understand, because the very word tends to stop people in their tracks. There's also no sense in alarming people, especially if they really *are* caught up in a demonic situation and don't know it."

Anyone who's ever witnessed the vile, ungodly phenomena

brought about by malicious inhuman spirits knows that a demonologist risks his life every time he enters a home to confront the forces of darkness. Yet that job must be done. Otherwise, individuals who unwittingly fall into the trap of the demonic will suddenly find themselves helpless and alone in the presence of powers that are merciless merchants of terror and violence. And with that, the strategy of the demonic will have just begun.

As Mr. Zellner so aptly put it when first describing his problem to Ed Warren, "There's an invisible being in my house with a deranged mind that's causing havoc and trying to overwhelm me." Though he didn't know it at the time, Mr. Zellner not only identified the problem, but defined the demonic's basic strategy in one fell swoop.

7.

Infestation: The Process Begins

"Long before we become involved in a case, in fact, long before we're even aware there *is* a case at all," says Lorraine, "strange occurrences will begin to happen. My word for them is 'little-big-things.' The telephone will ring in an odd way, and when I answer it, there'll be voices whispering in the distance, or animal growls, or bizarre sound effects coming across the line. Later on, when the case comes into the open, we're liable to hear these same whisperings or sound effects at the haunting site.

"Beyond that, other disturbing things are likely to happen to us before a demonic case approaches. Around midnight, we'll hear someone walking around in circles on the front porch, or pacing back and forth on the rear deck of the house. We'll check, of course, but no one will be there, though the footsteps may continue to be audible. Other times, we'll hear footsteps running up a stairway *inside* the house, trying to frighten us. Bright car lights will be seen pulling into the driveway, followed by the sound of footsteps, and then three knocks at the front door. But again, upon checking, there won't be anybody at the door, and there'll suddenly be no car in the driveway. Often, we're liable to hear a ruckus out in Ed's office, although the office door is locked and the sonic alarms haven't been tripped. We may be sitting quietly at home when a rush of freezing cold wind sweeps through the house, or there will be the rustle of clothes sounding like someone has just walked by. A black cat may saunter into the living room, sit down, and vanish—symbolizing demonic involvement.

"Two nights ago, Ed was called out of town on official business to the Midwest, and I felt terribly apprehensive about his safety. At *exactly* three o'clock in the morning, there was a tremendous, incredible crash, complete with breaking windows and the tinkle of glass. It actually sounded as though the roof had caved in! I got up and walked around the house using a flashlight—because light stuns the demonic—but there was nothing to be seen. Although nothing physical had happened, the thunderous crash still scared me to jitters. You just don't get accustomed to this kind of thing! Instead, Ed and I have come to understand that such negative 'set-ups,' as we call them, are part of a larger, more comprehensive demonic strategy that's already in effect before we are ever called in. It's only in retrospect, once the case is over, that these disturbing incidents tie in. What we do know beforehand, though, is that some person or family is being closed in by a spirit that wants no interference and will do almost anything to prevent detection."

As the time nears for the Warrens to become involved in a particular case, obstructions and interference in their lives become more and more overt. If someone desperate for assistance sends a letter, it is apt to be delivered to the wrong address. If someone tries to telephone, the instrument will not ring, although Ed and Lorraine are home and available. Messages spoken into their answering machine are strangely *not* recorded or distorted by overriding static. Once the message does get through, and the Warrens leave for the site, anything can be expected to happen to them on the way, including head-on collisions with phantom cars. And as Lorraine notes: "When viewed in isolation, none of these obstructions make any sense at the time; they amount to being no more than curious coincidences. Again, only after the fact, when viewed in totality, do the delays and obstructions tie in with a larger strategy."

Strategy, the dictionary tells us, means to outwit—by trick or artifice—in order to gain an advantage. The demonic spirit has classically proven to be a master strategist against man. Here one minute, gone the next, the complicated manipulations of these notorious spirits have long remained a mystery. In the past, facts about the *modus operandi* of the spirit were few and far between. Lacking books and detection instruments, monks and clerics could only keep longhand accounts of diabolical disturbances for possible use by future historians.

Now, however, after centuries of study and investigation, a pattern of demonic behavior has finally begun to emerge. As a result, the twentieth century demonologist—aided by books, technology, and mass communication—has the most thorough grasp so far on these elusive entities' overt motives and strategy.

"There are three distinct stages to demoniacal activity," Ed reveals, "*infestation, oppression,* and *possession*. In certain rare cases, death may occur as a fourth stage, or in lieu of possession. If no one is called in to stop the spirit, and the disturbance is allowed to run its course, then each stage can be anticipated to occur in 1-2-3 order.

"During the infestation stage, the strategy is to create fear—thus generating negative psychic energy—that starts breaking down the human will. The Foster children experienced the primary, infestation stage of the phenomenon, as did Mr. Zellner. The case with the rag doll, Annabelle, would also have to be categorized as infestation. Though these cases needn't have happened, they do illustrate that demoniacal phenomena won't tend to occur unless an individual grants some sort of 'permission' for a spirit to enter his life. *Doors must be opened for the phenomenon to occur,*" Ed states emphatically.

In everyday terms, therefore, the demonic spirit does not have free reign over man. Instead, through the exercise of free will, men or women *choose* to open the door to the unknown, and then follow the darkened path. As Ed explains, "The demonic is a spirit that people *don't* have to know. Specifically, it's a matter of need versus want. A ghost *needs* to communicate its own problem, or it visits as an apparition to give information that a living person may need to know. The demonic spirit is different: it's there because people, through their own free will, *want* or invite spirit contact when there's no need for it. With respect to this, two laws apply: the Law of Attraction and the Law of Invitation.

"The premise of the Law of Attraction," Ed now explains, "is *like attracts like*. Attention to the positive brings about the positive; attention to the negative brings about the negative. Therefore, people who do negative or patently unnatural things are essentially 'doing the Devil's work for him' and actually *attract* negative spirits to their side. They're on the same frequency, so to speak. The Annabelle case is a good example. Those girls had an innocent, though unnatural attachment to the doll; this lack of good judgment got noticed by the demonic. Once it was there, it went to work and oppressed them to consult a medium, then believe the bogus message. In short, the girls gave 'Annabelle' *carte blanche* to come into their lives. Had the case gone on, the young man, Cal, would have stood in real danger of being seriously hurt, if not killed; and the girls might likely have come under possession by the entity."

"As an extension of the Law of Attraction," Lorraine adds, "the demonic can also be brought in as a result of one's actions. Characteristically, wanton transgressions of the good—evil *deliberately* perpetrated by man against man—*is* a triumph of evil, and acts as a signal to negative spirits. When an individual derives satisfaction from committing cruel and malicious acts, his body vibration alters, resulting in an aura that is darker than normal in color. As a shark follows a trail of blood, the change in aura then attracts a negative spirit to one's side."

Attraction can also occur when an individual displays a lapse by letting self-control falter. As Ed puts it, *"If you can't control yourself, then something else will.* Hate, rage, despair, misery, drunkenness, and a suicidal sense of worthlessness will attract the demonic in a snap. Man gets no bouquets from the demonic: it's only there to promote his destruction." In short, the demonic tends to be attracted by actions or trends of thought that are inconsistent with healthy, positive well-being.

"By the Law of Invitation," Ed continues, "it's ask-and-ye-shall-get. An individual can deliberately summon the demonic through a ritual or via some channel of sincere communication. This is an open, voluntary gesture involving ceremonial magic, incantations, séances, use of the Ouija board, or secret profane rituals where an individual *voluntarily* invites a demonic presence to himself. Conducting one of the rituals is often the first step down a road of no return. The conjuring may be a private affair carried on in one's own home, or—as is the new fashion—to do it in public with one of the ever-growing cults of Satanists or covens of black witches who advocate this activity."

What is the relationship between witchcraft, Satanism, and the demonic?

"First, understand witchcraft," Lorraine replies. "Wicca—or witchcraft—is 4,000 years old, often called the 'Old Religion' because it predates both Judaism and Christianity. People who practice Wicca are known as white witches, and worship Mother Earth. They manipulate natural forces for positive results—healing, good luck, lasting love, and bountiful harvests. After that, however, you digress into gray witchcraft, black witchcraft, and Satanism, This is where problems develop because witchcraft goes both ways and can be used to bring about positive *or* negative ends.

"*Gray* witchcraft is named for its effects. The gray witch casts spells and manipulates the fate and fortune of others in a way that's neither totally good nor totally bad. Essentially, gray witchcraft is performed in order to give one person unfair advantage over another. The real problem, though, lies in black witchcraft and Satanism. The black witch seeks earthly rewards—money, sex, power, prestige—or the ruin of adversaries through the express help of diabolical agencies. Black witches may call on lesser demons and devils during their rituals; Satanists call on the satanic hierarchy— Astoroth, Beelzebub, even Lucifer—to intercede on their behalf. For their power and effectiveness, black witches work in legion with particular demonic spirits, while the Satanist goes all the way and worships Satan as a god.

"In the past, the negative rituals involved everything from the murder of babies to pacts with the Devil himself. In the more extreme rituals, celebrants would turn the Bible upside down and urinate on it, then begin a counterclockwise march, forming a magic circle while chanting blasphemies, renunciations of God and submission to the other-lord, Satan."

"Using profane rituals, Satanists and black witches are able to summon specific demonic spirits and command them to commit actions for either personal or group benefit," Ed notes. "Money, prestige, sexual conquests, material riches, great personal power, and the downfall of adversaries through spells and curses can all be brought about through the intervention of inhuman spirit agencies. But the demonic is a loan shark, and it not only collects before you're ready, it wants double in return for what it gives. Ultimately it wants the soul. That is why sorcerers, black witches, and Satanists will wind up paying a big price, maybe an eternal price, for what they do."

Nowadays, lone individuals performing rites gleaned from a drugstore paperback may not be prepared for the ghastly reality often bound, by what Ed calls cosmic law, to confront them. "This is what happened in the Foster case," says Ed. "The true beginning of that case would have to be placed on Christmas Day 1977, when the mother put a conjuring book, of all things, under a Christmas tree! High symbolism there. So, the mother gave the fundamental invitation to the demonic to enter her home. Be that as it may, Meg was the one who gave permission. Had she returned the book or thrown it away, then none of the bizarre incidents would have happened. However, through her own free will, Meg performed the formalized invitation rituals that set the process in motion."

When neither the Laws of Attraction or of Invitation apply, then spirit infestation may have already occurred in a home before new tenants move in. This happened in the Amityville case, for example, where the Lutz family walked into a supernatural bear-trap. Surprisingly, the Warrens claim this is the way most ordinary folks come in contact with inhuman spirit phenomena. Yet, even in an infested home, not all people may be vulnerable to negative interference. "A happy, well-adjusted person," says Lorraine, "virtually seals out negative forces with a positive disposition. On the other hand, just as a fly is attracted to flypaper, a dour, depressive person in an infested house can almost be guaranteed trouble. The majority of the time, though, the phenomenon is invited into one's life by granting permission for spirits to enter."

What are the ways in which permission can be granted?

"By opening channels of communication that should remain closed," Ed answers. "Ouija boards, séances, conjuring ceremonies, candle rituals, automatic writing devices are all doors that open to the supernatural and, more often than not, lead down a road of misfortune, terror, and ruin.

"The Ouija board has proven to be a notorious passkey to terror, even when the intent of communication is decidedly positive in nature," he stresses emphatically. "Of the cases we respond to, four in ten concern individuals who have raised inhuman spirits using a Ouija board. I was one of the few people who examined the official records of *The Exorcist* case. That case—which happened to a boy, by the way, not a girl—occurred in 1949, and do you know how it originally got started? By using a Ouija board!

"The Ouija is nothing by itself," Ed adds. "It's just a pressed piece of board with the alphabet on it. The same effect can be had with an upside-down wine glass on a waxed table, like they used in the 1930s. But in either case, it is a medium of communication. In other words, it's what you use the object *for*. When you use the Ouija board, you give permission for any unknown spirit to communicate with you. Would you open the front door to your house and let in anybody who felt like it? Of course not. Yet, that's exactly what you're doing on a supernatural level. Very seldom have Lorraine and I ever encountered anyone who's had a *truly* positive experience using the Ouija board. For those virtually addicted to the board who think they're in touch with the 'divine,' there has never been an occasion, to my knowledge, when a positive angelic spirit has ever come over a Ouija board with a true precognitive message. As we've said many times, doors have got to be opened before most of this activity can occur. The Ouija board is one way to do it."

"The same problem holds true for séances," notes Lorraine. "When everyday people become involved in communication with spirit entities, there is simply *no accountability* as to who, or what, is communicating from the other side. 'Blind' communication is a perfect opportunity for a deceptive spirit to enter the lives of unsuspecting individuals."

But isn't it possible to make contact with friends and relatives who have passed on?

"If you get six, eight, ten people focusing their minds on spirit communication," she says, "then there's a very great likelihood that communication will take place. But still, you *don't know* what you're communicating with. Very often, information can be verified by only one person at the table. Yet how do you know that the information wasn't passed on to the individual by a negative spirit—telepathically—before the question was asked?

"Furthermore, not every person who passes on is necessarily earthbound and ready to communicate with you at will. In order to conduct a séance properly, you should first have a darn good reason for doing it. You should have an experienced, professional medium who comes recommended by a reputable psychic research organization. A local do-gooder clairvoyant or amateur medium may make spirit contact, but won't necessarily be able to *discern* if the spirit in question is good, bad, or indifferent. In which case, again, you don't know who you're really talking to.

"Another point: a séance should be held during the *daytime* hours. Human spirits are usually just as capable of communicating during the day," explains Lorraine. "Séances held at night very often bring on negative-human or demonic spirits—sometimes because the individual holding the séance is oppressed beforehand to hold the sitting in the dark. How many times have you heard about séance tables lifting up and moving across the room? Ghosts don't have the power to lift tables even if they wanted to. Only two things could do that: either an inhuman spirit or, more likely, the psychic energy generated by the people sitting around the table.

"The point is, if you have a real need to communicate with the other side, then it should be important enough for you to consult a valid expert for help. Otherwise, you're going to get trouble if you aren't careful with séances beforehand."

With permission having been granted, through either the Law of Invitation or Attraction, it remains to be seen if infestation has indeed taken place. If it has, then the Warrens say it will be noticed, ordinarily, as a build-up of little incidents over a period of weeks or even months.

"During infestation, the strategy of the demonic is to generate fear through incidents of inexplicable phenomena," says Ed. "Activity will be especially prevalent during the psychic hours of night, between 9 P.M. and 6 A.M., with the peak occurring between 1 A.M. and 5 A.M. The very first incidents of activity will tend to occur at exactly three o'clock in the morning. This symbolic hour, the 'high noon' of the demonic day, is chosen as a mocking gesture because it is in direct opposition to the traditional hour of Jesus' death. Once the initial infestation has taken place, then phenomena will tend to erupt at any time after the sun goes down. If the infesting spirit can draw energy during the daylight hours, activity may also go on during the day, though to a diminished degree.

"During the early stages of infestation, however, the spirit often goes through great pains to cover its tracks," he adds. "It is not in the infesting spirit's best interest to be discovered prematurely. Therefore, activity will be low-key as the spirit takes hold. Individuals will often dismiss implausible phenomena as quirks, coincidence, or natural illusions. At most, unusual activity will be attributed to psychokinesis or to the work of restless human spirits. Most of the time, this judgment will be correct. In those rare instances when there *are* negative inhuman forces behind the activity, however, then a sinister intelligence at work will slowly become apparent."

Since the Foster case illustrates infestation in its most easily recognizable form, it is worth pausing to examine the case in greater detail.

"To begin with," says Ed, "there was no materialization of an earthbound human spirit before, during, or after the case. Instead, the external phenomena reflected an inhuman spirit's intervention, insofar as a ghost would not have been able to bring about most of the strange occurrences. Furthermore, there was nothing random about the activity. In fact, rather than being a chance manifestation-dissipation of a ghost, this activity was dynamic and goal-oriented, suggesting a negative strategy.

"In addition, great fear was aroused. This is a distinct sign of a demonic presence because inhuman spirits *need* fear to manifest, whereas ghosts do not. The violent and malicious phenomena in the Foster case was *meant to frighten.* This was evident when Meg told me 'the more scared I felt, the louder the activity would become.' You see, only when the individual notices that something bizarre is going on does the phenomena start to become frightening. In this case, Meg felt an icy touch, then her hair was yanked, then she was yanked, all by an invisible hand. Footsteps were also heard, causing the children to surmise that someone physical was in the house. They also experienced a fear-provoking round of crashing furniture, magical whisperings, and the manipulation of the radio, lights, clocks, water faucets, and room temperatures. Even the deaf dog responded to the presence!"

In addition, the girl spoke of seeing a dark form out of the corner of her eye. This would be correct, according to the Warrens because the physical eye is built to see natural images; supernatural images are often detected through peripheral vision. "The form itself was probably the early stages of the materialization of the spirit as a black mass," says Ed. "As the girl threw off more and more negative psychic energy, the spirit was being given the wherewithal it needed to manifest."

"Even in the infestation stage there is a method to the madness," notes Lorraine. "The phantom songbird that sang at night in the nonexistent tree outside the parents' window was an omen of dire events to come. When the phenomena did occur, it tended to happen in threes. The lights were turned off *three* times before the girl felt the icy hand. The clock in the girl's room was ahead by *three* hours; the clock in the boy's room was behind by *three* hours. The girl's hair was pulled not once, but *three* times."

"Phenomena that occur in threes are a signature of the demonic," Ed points out. "Often, the very first thing to happen in a case of infestation is that there will be three knocks at the door. There won't be anyone there, of course, at least nobody visible."

Yet why the use of three by the demonic?

"Three is used as a signal," he replies. "Three is *purposely* used as an insult—to mock the Trinity. But six is the devil's number. Demoniacal actions will often occur in groups of six so that it will be completely understood that the phenomena were not random, but rather *premeditated.*"

When the Foster children ran outside, they felt a malevolent force that let up under the street light. This is another significant fact for the Warrens, because negative forces prove unable to function in an environment of light. Not by coincidence are these known as spirits of darkness. Furthermore, the wildly screeching birds were active only on the left. In other cases that Ed and Lorraine have investigated, birds that screech at night on the left are often found dead on the ground the next morning.

As is evident in the Foster case, infestation activity does not come on as a quick, flamboyant assault. Rather, as noted, the phenomena will begin with three ominous knocks, or footsteps will be heard walking through the house. There may be the sound of scratchings inside the walls. Strange hot or cold spots will be detected in certain areas. A particular room or place in the house will repel, or seem "creepy." The sound of whisperings or heavy breathing may be audible to anyone present. Most notably, the individual in an infested environment will have an unshakeable feeling of another presence in the house. This sense of presence will develop to a point where the individual or family may begin waking up at fixed times of the night, or at precisely three o'clock in the morning.

As time goes on during infestation, things will begin to happen. The mewing of baby animals may be heard coming from that "creepy" room. The scratchings in the walls will change to knocks, raps, and then hard, percussive pounding. "Pranks" will occur that are intended to infuriate. Appliances will go on all by themselves. The phone will ring, but there'll be no call. The front doorbell will sound, at the same time there will be knocks at the back door. No one will be at either door.

"Another indication of an inhuman presence is the *unusual* movement of objects," says Lorraine. "A crystal water glass may fall to the floor by itself, but won't break—it will bounce! Food on the stove will not cook. The dishwater freezes. Keys will not open locks. Door handles will not turn, making the individual a prisoner in a cellar or washroom. Other times, things will simply not remain where they were left, no matter how many times the objects are put back.

"All this, of course, taxes not only the patience, but the individual's sanity, but at this stage, psychological effects are not a factor. Although the strange activity may arouse some anxiety and a great deal of concern, the individual's mind will not yet have been penetrated, as occurs in oppression. Children, particularly infants, are highly vulnerable to inhuman activity, even at the infestation stage. Infants one or two years of age in an infested home very often wake up screaming in mortal terror. The demonic has no compunctions at all about assaulting a baby. An alert person who is suspicious and can spot the early workings of demoniacal phenomena should seek help immediately before events move onto a more personal level, and then out of control completely.

"One question people often ask us," says Lorraine, "is 'How do you know that there's an inhuman spirit in a house?' The answer is that when an inhuman demonic spirit is present, you *know* it's there. Even before your five senses get into the act, your sixth sense is fully aware of its presence. When we interview people about these spirits, they most commonly say 'I felt a horrible sense of doom all around me.' Or, 'You could *feel* the evil in the room.'

"When you're in a spirit-infested environment and your five senses *do* become involved, you'll see, feel, and hear things that are distinctly foul or unnatural. But even that's not good enough for the spirit," she continues, "because this thing's *got to* make you afraid of it. So the frightening ruckus it brings about is part of the strategy. Granted, in the early stages of infestation, the phenomena will be ambiguous. A levitating teacup *can* be PK or a ghost—and a demonic spirit *knows* it's going to be called a poltergeist, instead of being named for what it is. The spirit *deliberately* hides behind ambiguity, in order to take hold. So it's not just the observable phenomena you look at. You can't point to any one levitating teacup and say, 'Ah ha! *This* is demoniacal phenomena!' You've also got to see the purposeful, directed complexity that goes along with the disturbance. The activity takes on a meaningful pattern. What seems at first to be a curious run of events turns out, after study, to be events that are integrally linked with one another, distinct from coincidence and arbitrary, random activity."

Although the terror experienced during infestation is bad enough, it's really only a warm-up to the pandemonium that's liable to happen with the next stage. Whereas the disturbances during infestation may be troublesome, annoying, or frightening, during oppression the spirit begins to take hold and use all the malicious power at its command. As Ed puts it, "During infestation, you've got a problem. With oppression, you've got real trouble."

THE BECKFORD CASE:

*Photographic Documentation
of a Demonic Attack*

At first, the Beckford family thought the destruction was being caused by neighborhood vandals. One morning, the first electrical pipe atop their house was found unaccountably bent at a 90° angle. As can be seen here, something is in the process of bending its replacement. A utility company repairman noted that it would take a jeep with a chain to bend an iron pipe this thick.

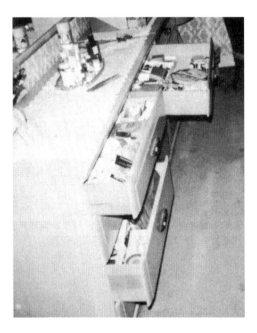

The bureau drawers in Pete and Sharon Beckford's bedroom would open and slam shut of their own accord. More than once, when their son Eric slept on the floor in a sleeping bag (letting the Warrens have his room), the drawers would become active and slam him in the head.

The day begins: each morning when the Beckfords woke up, the bathroom would be torn apart, and towels were often found stuffed in the toilet.

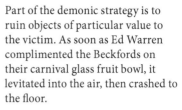
Part of the demonic strategy is to ruin objects of particular value to the victim. As soon as Ed Warren complimented the Beckfords on their carnival glass fruit bowl, it levitated into the air, then crashed to the floor.

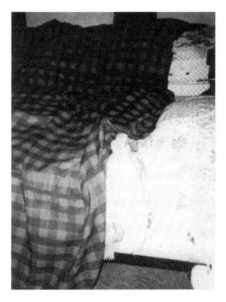

Part of the normal disarray: freshly-made beds have been partly torn apart. Later each day these bed linens would rise to the ceiling, then fall back in a heap on the bed.

The spirit Vicky Beckford contacted on the Ouija board left mementoes on her bed every day. Here it has teleported a door, removed a pocketbook from storage, and dumped garbage from the kitchen, bathroom, and laundry room.

Ed Warren inspects the refrigerator, which has spontaneously been levitated away from the wall at a 90° angle. The kitchen chair arrived atop the appliance courtesy of the same mysterious force. This was the second time the refrigerator had been moved; each time, a deep, baleful moan was heard just before the movement took place.

Preternatural entities can manipulate the physical environment to terrorize their victims. Here the kitchen table tips over as the Warrens watch.

In the basement,
a bottle of Coca-
Cola is levitated.

Throughout the house, bottles would rise into the air, their caps unscrew by
themselves, and the contents would spill. The hi-fi amplifier at left was part of
the second sound system to be destroyed by the infesting entities.

When this picture was taken, the recreation room's sofa cushions had just been dematerialized. A few hours later they were found in a closet.

Furniture levitating during a demonic rampage in the basement recreation room.

Ten minutes before, the room had been in perfect order. Note the plastic garbage can levitating upside down over the pile of furniture. When this photograph was taken, pandemonium was occurring throughout the house.

The first time the Warrens visited the Beckford home, Ed inspected the damage done to the basement recreation room. When he climbed back upstairs to the first floor, these bottles of bleach and detergent floated along behind him. Their caps were removed by unseen hands and their contents spilled on the cellar stairs.

In Lorraine Warren's presence, Eric Beckford's bedroom doors dematerialized. They were later found on the cellar stairs, as photographed. These dematerializations would happen in absolute silence. Physical objects would simply be there one minute, gone the next. Here, the shoes on the floor had been in storage, and for some strange reason, were placed in this ostensibly walking position.

The recreation room lamp being levitated.

8.

Oppression: The Strategy Revealed

Infestation essentially means a house is haunted; oppression means that the spirits haunting the house are trying to take over the people living there. On a practical level, therefore, one subject the Warrens emphasize in their lectures is oppression phenomena. They do so because infestation by spirits may have unknowingly occurred in a home, or it goes unrecognized, and the first time a problem is noticed is when oppression has already begun.

During infestation, the demoniacal strategy is to create fear in order to begin breaking down the human will. During oppression, the entrenched spirit tends to either launch a bombardment of incredible phenomena, or embark on a surreptitious psychological attack, dedicated to the complete domination of the victim's will.

"The prime objective of demonic oppression," Ed says, "is to cause the individual to lose control, or show a momentary lapse in free will, which then opens the door for possession to take place. The infesting spirit's strategy at this stage is to come on with phenomena so terrible and mind-reeling that it breaks down the person's will and tolerance almost completely. However, this wild activity is a *diversion*. The phenomena coming from two fronts—physical and psychological—weaken and disorient the victim, while taxing his emotions to the hilt. Furthermore, to make matters worse, if one or more entities have been successful during infestation, then additional, more powerful spirits are liable to come on the scene next, at which point the phenomena change from bad to worse, worse to terrible. Personal control is essential at this stage, because once the organized breaking down of the will starts, activity will not stop until it's made to do so. Perception of the problem is critical because negative activity will slowly build until it gradually transmutes into all-out chaos."

Oppression strategy can best be summed up in one word: the demonic spirit seeks to *dehumanize* the individual. By whatever means, it tries to reduce a human being—overtly or covertly—to his lowest ebb. Religious writers have long recognized this fact, and as a consequence divide oppression strategy into two forms: internal (through the mind) and external (through the senses). One is a psychological phenomenon; the other physical.

External oppression is an observable event: a negative spirit interacts with the physical world to bring about deceptive or frightening phenomena. At this stage, the Warrens assert, a person can see and feel the activity. "There's no mistaking it," Lorraine points out. "Brute force is used to terrify a person or family. Essentially deranged, the demonic spirit directs its rage into material destruction or attacks on people. In some cases there will be subtle hints of a spirit presence; in others, an all-out rampage. But, in most every case we examine, the spirits infesting the home *do* manipulate the physical environment to some degree."

What kinds of things happen to people confronted with inhuman spirit phenomena? Just how intense can oppression be?

"When Lorraine and I are called in on a case where external oppression is taking place," says Ed, "there's invariably great terror involved. The assault—and that's what it usually is—comes at the family on both a natural *and* a supernatural level. As for the kinds of things that are liable to happen, the victims' five senses will often be saturated with an input of frightening or repulsive phenomena: disgusting smells, ghoulish moans, bloodcurdling screams, knockings, rappings, poundings, heavy breathing and magical whisperings, disembodied footsteps, rapid changes in room temperature, ghastly visions, and so on. When a disturbance really gets going, say into what we call a diabolical *siege*, then you get phenomena like materializations, de-materializations, teleportations, levitations— of both people and objects—strangling sensations about the neck, arms being grabbed from behind, cuts, burns, gouges, wounds, sudden critical illnesses, blinding headaches, vulgarities and blasphemies written on the walls by unseen hands, spontaneous outbreaks of fire, inhuman voices calling on the phone, demon faces showing up on the television screen—you name it, I've seen it. Sometimes the victims are held prisoner inside their own home while being systematically overpowered, even killed, by these forces of inhumanity and evil. Mentally, the brain will be overloaded; physically, the body will be exhausted, and emotionally the person or family will be wrung-out, spent. It is then, when the activity is the *most* unbearable, that the victim gets awakened at three o'clock in the morning by an entity in black standing at the foot of the bed telling him to stop resisting!! This is terror: this is oppression!

"Take a good example," says Ed. "Every year millions of Americans change their residence and a significant number move into homes where there is the potential for activating a dormant spirit. This is what happened to the Carlson family. The Carlsons, a happily married couple in their thirties, bought an old coaching inn here in New England. It was a beautiful old house, right out of Currier and Ives which they moved into on a Good Friday. Now, Nathan Carlson traveled during the week, but his wife, Alexandra, was home all the time to take care of their infant and older daughter. Not long after moving in, Mrs. Carlson and her daughter began hearing footsteps on the second floor where, in the past, lodgers used to stay. During the afternoon and late into the night they'd hear dragging, heavy-booted footsteps move across the floor above them. The pattern of the sound was always the same.

"Mrs. Carlson's older sister, who lived nearby, occasionally stayed overnight in the house and helped take care of the children while Mr. Carlson was on the road. Both Mrs. Carlson's daughter and the sister slept on the second floor, and they too heard these footsteps. The Carlsons also had rooms set aside elsewhere in the house for live-in farm help, and these men would hear footsteps walking in circles around their bed. In fact, while Mrs. Carlson would be asleep at night, she'd be awakened by the spirits in the home which would actually yank the covers off the bed *while* she was in it. She later found out the very same thing happened to the farm help, which accounted for why the men tended to quit so soon after they were hired.

"Eventually, the infestation phenomena upgraded into whisperings that could be heard behind closed doors. However, when Mrs. Carlson or her older sister checked the room where the whisperings were coming from, there was never anyone present. Although these spirits projected words that were often audible enough to be heard, the women could never identify the language that was being used. Sometimes this mysterious language heard in infested homes simply proves to be English being spoken backwards.

"As time went on, the harassment continued. After she straightened up the house, knick-knacks and other little items would never be quite where she left them. Outside the house at night, lights would be seen in the attic—although there was no electricity up there. While painting a room one day, the heat was suddenly drawn away, and she felt a hand touch her shoulder. Mrs. Carlson said she became so angry, she hauled off and threw the paintbrush in the direction where she believed the entity to be, and told it out loud, 'I don't know who you are or what you want, but you're not going to get me.' Mrs. Carlson, of course, told her husband about these disturbances. But Mr. Carlson, having never experienced the sounds or phenomena, shrugged them off, telling her they were the creakings of an old house.

"This is part of the strategy of the demonic, of course—to direct phenomena at specific persons, when others experience nothing at all. Typically, oppression will focus on one or maybe two members of the family group. It really doesn't matter whether the spirit was on the premises when the house was bought, or whether the kids brought it in using a Ouija board. If there's a negative spirit in the house, it's going to pick on someone. Usually the entity will pick on the most psychologically vulnerable person or the one who spends the most time in the house alone. Needless to say, that's usually the housewife. Four out of five oppression and possession cases we investigate involve women. The demonic finds it easier to oppress women because they are generally more open and sensitive than men—not to mention the fact that they're physically on the scene where the infesting spirit is active while their husbands are away at work.

"The reason the demonic spirit singles out one person is obvious: two people could compare notes and recognize an external influence. On the other hand, one person has no way of proving what's happening. Feeling a tap on the shoulder by an invisible hand, hearing a door slam in an empty room, finding a wedding ring at the bottom of the toilet bowl can be quite upsetting, but it doesn't indicate anything supernatural. So, to avoid ridicule, the person keeps quiet about the problem. Rather than making two problems out of one, the oppressed individual simply internalizes the experience.

"Sooner or later, though, self doubt arises and in time the person begins to question his own sanity. He cannot find an origin for the car horns blowing in the living room at night. He sees no one behind him after feeling his hair pulled. He can find no dead animal to account for the revolting smell that comes up after sunset. *Am* I really experiencing this? the victim honestly asks himself. Naturally, the oppressing spirit preys on the doubt it has created, then enlarges upon that doubt until the person doesn't know whether he's coming or going. This is why the phenomena is considered to be a diversion. It is brought about to destabilize the victim. Therefore, under oppression, the self is purposely attacked by an external force, and should the victim start to lose control, then he's one step into possession—the goal, of course, of the inhuman possessing entity.

"In the Carlson case," Ed goes on, "external oppression phenomena went on almost daily, insofar as infestation had occurred in the house long ago. Both the kitchen and bathroom water faucets would suddenly turn themselves on, full force, at the same time. Tappings were incessantly heard at the windows, doors creaked open, and always the bootsteps and walking-around upstairs. A *real* haunted house! On occasions, Mrs. Carlson would hear three knocks at the front door—a conventional sign of an inhuman presence. But whenever she'd go to the door, there'd be no one there. On the second floor, a visitor reported seeing a snake on the window ledge after hearing three taps on the window, yet there was no nearby tree the reptile could have climbed.

"One time when Mrs. Carlson heard the sound of three knocks, she also heard the front door open, then slam, followed by the stomping of bootsteps upstairs. 'Now I got 'em,' she thought. With all the courage she had, Mrs. Carlson went upstairs, armed with her husband's pistol, and systematically checked every room, determined to find the malicious intruder. But, of course, no one *visible* was there. As happens so often when the demonic is involved, she'd been made a fool of.

"Yet," continues Ed, "these were basically little incidents compared to the tragic, sinister things that followed later. While living in the house, the Carlsons had another child. One night, while she and a farm hand were watching television in the living room, they suddenly heard a tremendous, powerful explosion. When they jumped up to check, thinking the furnace had blown apart, they found the door to the infant's room violently torn open. Objects were still swinging and vibrating by the time they arrived, and the temperature in the nursery 'was equal to a meat locker,' she said. Her baby had been born premature, and until only a few weeks before had lived in a hospital incubator. Though the spirits in the home had evidently tried to kill him, the baby managed to live through the experience. However, when the baby boy was three years old, Mrs. Carlson made another startling discovery. As she walked past the child one day, he suddenly let go with a loud shriek. 'You stepped on Beatrice!' he told his mother in no uncertain terms. Being this was a terribly sophisticated name for a three year old to know, let alone pronounce, Mrs. Carlson put down the laundry she'd been carrying and asked the child who was. 'She's my friend,' he answered, 'she tells me what to do.' Mrs. Carlson then told her son to ask *Beatrice* who she was. The little boy did just that, and a few seconds later, after he waited for her reply, said to his mother: 'Beatrice told me to tell you that she's a witch!'

"Like most people, the Carlsons had no belief or knowledge of spirit phenomena, so these invisible entities in the home exerted almost free rein over the family. That was the case, until finally one night things came to a head. Mrs. Carlson was in bed by herself when she saw a large black form in the room with her. She described the entity as being 'blacker than the blackest night.' She said this because the lights in the bedroom were off, and where they lived there were no streetlights to cast weird shadows. The entity moved slowly around the room, transfixing her with fright. Technically, Mrs. Carlson was a victim of phantomania. Before the black mass went away, it transmuted into a globe of synthetic light about the size of a basketball, while producing a deafening roar which she compared to a blast furnace. The phenomenon grew in intensity until suddenly it vanished, leaving Mrs. Carlson absolutely fatigued, whereupon she immediately fell into a deep sleep. This happened twice more—*three* times in all.

"The next two times, Mr. Carlson was home in bed with her, but he didn't see anything. As Mrs. Carlson told me—and mind you, this was a sensible, aware woman—'I knew in my heart this terror was meant exclusively for me, not for anyone else.' When the spirit came the second time, she was suddenly awakened by the presence of the same black entity near her side of the bed. This was followed by the manifestation of the large orb of light, again accompanied by the roar of a blast furnace. The phenomenon peaked, then vanished, leaving her completely drained of energy. The third night the spirit manifested to her in the bedroom, she tried to rouse her husband, but to no avail. She shook him and pounded on his back, but he wouldn't—or rather *couldn't*—wake up. In the meantime, the spirit remained menacingly present in the room with her, its very being scaring her senseless. Ultimately, the message the demonic projected to her was 'Get out!' And they did. Today, the Carlsons live in the same town, but now they know all too well about the coaching inn, and the deadly, oppressive spirits it contains."

Does the demonic spirit always manifest as a black, cloud-like mass?

"The 'black mass' I speak about," says Ed, "is the most common way the demonic introduces itself into the physical realm. I don't know if this represents the mechanics of its manifestation, or if it's peculiar to certain kinds of demonic entities. But a demonic spirit can ultimately manifest as Jesus Christ himself! It may be seen as a ghost; it may come as a hooded specter; even in the form of an animal. A few years ago, sitting in my office here, I happened to catch something move out of the corner of my eye. When I looked,

I saw a black animal I have never seen before about twice the size of a woodchuck, walking across the rug. It was furry and fat and waddled when it walked—as though its body didn't belong with its legs. I didn't know what it was and presumed that it had walked in through a door out of the woods. But when I got up, I saw no door was open. By that time, though, the animal was heading for the passageway. It seemed to have a snout for a face—like a skunk. I followed the thing as it waddled down the passageway. Since the door was closed it couldn't go any further, so as not to corner the thing, I stopped—but it kept going and walked right *through* the closed door. A second later, when I swung the door open, the animal was gone. It was then I realized it was a spirit—or at least the monstrous creation of one. The room it entered—if it did enter the room—was self-contained with no access doors. Whatever the thing was, it vanished. In effect, the inhuman demonic spirit can take on any form it chooses."

If that is so, then why does it come as a black mass?

"Because the watchword of the demonic spirit is *anonymity*," Ed replies. "The spirit comes across as a large, undifferentiated black mass that is easily visible on the rare occasions when it is seen during the day, though it will more likely be witnessed during the psychic hours of night. Only rarely, though, will it show itself in preternatural form. Why come comprehensibly, it reasons, when the spirit's best protection—in fact its ultimate protection—is anonymity and disbelief in its existence? As a physical phenomenon, though, the black mass *is* the spirit, and as such it is perfectly dangerous. When it corners a person, as it did, say, with the Foster children, the individual then reports a critical lack of air, incredible coldness on his body, and a pressure like the weight of a boulder bearing down on him.

"When the person can't get away, then that's it: one of two things will tend to happen. Either spontaneous combustion will occur—the person bursts into flames and is reduced to ash—or he'll dematerialize completely, sometimes forever. Incidents of human combustion are very rare: there's only about twenty cases on record. More likely, though, the individual will dematerialize. In the Carlsons' house, Lorraine was able to discern that the black mass engulfed two people there. The first to be literally spirited-away was a soldier's lackey who was approached by the black mass in the stable behind the house in the year 1776. He was never seen again. The second to vanish was a little girl about 14 years old, named Laura DuPre, who ran into a closet in the house to escape from the black mass, but it subsequently enveloped her too. This occurred around the turn of the twentieth century, and she is still listed by the state police as a missing person. The third to go might have been Mrs. Carlson, if she hadn't the foresight to get hold of us before the spirits in the coaching inn did the same thing to her too."

Ed speaks of the demonic spirit showing itself only rarely in preternatural form. What *does* the demonic spirit look like? The question is an uncomfortable one for him to answer.

"Although the spirit can project itself in any form it chooses," says Ed, "its appearance is an abomination, a monstrosity. To see what's really behind the phenomenon is not something to be desired. To actually *see* the demonic is to feel ruin. What shows is something distinctly preternatural in appearance: something real enough as you see it, but yet something not of this world."

But what does it ultimately look like?

"Ultimately," Ed answers with great reluctance, "it is not human. It *is* inhuman. It has scales. It looks . . . like a reptile. That's it," he cautions. "I won't complete the rest of the image."

Oppression is not always external and observable, however. It is just as often subjective. *Internal oppression* is an emotional and psychological demonic intrusion, dedicated to bringing about an overall change in the person's way of thinking. Here the oppressing spirit's strategy is to so manipulate the person's will that bad habits become worse, and worse habits become impulses toward "sin" or self-destruction. As a creature of sin, the demonic spirit seeks to make the human being culpable, by dragging him down to a level that rejects all life. Writing on this very point in the fifth century A.D., Saint Augustine noted that a habit unchecked becomes a necessity. "This," says Ed, "is precisely what happens during psychological oppression. The individual stands in jeopardy of becoming a stooge, if not a slave to the spirit oppressing him. In advanced stages of oppression, the spirit may so dominate the will that the person has no autonomy at all. At which point, of course, you're at the doorstep of possession."

"The objective of the oppressing spirit," Lorraine adds, "is to possess the person's body, or failing that, to drive the individual to commit murder, suicide—or both. Before that point is reached, however, the individual under oppression will already have been the victim of a *very* complex strategy. Let me give you an example of just how comprehensive internal oppression strategy can be.

"In April 1978, we received a call from an articulate, well-educated woman of about thirty-five who was beside herself with fright. This woman, Patricia Reeves, was under oppression, but she didn't know what was happening to her. She had extreme difficulty getting hold of us, while Ed and I had just as much trouble getting up to see her. Patricia and her friend had bought themselves a bona fide haunted house in New England. Although the events of the case are interesting, what is significant here is how demoniacal strategy figured so prominently in their purchase.

"Patricia was born and raised in Ohio, the daughter of a long line of Baptist ministers. Patricia wasn't married; instead, she split the rent with another woman named Melinda. Though she was a capable adult in every way, money, happiness, and contentment seemed to be withheld from her, and she got to the point of even planning her own suicide. In utter frustration, she purchased a book on witchcraft. Out of that book, Patricia selected one ritual: for prosperity. A few months after she performed the ritual, she received a well-paying, high-prestige job.

"Interestingly, ever since the age of twelve, Patricia had a vivid recurring dream about living in an old colonial farmhouse. Getting this 'dream' house was a lifelong goal. For Patricia, it meant 'going home.' The house was in a rural, upper New England setting and *had* to have been built no later than the early 1800s. So every week without fail, she'd go downtown to the city library and scan the Boston paper for its real estate ads. Using her own word, she did this 'obsessively.' Insofar as oppression is also called obsession, this whole process was going on right under her nose, though she didn't know it.

"One day, about two years after taking over her position of employment, Patricia found an old farmhouse listed in the paper that seemed made to order. Desiring to see it, she and her roommate Melinda took a joint vacation and drove East. They first saw the house on January 1, 1977.

"The place was quite lovely, down a long, wooded lane almost a mile back from the main road. Though the place seemed perfect," Lorraine says emphatically, *"it was a setup."* The previous owner of the house, it turned out later, was a Satanic black witch. Rather odd, don't you think, that they should be drawn three thousand miles from the sunny Southwest to the middle of the New England woods to inhabit *this* particular house? Well, it might seem odd, but by performing the black witchcraft ritual, Patricia and to a lesser degree Melinda, were in debt to the demonic. And what better way to draw them to their doom than by making a dream come true?

"Over the course of a year, the two women drove East a total of not once or twice, but *three* times before ratifying their desire to own the place. On one occasion, Patricia's sister Susan also came along for the ride. During that period, none of the women suspected there was anything wrong.

"When the process of internal oppression first begins the problem is almost impossible to recognize because the shift occurs slowly, one step at a time. Essentially, the person is being groomed or 'prepped' for the day when possession can take place. On December 31, 1977, Patricia made a major decision: to resign her job and buy the house. Both she and Melinda were independent sorts and said they wanted to 'get back to nature and raise animals.' In reality of course, this was the Law of Attraction at work.

"By the time she resigned," continues Lorraine, "Patricia had been through all the paperwork needed to buy the farmhouse. But no bank on either coast was willing to give a large mortgage to two unmarried women. Buying the house would require them to put up a substantial down payment, and they didn't have the cash. No problem, though! While visiting Los Angeles, Melinda got herself on a television game show, and on her birthday, won *ten times* the amount needed for the down payment. In fact, her winnings virtually paid for the house. Yet when they went back to the bank, the lending officers for some reason wanted *three* signatures on the mortgage. Because of this, Patricia's sister Susan was brought in and co-signed the mortgage with the other two women. Traditionally, when a pact is signed, the demonic often arranges for three people— three human wills—to participate in the commitment, again as an insult to the Trinity. To Susan's misfortune, her fate was now formally tied in with that of the other two women.

"The night the mortgage was signed, heavy-booted footsteps entered Patricia and Melinda's apartment in New Mexico. What sounded like an intruder pounded on the doors to the women's respective bedrooms. Cut off from the living room phone, both women spent a night of dread terror, each huddled alone in fear. What they didn't know at the time was that this was the classic entrance of the demonic. The bill for the prosperity ritual had now come due.

"With the mortgage secured, Patricia and Melinda moved East to the farm at the end of January 1978. As soon as they took up residence in the house, they had a terrible feeling of being watched. The feeling was so intolerable that they both often slept at a nearby motel, while fixing up the inside of the house during the day. They also had two dogs, Corgis, that'd always gotten along well before. But just as soon as these two dogs were brought onto the property, they began attacking one another. The women had to keep them separated lest they tear each other apart.

"Around the same time, Patricia and Melinda also started to argue and fight with each other over petty, inconsequential things. Rather than work, they'd argue for days on end over who would paint a window and who would paint a door. These women, you see, were unknowingly oppressed into this behavior, as were their dogs. In fact, oppression was all set, waiting for the group to arrive.

"Eventually—under oppression—the women decided it was their house and they were going to sleep in it and not patronize the expensive local motel. At that point, the feeling of being watched turned sour, into an atmosphere of evil in the home. Believing their feelings were only psychological, the women did their best to play down these emotions, but then strange things started to happen. At night, from outside the house, they heard ominous chantings that turned their blood cold. During the day, ammonia and cleaning agents disappeared; in their place would be drops of blood. Inside the house, money and personal items also vanished and were never found again. One afternoon, there were knocks at the back door. When they answered it, no one was there. Instead, what the women found were a series of *left* footprints—a sign of the demonic—in hip-deep snow leading to the barn. The prints were spaced three feet apart, yet they'd penetrated only a half-inch into the soft powder.

"A few months after they purchased the house, Patricia's sister Susan came to help with the fix-up job. Susan was a sensitive woman in her twenties. When she arrived at the farmhouse this time, the place overwhelmed her with morbid terror, and she immediately flew back to her home. Yet, she was still affected by the oppressing spirits, because a few weeks later, out of nowhere, Susan brutally stabbed herself with a butcher knife. The doctor who worked on the young woman said her wounds—and there were three stab wounds—should have been mortal, and he didn't understand why she hadn't died.

"For leaving the farmhouse, Melinda, too, received a similar penalty. No more than a month after they moved East, Melinda became so totally repelled by the evil in the house, that she also returned to Ohio. But Melinda was there no more than a few days when she was forcibly and violently raped by an unknown intruder. At that point, she succumbed. Believing mental terror preferable to gross physical violence, she returned to the New England farmhouse.

"By the spring of 1978, after experiencing a catalog of horrors for months, these poor women had now fully come under oppression. Both developed wrinkles on their faces, their brown hair turned to gray, and, physically their features aged twice their years. 'I couldn't recognize myself in the mirror,' Patricia told me. 'The look in our eyes was one of emptiness and death.'

"Now and then, Melinda would be involuntarily overwhelmed by an evil personality, especially when Patricia wanted to make any radical change to the house. The worst episode came when Patricia rented a chainsaw and was about to cut down the pine trees in front of the house that kept the interior dark. 'Melinda came running out of the house like she was on fire,' Patricia said to me. 'She had the most incredibly wicked face—the face of *someone else!* She threatened to kill me if I put so much as a nick in one pine tree!' Patricia now understood there was something wrong—*metaphysically* wrong—

and saw the need to get help. After having an incredible time getting anyone to believe her, someone finally gave Patricia our name and she called on us.

"I couldn't tell them at the time," Lorraine goes on, "but for these women, death was really just around the corner. That farmhouse was a killing place. When Ed and I drove down the access road to the property, I saw—through second sight—people in robes performing some kind of profane ritual in the meadow by the house. There was chanting, and the whole show was going on at night; they were using a human being as an altar—or victim. When we got into the house, it was apparent to me that whoever lived there before had engaged in the slaughter and mutilation of animals. I could feel the sorrow of many hundreds of animals, large and small, that had been killed there. And in the house, the atmosphere, the very air you breathed was thick with evil and perversity. The place repelled me too, and it was evident that only through demoniacal oppression could anyone ever live in such a hellish domain.

"I think what we've said makes it quite clear that an invisible, negative intelligence was guiding events here. But I'd like to make the point that in this case, in this house, it wasn't just invisible. While Ed was interviewing the women, I decided to walk through the dwelling. One of their Corgis came with me. The place was like most of these infested homes—uncomfortable and threatening, with an overlay of sadness. Suddenly, the dog bolted and ran down the hallway, skidding to a stop at the closet door, where it began growling viciously. I opened the door. The closet smelled like a cesspool. The dog lurched at something in the closet and then a few seconds later, to my astonishment, a totally black figure—in the crude form of a man, but having no features— ran right past me out of the closet and scurried up the stairs, with the Corgi in hot pursuit. In all my days, I have never seen the demonic take on such an overtly humanoid form.

"In this case," Lorraine concludes, "the thrust of oppression strategy by the demonic was subtle—more psychological than physical. Either way, though, the strategy of the demonic remains the same: to break down the will of the human being in order to possess the body, or to oppress the individual to commit some negative act, preferably one involving bloodletting and death. And here, it was nearly successful. Both women required a form of exorcism to be performed on them in order to be freed from the influence and physical distortions brought about by the inhuman entities that inhabited that place. In the end, Patricia and Melinda sold the farm for what they paid for it, and returned to New Mexico where they both live sadder but wiser today. Although Ed and I could go on and on with all the densely knit factors that make up this individual case, I think it's quite apparent there's more than coincidence involved in a case such as this. Lurking in the background is a negative intelligence *directing* the activity."

"By the time the phenomena move from the infestation to the oppression stage," Ed agrees, "the demonic spirit is really no longer able to veil its presence. Instead, out of pride in its own effectiveness, it begins leaving calling cards—some literal, some symbolical.

"Often the demonic spirit likes to make its presence known in writing. It particularly likes to write on walls and mirrors, even going so far as to prefer lipstick or crayon as a writing implement. The demonic spirit tends to write backwards, from right to left, so the script has to be read in a mirror. The words and phrases appear as though someone has written on the walls with the 'wrong' hand. As far as *what* they say, about all these spirits tend to write are vulgarities, smut, and blasphemies, usually in the language spoken by the person or family being oppressed. Other languages may be mixed in, though the mixing of languages more often occurs when the spirit speaks during possession. In later stages of oppression, or in situations where devils are at hand, more sophisticated languages may be used."

Ed and Lorraine speak almost exclusively about demons. If there are devils—a separate hierarchy of spirits, why not speak about them too?

"Although much has been written about devils by laymen," Ed claims, "my knowledge comes either from my own experience or from the study of authentic religious documents. Based on my work, what is *properly* known about devils is minimal compared to what's known about the demonic spirit. It's the demonic we see carrying out all this incredible phenomena. True, during an exorcism a demonic spirit will carry on and brag that it is this or that devil, but the spirit is usually lying. In the end, the distinction between demons and devils is like labor and management: one works, the other supervises. Demonic spirits of a higher order bring about internal oppression, because lesser, bestial spirits lack the wisdom and ability to follow through with possession. The lesser entities are content to bring about external havoc to break down the will through fright, while higher entities break down the will by diminishing internal psychological resistance. Theologically, you see, devils were a higher order of angel before the Fall, and have greater knowledge and power than the spirits below them. The writings of a devil tend to be neat and orderly, for example, written backwards from right to left, in a rather attractive script. Moreover, these more knowledgeable entities often rely on classical languages—mostly Latin, though sometimes Greek or ancient Hebrew. As opposed to demonic spirits, devils seem inclined to write only on paper or parchment and only when a pact with Satan is involved. More often than not, in the cases I work with, the scribblings and scrawlings and blasphemies are done by demonic spirits."

When the demonic does not literally sign its name to its loathsome handiwork, then the Warrens must look for more symbolic, intellectual traces of its presence.

"For one thing," says Lorraine, "this is a negative spirit, so it's something that's literally 'going the other way.' The demonic tends to work in direct opposition to principles of the positive world. When the spirit moves, it tends to go right to left, counterclockwise, or in circles. When the spirit approaches you, it typically moves from the left or from behind. Hate, filth, and death invigorate the demonic; goodness, light, and prayer immobilize it. The spirit comes in black, accentuates evil, and seeks to destroy rather than enhance. The residue it leaves behind is foul and offensive. Bloodletting and physical injury are part and parcel of the phenomenon. It befriends the mean and the ignorant; it attacks the innocent, the unwary, and the pious. It is a sneak, it is deceptive, and it comes like a thief in the night. It veils its presence through lies, and preserves its anonymity through duplicity and invisibility. As religious writers have said, 'the spirit has no positive nature; its being is based on the *lack* of something that is good.'"

The spirit's symbolic workings are no less an indication of its presence. Customarily, the demonic will choose a significant day or time of year to launch its siege. The Warrens have found that favored occasions include Christmas, Easter, Good Friday, the beginning of Lent, the first night of Passover, the month of November (the astrological period of Scorpio), Sundays, Fridays, and individuals' birthdays.

"The phase of the moon may also figure into the formula," Ed notes. "A new moon is the preferred phase, because there is a total absence of natural light—plus a new moon has long been a symbol of death. Events may often peak or begin on a full moon, though. This occurs because, by nature's clock, what is started on a new moon comes to a head on a full moon. But let me stress, when dealing with spirit phenomena, this symbolism can be taken too far. Again, only in retrospect, upon analysis, will a particular number, date, or time of year reveal itself as being part of the overall strategy of an oppressing spirit.

"When all the factors are assembled," Ed continues, "after we interview the principals, and witness the activity ourselves, it will become apparent that there is an order to the pandemonium. If you had to reconstruct a typical case of demonic oppression, you'd have something like a thousand separate factors. Therefore, the case has to be looked at in totality so the interplay of all factors—the history, the phenomena, the signs, symbols, strategy, and synchronicity—can be viewed as working in unison. When viewed in totality, a progression of events will become apparent, with each individual bit playing its own part. You'll notice the origin of the problem, preliminary setups, infestation strategy, oppression strategy, symbolic events, and so forth. There'll be signs of deliberateness—events occurring at precise times of the day, or only on certain days of the week. Although we couldn't possibly repeat all the details in *The Amityville Horror,* for example, let's look at some of the similarities between what the Lutzes reported and what we've experienced in our own investigations.

"First," says Ed, "take the background to the case, before the Lutz family moved in. A normal family of seven, the DeFeos moved into that home in the early 1960s.

Around three o'clock in the morning on November 13, 1974— the worst time of day on probably the most troublesome day of the year—the son murdered the six members of his family, including his father, with a high-powered rifle. Not one of the neighbors heard the shots. Thirteen months after the murders occurred, George and Kathleen Lutz moved into the home during the Christmas season— often an active period for the demonic. Our knowledge of what happened next is necessarily secondhand—we weren't there with the Lutzes. But according to what the Lutzes told Jay Anson, George, who was usually clean, well-dressed, and a bit of a workaholic, turned lazy and sloppy. He sat by the fireplace throughout almost the entire episode. He could never get warm, although the thermostat in the house was always in the eighties. In cases we've investigated, when a spirit draws thermal energy, it also removes all the heat from the rooms as well. This is what we call the *psychic cold.* You can wrap yourself up in a dozen blankets, but it won't do any good, because your body heat is also being robbed.

"Of course," says Ed, "a spirit draws this energy for a reason: to use it *against* the people in the home. Given that this is a negative entity, it thinks negatively, so these forces are used for brutal, negative purposes.

"Kathy, meanwhile, told us she was 'unlike herself,' and became cranky, argumentative, and impatient with her children. According to *The Amityville Horror*, she had a number of dreams that seemed to correlate with certain facts in the DeFeo murder case. The children also became quarrelsome, and the family dog acted peculiar as soon as the family moved in.

"What happened next?" Ed asks rhetorically. "Only those who were there can say for sure. But George and Kathy said that hundreds of flies appeared in the upstairs bedroom. The toilet fluids turned black. A ceramic lion teleported itself around the house. Furniture moved on its own accord. One of the children's hands was squashed flat, yet he suffered no physical damage afterwards. And, of course, in the middle of the night, George heard the sound of a marching band.

"Ironically, while the Lutzes were living in the house, we'd delivered lectures to two college audiences detailing the kind of phenomena victims encounter in demoniacally infested environments—including the sound of marching bands playing Sousa in the middle of the night!

"Activity bearing the stamp of demoniacal powers is *meant* to frighten. In addition, the Lutz family claimed they also experienced psychic cold, stiflingly hot temperatures, and the repulsive smell of excrement—a conventional sign of a demonic presence. The Lutzes were also subject to obstructions while using the telephone; and Kathy Lutz's brother discovered $1,500—money he intended to use for wedding expenses—missing from his pocket."

Did that money really disappear?

"I can't say," says Ed. "But money often disappears in homes infested by malevolent spirits. Loss of a paycheck or large sums of money will disturb an individual. It's just one of many ways negative spirits try to break a person or family down. But, I think it's unlikely that such 'lost' money just disappears into thin air. Instead, between you, me, and the lamp post, I'd say there's roughly a hundred percent chance that the money gets teleported to a sorcerer or someone else involved in the black arts. I say this because I know sorcerers who have never worked a day in their life, yet they're financially well-off. For them, everything falls into place. Life is easy; good things always come their way. They have no troubles at all. *Money finds them.* Why? Because they've made a metaphysical arrangement and work in league with the demonic.

"Though that may *sound* harmless, there's a hitch. These sorcerers or witches are usually in debt to the demonic to the tune of their soul; indebtedness to the devil in a future life; or perhaps the sacrifice of someone close to them, like a child. For these people, it's your basic Faust trip. Life is short, and they don't respect it. They sell their soul for a penny when it's worth a million later on. So, yes, when money disappears in an infested house, I'd be willing to bet it reappears in the wallet of a sorcerer!

"All these factors set the Lutzes' emotions on edge and put them in a position where they began to doubt their own sanity," Ed resumes. "Nevertheless, these disturbances, plus a lot more I've left out, like a crucifix being symbolically turned upside down, resemble what we have seen in *external* oppression phenomena. Going further, though, the Lutzes said a demon form burned itself into the back of the fireplace. Typically, these spirits manifest themselves in fire or in fireplaces. There was also a hooded monstrosity that showed itself on the stairs. These spirits are often seen in monks' robes. And, of course, the youngest child, Missy, talked about a pig that called itself Jodie, and *told* the child that it was an angel!"

There seems to be some question about Jodie the pig. Could it have been a real, physical entity?

"I never saw the entity myself," Ed replies. "However, it isn't necessary for a spirit to be physical. Spirits can also project themselves through a process we call *telepathic hypnosis*. That mouthful of syllables simply means the spirit can project its image in any form it chooses, through a process one might call three-dimensional ESP. The spirit merely *thinks* of how it wants to display itself, and that's how it will look. Using this method—and both human and inhuman spirits can do this—the entity bypasses the physical eye and projects the desired image directly to the 'mind's eye,' or third eye as it's called in Eastern religions. The result of this telepathic transfer of vibrations from one intelligence to another may have all the trappings of a physical being. In reality, however, the spirit may never have physically manifested at all. One way or the other, though, something has to be *there* to be perceived."

The Amityville case took place during the Christmas season. A no less horrendous case of true demoniacal phenomena occurred during the Easter season of 1974 and went on for eight-and-a-half weeks before it was finally brought to a stop by a church-sanctioned exorcism. Except for the Warrens, the exorcist, and the principals involved, few people until now know that a supernatural battle took place in the home of this otherwise normal American family.

Behold the Beckfords.

9.

A Family Under Attack

On March 3, 1974, Mr. Peter Beckford, age fifty, made a note on the kitchen calendar: his daughter Vicky's car had just gotten a flat tire on a trip to the drugstore. Pouring himself another Sunday morning cup of coffee, Pete Beckford could hardly have imagined that this seemingly ordinary event was the beginning of an all-out siege by violent, inhuman spirits that would begin with acts of vandalism, and end in the near-total destruction of his small ranch house.

Hell would break loose in the Beckford household because the night before, nineteen-year-old Vicky Beckford had crossed the line: she invited a demonic spirit to manifest. Though the deceived girl gave this permission unwittingly, she nevertheless committed a supernatural transgression of the highest order. What resulted was perhaps the worst case of diabolical attack the Warrens have ever experienced.

"The actual beginning of the case would have to be dated a year earlier, though," Ed states. "That's when Vicky began using the Ouija board." In this day and age, her motive for seeking spirit communication was somewhat understandable. Bored and lonely, she was seeking excitement. Her family was strict and religious and kept a tight rein both on her and her fifteen-year-old brother, Eric. A brooding adolescent, Vicky had few friends and withdrew into herself. One night, in futility, she decided to try to find a friend on the Ouija board. After everyone had gone to bed, she placed the "magic talking board" on the floor, put her fingers on the planchette, and began asking questions.

"Is anyone there? My name is Vicky Louise Beckford. Is there a spirit who can hear me?" Suddenly the planchette whizzed up to YES. To Vicky's eventual misfortune, she now had a disembodied acquaintance.

From then on, Vicky contacted the same spirit every night. She looked forward to the nightly communication with her patronizing ethereal "friend" and would spend hours conversing on the board with it. And no wonder, the spirit played on her vanities, always making a point of complimenting the girl: YOU LOOKED BEAUTIFUL IN THE BROWN DRESS TODAY, VICKY. YOU'RE SO PRETTY COMPARED TO THOSE OTHER GIRLS. TOMORROW WEAR YOUR HAIR UP. IT LOOKS GOOD THAT WAY. Night after night, the spirit on the board accented melodramatic issues that would lead to emotional excesses later on. YOU MAKE ME SO HAPPY, HONEY, the board would perversely tell the lonely teenager. I'D LOVE TO MARRY YOU, IF I COULD.

YOU'RE SO LUCKY TO BE ALIVE, was another ploy. TELL ME WHAT IT WAS LIKE TO BE ALIVE TODAY, it implored. In response, Vicky Beckford would sympathetically recite the events of her day. Following that, she'd then ask the thing questions. The spirit responded with stories about its death, and how lonely it had been before "meeting" her. Vicky believed every word. Cunningly, the spirit strung the girl out emotionally every night. Then it would abruptly stop communicating and say teasingly, SEE YOU TOMORROW.

Over the course of many months, the entity led Vicky to believe it was the spirit of a teenage boy, a sort of "teen angel," who'd died when she herself was just a little girl. Gullible and unsuspecting, Vicky replied by telling "him" all about herself and her feelings. In turn, the spirit on the board fed her similar "intimacies." Yet, on the one occasion she asked the spirit to tell her its name, the oppressing entity backed off, giving the lame excuse that it "must never reveal its name to a living person, or else be forced to return to the mists."

As time went by, Vicky nevertheless became infatuated with the spirit on the Ouija board, which she came to view as a boyfriend. To acknowledge her affection, the spirit gave Vicky information about insignificant future events. Later, she would witness incidents around town that the spirit told her would occur. Overall, the spirit on the Ouija board became extremely credible to Vicky Beckford.

After a year of trading intimacies on the board, Vicky became emotionally dependent on the spirit. During the last week of February 1974 Vicky went a step further. "Can you reveal *my* future?" she asked.

The spirit was only too happy to comply. In a long, involved session, it laid out a scenario of Vicky's life for the next six years, providing specific details, right down to the date of birth of her first child, and the fact that she would have a total of three children by 1978 (all information that would eventually prove correct!).

Vicky's overwhelming involvement with an unknown spirit soon made her even more curious and impatient. She craved to *see* her invisible boyfriend. Late Saturday night, March 2, she pleaded for him to manifest. Just once, she told the spirit, she wanted to see what he looked like.

The next day, Sunday morning, Pete Beckford went out and tried to start his car. It wouldn't turn over. Lifting up the hood, he found the sparkplug wires pulled out, the rubber hoses unfastened, and the fan belt cut. Not much later, Vicky tried to start her car too. It wouldn't start either, and finally had to be towed away to a local garage. The next day, mechanics surmised that internal engine parts had been disassembled.

That week, other incidents of apparent vandalism occurred around the Beckford house. The back doorbell was torn out of its housing. Foundation shrubs were yanked out of the ground—roots and all. On the roof, a six-foot cast-iron pipe, housing electrical wires, was unaccountably bent at a ninety-degree angle.

On Friday, March 8, Pete Beckford marked "1 flat" on the kitchen calendar. No sooner did Vicky get her car back from the shop than one of her other tires lost air. The next day, Saturday, her father made the same entry on the calendar; although this time, it seemed the tire had been cut with a knife.

In the meantime, inexplicably, Vicky could no longer raise her invisible boyfriend on the Ouija board. Night after night, she tried to communicate, but the planchette would simply slide over to GOODBYE. She had no idea that her ethereal beau *had* actually manifested: in the form of a supernatural vandal.

By the second week of March, material damage to the house and cars had become so troublesome that Pete Beckford complained to the police. When the law arrived, Pete pointed out the destruction done to garden plants and shrubs, the exterior of the house, and the apparent intrusion into a locked garage to puncture tires and tear engines apart. Once he'd even heard someone pound on the house from outside! Before leaving, the policeman assured Pete—a respectable member of the community—that they'd keep an eye on the property during night patrols.

Later that second week, however, came the first indication that the damage had nothing to do with prankish neighborhood kids. After work, Pete and his wife, Sharon, were sitting in the kitchen questioning Eric about his friends. Were these incidents of vandalism the outgrowth of some sort of high-school feud? Suddenly, all three heard something smash against a wall somewhere *inside* the house.

Cautiously moving to investigate, they found a gaping eighteen-inch hole in the plasterboard wall in Eric's room.

Just as upsetting was the fact that the jagged edges of the plasterboard were pointing *inward*. The blow had been delivered from inside the house! For the Beckfords, the strange vandalism suddenly took on a sobering new dimension.

That night when they went to bed, the Beckfords could hear scratchings inside the walls. It sounded like a squirrel had gotten into the house. Listening in the dark, Pete also heard the sound of a board being pried loose. Leaping out of bed, he switched on the lights and spent the next half hour checking the house from cellar to attic. He found no loose boards; in fact, he found nothing out of place. Yet the same weird, troublesome noises continued all week long.

In the meantime, Vicky's car had already suffered three flat tires, so Pete bought her a new set of radials. On Tuesday, March 19, in the locked garage, one of her new radial tires went flat. It seemed to have been slit with a knife.

That third week of March the phenomena began to intensify. After nightfall, something again began to pound on the Beckford house from outside. The hard, ka-*boom* type wallops came in series of threes, hitting with so much force they shook the house. Naturally Pete went out to investigate, but there was nothing to be seen. At least a dozen times that week, he and Eric went outside with flashlights, vainly trying to find the source of the pounding.

As the third week wore on, sharp, jarring raps were heard inside the house as well. This quickly upgraded in power, until the sound was like that of a grown person beating on the walls. When the family went to bed, the random poundings and scratchings continued. Around midnight, the sound of boards being torn off the walls could be heard throughout the small ranch house.

The weekend of March 20 and 21, the pressure valves on the

steam radiators somehow became unscrewed, spewing hot water all over the walls and carpets. Pete's first inclination was to blame Vicky or Eric, but they weren't home when it happened. Puzzled, yet upset, he methodically replaced the radiator cylinders, but every few hours they came loose again, inflicting more water damage. Finally, he turned off the heat in the basement.

Meanwhile, the pounding was becoming more frequent—and intense. Rather than relax that weekend, Pete Beckford, a man with twenty-three years' experience in machine design, nearly tore his house apart looking for the source of the noises. After wasting a whole Sunday, he gave up. The next morning, desperate for peace and quiet, Pete capitulated and called both a furnace repairman and a plumber.

The furnace repairman arrived early in the morning on Tuesday, the fourth week of March, and declared the furnace to be in perfect working order. But he too heard the pounding noises and ultimately spent some nineteen hours in the Beckford house trying to stop the intermittent poundings. In the end, all he could tell Pete and Sharon was that "the sounds *are not* being caused by the furnace."

On Wednesday, the plumber came to examine the radiators. Pete was at work at his manufacturing plant, but Sharon explained that every day one or two pressure valves would unscrew themselves, spewing out steam and hot water. She also told him about the poundings on the walls and the nocturnal scratchings. The plumber tested for pressure leaks, but the radiators were also in perfect working order. As a precaution, he replaced the old valves with new ones, cinching them down with all his strength. Yet strangely, no sooner did he move on, than the new cylinder would be found lying on the floor beside the radiator. After testing and repairing the radiators two full times, he finally put the old cylinders back on. He then packed up his tools and said to Sharon Beckford: "Lady, you got yourself a problem!"

That same week, another of Vicky's new tires was slashed with a knife, although the car was parked inside the locked garage as usual. However, flat tires had become insignificant compared to the turmoil going on inside the house. Each day—particularly after sunset—the poundings on the house and walls grew louder and louder. The percussive blows often went on for hours on end into the night. Pictures and decorations fell off the walls from the force of the impact.

Valiantly, the Beckfords tried to cope with the unreasonable problem by going out to dinner, milling through shopping malls, or frequenting drive-in movies that could keep them away as late as possible. Though the family's early attempts to avoid the ruckus provided some temporary respite, what had happened so far was really only a prelude to the pandemonium that was in store.

On Sunday, March 31, yet another knife hole appeared in one of Vicky's new radials. This was the sixth time a tire had been cut or gone flat; it was also the last time she would have tire problems. Because that night, the unexplainable vandalism of the past month transformed itself into overt supernatural activity.

Around ten o'clock that Sunday night, with the unstoppable pounding going on, Pete and Sharon were watching television in their bedroom, the quietest place in the house. Eric and Vicky, afraid to be by themselves, sat on the floor nearby. Suddenly the lights went off and on by themselves three times in succession; then the television set went dead. As it did, the Beckfords watched as the heavy wooden bedroom dresser eerily began to levitate a few inches off the floor.

Aghast, they watched as the loaded dresser—six feet long, weighing some two-hundred-and-fifty pounds—began violently twisting back and forth. Perfume and cosmetic bottles fell over and dropped to the floor and broke. The dresser was then set down. A moment later, however, one of the drawers slid open. The drawer hovered for a second, then slammed forcefully shut. Soon, all the drawers were slamming in and out by themselves.

As the Beckfords sat frozen in terror, the drawers came to rest. Promptly, a heavy chair, laden with folded clothes, lifted some three feet off the floor, tilted on its side, dumped the clothes, and then fell on top of the linen with a heavy thud. Next, one after the other, pictures lifted from their hooks, drifted away from the wall and then floated in a circle around the room.

"My God," Sharon cried out, "what have we done to deserve this?" With that, the bedboards fell to the floor. The double bed, with Pete and Sharon on top of it, collapsed. The pictures then dropped to the floor, and all activity ceased.

Later that night after cleaning up the mess, the Beckfords tried to go to sleep. When the lights were turned off, however, they heard the sound of a kitten mewing in the spare bedroom. Minutes later, the sound transmuted into that of a crying baby. Pete wanted to check out the room, but common sense told him to stay away. The ever-present scratching sounds changed into ripping and tearing noises. Again the sound of planks being torn off the walls was heard; indeed, it seemed as though the whole house was being dismantled.

Poundings picked up on the roof and the outside of the house, which then transferred themselves to the inside walls. Over the course of an hour, the poundings made their way up the hallway, then ominously stopped. All of a sudden, sharp, jarring raps sounded on Pete and Sharon's headboard; as though the headboard was being hit with a hammer. Pete and Sharon jumped out of bed, but the noise continued. At one point, Pete counted eighteen continuous bangs on the wooden headboard.

As fear permeated the house, the activity grew even more powerful and intense. When furniture was heard to fall over in the living room, Pete was about to investigate when a bloodcurdling scream came from Vicky's bedroom.

"Something was here!" the girl said in a breathless panic. "Something was *in this room* with me!"

On April Fools' Day, it rained rocks! The rocks descended right out of the blue sky, pelted the Beckfords' roof, and rolled off onto the lawn. Terrified when one of the rocks crashed through the back window, Sharon Beckford telephoned her husband at work. Fatigued from the night before, Pete told her to call the police and said he would be home right away.

By the time Pete Beckford got home, the police were on the scene, also watching the incredible spectacle of stones falling out of the sky onto the trim ranch house. The stones fell for about one hour, in all, then stopped. Desperate, Pete asked the police what to do. "Call a priest," they suggested.

How could a priest help? Pete wondered. There was nothing "religious" about their predicament

Pete Beckford stayed home the rest of the day. That night, when the sun went down furniture and objects in the house began levitating in the air in full view of everyone. Some of the items dropped to the floor while others were slammed up against the walls. This terrible, insidious activity went on all night long. The best the Beckfords could do was stay out of the way, because some of the objects seemed to be thrown directly *at* them.

The next morning, with the house a shambles, Pete was exasperated enough to take the policeman's suggestion. Being Roman Catholic, he telephoned the rectory of the local Catholic church and spoke with the priest who was on duty. Furniture in the house was levitating, Pete explained; expensive objects were being thrown down and broken; poundings and scratchings and other frightful noises went on all night; stones had even fallen on the house! The priest took the Beckfords' address and promised to be there within an hour.

The disturbance came to an abrupt halt when the priest arrived, but Pete escorted him around the house nonetheless. Stepping over the breakage and overturned furniture, the priest's only assessment was that someone in the house was "disturbed" and Pete had better call a psychiatrist. The clergyman then left, whereupon the poundings and levitations started up anew.

Tormented and confused, Pete went into work late that day. Fully exasperated, he decided to go ahead and confide in the one man he trusted and respected: his supervisor. In a glass-enclosed cubicle, Pete explained why there were so many absences on his previously excellent attendance record. For the better part of an hour, Pete disclosed the whole bizarre story to the man. The supervisor believed Pete and wanted to help, but he had no idea how he could be of assistance. He did, however, recall the name of some people whom he'd heard speaking on the radio. "Their name is Warren, I believe: I remember them saying that sometimes only a blessed object placed in a home will stop weird goings-on. I don't know how to get hold of these people, but I do think they're your best bet."

The conversation did much to bolster Pete Beckford. That evening, he went down to the basement and unpacked an eighteen-inch plaster statue of Saint Anne that Pete hoped would solve the problem. However, no sooner did Pete bring it upstairs than he heard a tremendous commotion downstairs. When he ran down to investigate, he found the recreation room furniture *floating* through the air. To the left, soaps and detergents in the laundry room were also levitating, spilling their contents on the floor. The irrationality of the whole thing overwhelmed Pete. He trudged back upstairs to find the statue missing. Later he found it in the bathroom, beside the toilet.

That night, along with all the other intolerable phenomena, shrieks and hellish noises filled the Beckford house. After a search the next morning, the statue of Saint Anne was discovered under the covers of the bed in the spare bedroom.

Before uncovering the statue, however, Pete found obscenities written in pencil on Eric's bedroom door; the same foul-minded filth one encounters in a public lavatory. Believing Eric might somehow be behind it all, Pete flew into a rage and laid into the teenage boy. But Eric just collapsed into despair and began crying from the bottom of his heart. The boy had done nothing wrong. Pete apologized to his son. Though perplexed, Pete Beckford was slowly becoming aware that for some unexplained reason his whole family had fallen victim to the same thing—whatever it was.

As the first week of April wore on, sleep was impossible. Fed up, Pete decided to move his family out of the house until some solution could be found. Maybe they were just imagining it all, Pete thought, or perhaps by staying away, the "spell" would be broken. Taking toilet articles and a change of clean clothing, the Beckfords went to a nearby motel.

That night at the motel, the Beckfords all slept in the same room for safety. However, they soon learned there was no escape from their troubles. Lights switched themselves on and off. Pictures left the walls, and once more the pounding started up.

The next morning, when the Beckfords came back to their room after breakfast, everything was topsy-turvy. Furniture was tipped over, drawers were pulled out. Sheets and clothes, mattresses and box springs were strewn around the room. As they set about straightening up, the manager appeared to say that other guests had complained about the Beckford "children" banging on the walls all night, and the maid had pointed out the ridiculous vandalism to the room.

Pete Beckford took the blame for everything, apologized, and assured the manager that it wouldn't happen again. But that night, it did; the next day the Beckfords had no choice but to return home.

Saturday, April 6, when Pete opened the front door, the mixture of smells was unbelievable. Rugs and beds were saturated with spilled food, cleaning fluids, liquor, shoe polish, cologne, and perfume. Towels were stuffed in the toilets. Furniture in every room was knocked over, some of it broken. Across the walls were scribbled truly demented blasphemies in blood-red ink, and obscene accusations against God and Christ. It took the Beckfords the rest of the day to clean the walls and put the house back in order.

In particularly violent cases the Warrens have investigated, the most outstanding feature of oppression strategy is this kind of systematic destruction. The aftermath of these invisible vandals' onslaught is enough to leave an observer dumbstruck with amazement. It truly looks as though a platoon of morons has marched through the house. Wreckage is everywhere. Foul writing is scrawled on the walls. Cherished items and religious objects are singled out for particular besmirchment and ruin. In terms of dollars and cents, it can be very costly to play host to the demonic. Yet why the destruction? Why should these incorporeal entities care about destroying material items?

"These spirits are the essence of cruelty," says Ed. "If you've spent half your life trying to assemble a nice home for your family, then it's very distressing to stand by and watch $5,000 worth of furniture get trashed in five minutes. Usually many spirits will be responsible for a rampage—and they'll ruin whatever is worthwhile to you. And you can't do anything about it. If you try, you'll either be held back, incapacitated by some invisible force, or else you're liable to get hit over the head with something. Many times, as in the Beckford case, people aren't even home when the destruction occurs. They'll just walk in and find everything they own wrecked, destroyed, or broken. It's so inconceivable that a nonphysical being could cause such damage, that people's first response is to pick up the phone and call the police, believing their home was ransacked by burglars. Nevertheless, the net effect of the destruction is psychological. The spirit is attempting to penetrate the individual's will.

"Don't forget," Ed goes on, "that the external phenomena is used as a diversion. While breaking furniture, the spirit devotes just as much energy to breaking a person down internally. To keep your emotions under control during oppression, you'd have to have the patience of a saint. Whether the disturbance leaves you scared, depressed, angered, or whatever, you can't help but become upset emotionally. It's nothing to be ashamed of—it's called being human. Although it's quite all right to be emotional as a result of the situation, it's something else again to fully lose control because, ultimately, that's what the demonic is *trying* to make you do."

On April 7, Palm Sunday, Pete's brother Terry was bringing his family over for dinner. Unlike Pete, Terry was a professional man, yet both brothers were hard-working men who had helped each other all through life. Perhaps now, Sharon thought, they might be able to solve this problem together,

She and Pete explained to Terry the terrible ordeal they'd been through; however, no unusual activity occurred that Sunday as the Beckford clan sat down to dinner. Terry Beckford's only response was to say there had to be a rational explanation for the whole thing.

After dinner, both families adjourned to the recreation room. Terry had brought slides of his family's recent vacation, including shots of Holy Land, a roadside tourist attraction.

When a slide depicting crosses and statues and shrines came up, Vicky leaped to her feet and pointed. Incredibly, water was flowing *out of the wall* in the basement!

Suddenly, the lights went off and on by themselves; a moment later, the pounding started upstairs. Together, Terry and Pete ran up to the first floor to find out where the pounding was coming from. But each time they drew close, the noise would simply take up in another part of the house. Then, up on the roof, it sounded like carpenters were on top of the house swinging hammers with all their might. The whole house vibrated, and again pictures fell off the walls. Meanwhile, Terry's wife and young children, seized with terror, had followed the men upstairs. Pete insisted that Terry get his family out of the house. Terry hated to leave his brother in such an appalling situation, but that night he had no choice.

"There's nothing natural about this," Terry finally admitted at the front door. "You'd better go find another priest who'll listen to you!"

That Sunday night the reign of terror continued. Yet, beyond that, it seemed as though everyone in the house had gone haywire.

"I'm gonna kill you!" Vicky screamed at her brother.

"Yeah? I'll kill you first!" Eric snarled back.

"I'm going to kill both of you!" Sharon shouted at the two of them.

In the midst of the fighting and arguing, the percussive pounding went on unabated. Now Pete Beckford, his mind aswirl, his house a wreck, broke down. With tears glistening in his eyes, he commanded everyone to stop! When Eric saw his father, he broke down in tears, as did Sharon. Vicky, however, was indifferent and unaffected. She locked herself in her bedroom until morning.

The next day, April 8, Pete Beckford was drawn and pale. He'd already used up all his sick days babysitting the pandemonium. Something had to be done, yet who could he turn to? Repairman couldn't help; neither could the police, the church, or even his own brother. As Pete stood at the kitchen window, he found himself staring at the large cross atop the monastery retreat house that bordered his property. Hope suddenly flooded into Pete's heart. The monks would know!

Pete waited until after the breakfast hour and then walked up the road to the retreat house, where a kindly, middle-aged monk ushered him into the foyer. Pete quickly did his best to explain the problem and asked desperately, "Would you please come to my house and see what I'm talking about?" The monk agreed. Together they walked back down the road to the Beckfords' ranch house.

Inside, the monk surveyed the damage done to the furniture and walls. He listened to the random poundings and read the obscenities scribbled about the place. Yet despite it all, he was distinctly unperturbed by what he saw. Instead, he sat Pete down.

"Let me explain what I believe is happening here. There are things that go on in this world that are deliberately kept secret—things that one learns about only through experience. In my opinion—and of such things I have only limited knowledge—this terrible problem you are suffering is being caused by spirits. Do you believe in such things, Pete?"

"These days, Father, I'm open to suggestions."

"Very well, then," resumed the monk. "This kind of spirit, which delights in tormenting people, is not a ghost, but a spirit of a special order. We know almost nothing about them except that they are *truly mean* spirits; judging from the intent of their actions, it would seem there is something wrong with them. I myself cannot challenge the type of spirit that appears to have entered your home, though there are other priests who can. But be reminded," the monk stressed, "there are other mysteries in the world. The mysteries of science unfold before our eyes every day. Not every strange question has a strange answer. The mind plays tricks on us, nature plays tricks on us. Before the Church will assign clergy to a case such as yours, the matter must first be proven *genuinely* spiritual in nature. What is your opinion?"

"I think you might possibly have hit upon the matter, Father. I would like to pursue it," Pete concluded.

"Then let me give you the name of someone who may be able to help you sort this thing out. His name is Ed Warren."

This was the second time someone had referred Pete Beckford to the Warrens. When the two men walked back to the retreat house, the monk made a phone call and got Ed and Lorraine's telephone number. "You'd better get in touch with these people as soon as possible."

"That's precisely what I'm going to do," Pete assured him.

At work later that morning, Pete telephoned the Warrens and spoke with Judy Penney, a young woman who works as a liaison when Ed and Lorraine are out of town. Judy has heard some hair-raising tales over the phone, but this one particularly scared her. "The Warrens are out West," she told Pete Beckford, "but I'll relay the message to them. I suggest you call back Saturday; by then they'll have returned home."

Saturday, however, was a long five days away: it was Holy Week, the most notorious time of the year for demoniacal activity. The next morning at daybreak the Beckfords awoke to the sound of objects pelting the roof. Going out to investigate, they once again saw stones falling onto their house out of thin air. All week long, stones began falling on the Beckford house at dawn—and stopped at dusk. Their number and velocity varied. Some fell slowly, as though sinking through water. Others came down in erratic zigzags. Every so often there'd be a violent deluge of rocks and stones, some falling hard enough to imbed themselves in the roof. When they hit the ground, about half the stones would vanish, the others remained for the family to clean up later. Inside the house, the antireligious activity had become as violent as the stones falling outside. Crucifixes were turned upside down. Pictures of saints were torn up—the minute shreds left defiantly in a pile. The statue of Saint Anne, which the Beckfords now kept in the living room, was constantly being hidden, as though something could not bear to see it.

Indeed, the antireligious activity reached a ridiculous extreme. One night the Beckfords heard a tremendous commotion in Eric's bedroom. When it died down, they went in to find one of the twin beds torn apart. The mattress was under the bed frame; the box spring, however, was propped up against the wall, covering a framed picture of Jesus.

On another occasion, while sitting in the living room, the Beckfords heard a hellish, woeful moan resonate out of the kitchen. Ever so cautiously, Pete walked down the hallway. Sitting in the middle of the kitchen floor was their big double-doored refrigerator: it had been moved away from the wall the exact limit of its power cord. The next night they heard the same lingering moan; again the refrigerator was found sitting in the center of the room.

Perhaps even more intimidating was the observation that even physical matter presented no great obstacle to the oppressing entities. Pete had the only key to the deep freezer located in the basement. Incredibly, when he opened the freezer one afternoon to take out provisions, he found inside the big iron blacksmith's anvil he kept in the garage. Later, Pete also discovered that his huge steel toolbox had mysteriously been teleported to the attic.

Worst of all, there now seemed to be a physical presence in the house. When alone, members of the family had the unshakeable feeling that someone was in the room staring at them from behind. The terror was enhanced by footsteps, the rustle of clothes, and heavy breathing. Once when Sharon Beckford quickly turned around, she saw a black form standing in the room behind her.

For the Beckfords that year, Good Friday—April 12—was a day of abject fear. A forbidding atmosphere enveloped the house. Indeed, it seemed as though the whole place might suddenly explode as the berserk rampage continued unabated. Stones mysteriously pummeled the house outside, while unrestricted bedlam went on within, all of which was now compounded by an evil presence so increasingly real and physical that no one dared be alone in the house for even one moment. The Beckfords, frightened and tormented, now had only one hope left—the Warrens, whoever *they* were.

10

Deliverance

April 12.

Inside, the LaGuardia Airport terminal, enough people to fill a small town milled around, waiting for planes. Outside, on the observation deck, the air was thick with diesel fumes and the screaming whine of fan-jet engines. Off to the left, the Manhattan skyline was silhouetted against the setting sun. Above, in the twilight sky, incoming jets approached from the west, turned right over the Whitestone Bridge, then, one by one, drifted slowly back down to earth.

On board the big tri-jet touching down just after six that evening were Ed and Lorraine Warren, coming home after a ten-day speaking tour. They'd delivered six lectures in four states, appeared twice on television, answered three hours of questions on a radio call-in show, visited a not-very-haunted house, and granted four separate interviews to student newspaper reporters. They were glad to return; the Warrens looked forward to spending Easter Sunday with relatives. On Monday they'd be off again, this time to Vermont.

Around noon on Saturday, the following day, Lorraine received a call from a man beside himself with fear and anguish. In her pleasant way, Lorraine calmed him down. "Could you explain your problem as specifically as possible?"

For a quarter of an hour, Pete Beckford unfolded a tale almost too incredible to be believed. He told her of the slashed tires and the vandalized engines that had cost him over five hundred dollars to repair. He told her of the ketchup, salad oils, bleaches, and perfumes that floated down the hallway and dumped their contents on the rugs and expensive furnishings. He told her that a statue, an anvil, and a refrigerator had moved on their own accord; that heavy furniture had levitated; that stones had fallen on his house, and that water flowed from the walls. He couldn't stand it anymore. He pleaded for help and offered to pay anything for it.

At first, it struck Lorraine that Pete Beckford's imagination had run wild. But by the time he finished, it was evident to her that this man's home was under diabolical siege. "Ed is involved with another case this Saturday," she had to tell him. "However, we would be able to come to your home tomorrow, Sunday."

Pete agreed immediately. After the anguish of the past six weeks surely, he reasoned, one more day would be inconsequential.

Demonology is not just a matter of chasing down spates of weird activity. Wherever they go, and despite their often busy schedule, the Warrens' first priority is to assist those who are being oppressed, assaulted, or even possessed by the forces of darkness. That night, Lorraine repacked their traveling bags, and early Easter morning, they were on their way to Vermont via the home of one Pete Beckford. They arrived at the Beckfords' house on Easter afternoon. "The place looked fairly placid," says Ed, "except for those stones littering the lawn." Inside, however, things were just the opposite. Evidently expensive furniture stood chipped and stained. Marks covered the walls, and a foul odor permeated the air. Lorraine said nothing, although at the time she sensed in the home the presence of entities so numerous and threatening that she had to fight with herself to keep from going back outside. It seemed to her that a wild fury was building; that, indeed, the worst was yet to come.

Having introduced his family to Ed and Lorraine, Pete then showed them the rest of the house. In every room, he stopped to recount at least a dozen incidents, to which the Warrens listened attentively—taking mental notes of the activity he described, while keeping an ear cocked for any exaggeration or salesmanship in the man's rendition of events.

When the tour was over, Ed and Lorraine conducted an investigative interview with the four Beckfords. First, they asked Pete to speak for the family and give a chronology of events that had occurred in the house since the siege began. For over an hour, Pete provided meticulous details of events that were—in the Warrens' estimation—potentially spirit-induced.

"Do any of you *know* what may have caused this problem in your house?" Ed asked.

"No," they answered.

"When did you notice the first occurrence of unusual activity?"

"We figure it was on March 3, when Vicky's car tire went flat at the drugstore. Though that may have been a coincidence, it seems to have been the first incident," Pete replied.

"Has anyone in the neighborhood, or your immediate family, recently passed away—perhaps someone you didn't get along with very well?"

"No."

"Is anyone in the family seeing a psychiatrist?"

"No."

"Did you purchase an antique or secondhand piece of furniture—from a tag-sale, say—before the ruckus began?"

"No."

"Has anyone in the family bought or received an unusual gift or figurine from abroad? Carved statues? A Haitian voodoo doll? A picture of a deity from another religion?"

"No."

As Ed and Lorraine interviewed the Beckfords, intermittent knockings began to occur. The sounds could be heard in the walls for a few minutes, then they'd stop. The noises started up again a few minutes later, this time erupting from various points on the floor. The sounds were audible enough to be picked up on the tape recorder.

The Warrens pressed forward with the questioning, giving no recognition to the activity. Ed then began to ask specific questions which would hopefully pin down the origin of the problem.

"Are you people interested in the occult as a pastime? Have you been attending sessions with consciousness-raising groups?"

"No."

"Has anyone bought or withdrawn from the library books on Satanism or witchcraft rituals?"

"No."

"To your knowledge has a séance ever been held in this house—even years ago?"

"Never," was the firm reply.

"Eric, Vicky, are any of your friends interested in the occult, who maybe perform rituals, or ceremonial magic?"

"No."

"Has anyone here used a Ouija board or automatic writing device?"

"Oh," Vicky said, just above a whisper.

"Have *you* used a Ouija board, Vicky?" Lorraine asked pointedly.

"Yes," the young girl admitted, to her family's amazement.

"All right, dear, you'd better tell us all about it then." Lorraine said. "Start right from the beginning, please."

With that, Vicky Beckford told how she'd been using the Ouija board to communicate with the spirit of a "teenage boy" who supposedly died in the area some ten years earlier. Vicky admitted that she never actually saw the spirit, though she once asked it to manifest. She also defended the spirit as real, citing how it accurately predicted future events days before they happened. She denied her spirit friend could have caused the gruesome activity in the house. He was "kind and understanding," *not* cruel and destructive.

"Did this spirit tell you its name?" Lorraine asked the girl when she'd finished talking.

"No, he told me he wasn't *allowed* to," Vicky replied.

"I presume you are still communicating with this spirit?" Lorraine said.

"No," Vicky admitted somewhat dejectedly. "I must have done something wrong. I've never been able to talk to him again after I asked if he'd show himself to me that night."

"When was *that night?*" Lorraine pressed her.

"Just a minute," said Vicky, who got up and went into her bedroom. "March 2," she called out, then returned to the table.

"And the activity began . . . ?"

"On March 3!" Pete Beckford said, looking at Ed.

Pete, Sharon, and Eric had listened in astonishment to Vicky's bizarre tale. How could something so trivial as a Ouija board cause so much calamity? Accordingly, amidst the knockings, Ed had no other choice but to spend the next half hour explaining the gruesome reality of demoniacal phenomena to them.

After Ed finished his explanation, the Beckfords sat dumbfounded and silent "Mr. Warren," Pete finally felt compelled to ask, "how do you *know* all this?"

"Mr. Beckford," Ed replied, "this is my work. I have done it all my life. I am a demonologist."

"My God," was all Pete was able to utter.

Completing the interview with the Beckford family, Ed and Lorraine excused themselves and held a private conversation outside on the front lawn. The case, they agreed, was far more serious than they'd first imagined. Certainly the siege would never stop of its own accord. In fact, the activity was now reaching a dangerous stage. And as the family had already learned, they could not avoid the problem by running—it would follow them wherever they went. The Warrens decided the quickest solution was to get the Church involved immediately—so the phenomena could be verified and then acted upon.

Somewhere along the line, Ed knew a clergyman would have to bear witness to what was happening, and he specifically wanted Father Daniel to be that witness. With the Beckfords' permission, he telephoned the same priest singled out as an enemy by the spirit associated with the rag doll, Annabelle. Father Daniel, a learned young priest in his early thirties, had recently studied demonology and over the past year Ed had been tutoring him on the practical aspects of the discipline.

A few hours later, just after sunset, the priest arrived at the Beckford house. By that time, activity had already begun afresh, with scratchings and poundings, and the levitation of small objects. To test whether the pounding was being caused deliberately, Ed pounded twice on the wall. There came two poundings in reply! He then pounded four times in quick succession. Four quick raps sounded on the floor, then on a table. Obviously there was an intelligence behind the activity.

Ed asked Father Daniel to perform a blessing in each room which, when accomplished, reduced the power and frequency of the poundings—the most annoying aspect of the disturbance. When that was done, Ed and Lorraine sat in the living room and briefed the priest. The Warrens had to leave for Vermont that night, but Father Daniel would be staying on with the family in their absence.

"You will now be the object of hatred," Ed told the young priest in no uncertain terms. "Under no circumstances must you challenge the undiscerned spirits that are here. You are in both physical *and* mental danger in this house. If you're not careful, you can be hurt seriously. So don't try to resolve the problems yourself. Just be strong, and don't let your emotions get the best of you. Use the rosary, not your temper." Ed handed him a card, "Now, here's the phone number where we'll be. Don't take anything for granted. If there's something you don't know, or can't handle, call us day or night." Writing down another phone number, Ed added, "Father Shawn McKeegan will be your immediate superior in this case. I have already contacted him. Call Father McKeegan every day and give him an update on the activity occurring here.

"In the meantime," Ed told Sharon Beckford, "we know you're in the best of hands, and there's always the possibility the presence of a priest will cause the phenomena to stop."

After doing everything they could that night, Ed and Lorraine left for the airport. They would remain in constant phone contact and return from Vermont immediately if Father Daniel needed them.

After the Warrens left, Father Daniel was offered the spare bedroom. That night, after turning out the lights, the priest lay in bed and listened to all the terrifying sounds the Beckfords had been hearing over the past month.

During the next few days, activity went on as usual. Father Daniel continued to witness the noises and strange movements of objects. Yet by Wednesday of Easter week, it was apparent the activity was occurring in defiance of the priest, if not in contempt of him. Whenever Father Daniel asked for a pencil, a glass of water, or a book, that object would either rise up and float over to him; or, more often, would simply be there the next time he looked. On a few occasions, the object would already be on its way to him before the priest even asked for it. Such actions seemed amusing, but Ed warned Father Daniel not to take them personally. These sarcastic challenges were intended to try his patience, if not lure him into an emotional involvement he might not be able to control.

When they all went to bed that Wednesday night, the atmosphere in the house was anything but playful. The fury of the noises made it impossible to sleep. But beyond the havoc, an appalling evil presence was quite evident in the house. All night long Father Daniel could feel its violent, passionate enmity.

On Thursday, April 18, when the Warrens returned, Father Daniel was ashen and drawn. After four days and nights with the Beckfords, he had to get away from the intense demonic turmoil. That afternoon he returned to his rectory to recompose himself for a few days. He would also report to Father McKeegan that an exorcism might have to be performed in the house.

Meanwhile, Ed and Lorraine stayed the night with the Beckfords to verify the phenomena for themselves, as well as try and discern the precise nature of the spirit presence. Out of fear, Eric and Vicky settled down on the floor of their parents' bedroom. Sleeping in their clothes like everyone else, Ed and Lorraine would rest in the twin beds in Eric's bedroom, across the hall.

When the Warrens' lights were turned off that Thursday night, the phenomena rose up in full strength, beginning with gruntings and other bestial noises, followed by the sort of piercing, bloodcurdling screams one associates with a horror movie. Added to that were ripping and tearing sounds, which then changed into the noise of boards being wrenched off the walls. Soon the familiar pounding started up. This upgraded into what seemed like the blows of a gigantic fist pounding on the house. The force of the blows made the whole building shake. Ed worried whether the structural integrity of the home could withstand much more abuse.

Over the better part of an hour, the phenomena grew in power and intensity, with all the mad sounds going on at once. Suddenly, terrified yells erupted from Pete and Sharon's bedroom. When Ed reached them, the hysterical family claimed that some sort of ultra-black figure had manifested and begun to move in the room.

Disgusted with the abuse being heaped on the family, Ed decided to go ahead and challenge whatever was in the house to reveal its identity. Sending Eric into the bedroom to stay with Lorraine, he had Vicky and her parents sit on the bed.

Then, he traced a large cross in the air with his right hand. "In the name of the Father, the Son, and the Holy Ghost, I demand that you reveal your identity. In the name of Jesus Christ, *are* you a demonic spirit?"

With that, the double bed with the three Beckfords on it rose eerily into the air and remained suspended, some two feet off the floor. Suddenly the dresser careened across the room as though on rollers. Ed managed to step out of the way just before it smashed into the wall, whereupon the double bed crashed to the floor.

At the same time, Eric lay quietly sobbing on the other twin bed in his own bedroom. When Lorraine looked over to comfort the young teenager, to her astonishment, Eric was *levitating* some two feet above the bed! A second later, she watched as the boy was propelled with tremendous force against the far wall, five feet away. The boy then fell to the floor in a crumpled heap.

Lorraine leaped off the bed and switched on the light as the others entered the bedroom. Dazed and trembling, Eric had suffered no broken bones, but his face and chest were bruised and swollen.

The sign Ed asked for had been given. The demonic was indeed at work! This was made even clearer the next morning, after the sun came up, when Lorraine looked outside the bedroom window. Upside down, stuck in an unmelted pile of snow, was the foot-long walnut crucifix that had been a fixture in Pete and Sharon's bedroom from the day they were married.

On Friday, April 19, as Ed and Lorraine continued their stay with the Beckfords, the phenomena became more and more a display of preternatural power. Obscenities and blasphemies showed up on the ceiling of the parents' bedroom, written in indelible red ink. More astounding still, as everyone watched, the wallpaper began to peel off the walls, one sheet at a time, revealing foul language and blasphemies, again written in blood-red ink, on the wall underneath! Pictures not only moved on their own now, they began to smolder and break into flames. Doilies and towels and scarves would suddenly ignite, and then, flaming, hurl themselves at someone in the room.

The fierce activity continued into the weekend. The Warrens canceled all commitments so they could stay with the Beckfords until Father Daniel's return on Sunday. Meanwhile, the rampage continued unabated. In the downstairs rec room, heavy recliners floated up into the air, drifted to the middle of the room, then piled atop one another in ostensibly sexual postures. Eventually, the rest of the furniture floated to the same area, then dropped haphazardly to the floor. Upstairs, the wallpaper continued to peel itself down, exposing the hateful sentiments of the demonic. And throughout it all, fires started spontaneously, requiring everyone to be on guard to prevent a sudden conflagration.

By Sunday, when Father Daniel returned, it was apparent to Ed and Lorraine the fury could be stopped only by exorcism. Ordinarily, a priest does not need permission to exorcise a house. However, *The Exorcist* had just been released as a movie, and the Church was extremely sensitive to criticism at the time. Therefore, the priest's instructions from Father McKeegan were explicit: be able to support your request for exorcism with documented evidence of *supernatural* activity!

The Warrens had anticipated this paperwork complication, and were already collecting the necessary evidence by the time the priest arrived. The bulk of the work would still have to be done by Father Daniel, though. The Warrens, unable to postpone other important commitments to people involved in other cases, had to leave that night for upstate New York. Therefore, the priest would again have to remain in the home—to interview the family and list all incidents of phenomena that had occurred, while keeping a record of the ongoing activity now taking place with even more force and violence.

On Monday and Tuesday, April 22 and 23, Father Daniel set about documenting the activity. Assembling a personality profile of each member of the family, the priest came to see the human cost of a diabolical siege. Perhaps the worst affected was Pete Beckford. Right from the very beginning, every sound, every movement, had filled him with fear that rose up from the soul itself. He could not, moreover, bear the thought that his home was now apparently the abode of the devil. How inconceivable, how unwanted it all was! Tired, humiliated, and emotionally spent, Pete Beckford was also physically ill with a painful ulcer for which he took expensive medicine. Even though he kept the pills hidden, the medication was found dumped in the toilet every morning, and he could no longer afford the luxury of renewing the prescription. He had not been able to work in over a month, and the ongoing expense of damages and repairmen was now eating into his meager savings.

"Internal oppression can be seen as a building process," Ed explains. "When it starts out, it's basically a stimulus-response situation. The spirit stimulates a particular emotion—say, depression. If the person responds to the impulse, then the spirit stimulates it again and again. If the person keeps on responding, then eventually that emotion will be accented so often and so intensely until one day there's either a breakdown or a catastrophe. Many times, though, the individual won't even know he's being programmed to destroy himself, because oppression can be external as well. So, while the spirit is turning internal depression into deep despair, it's diverting the person's attention to his thousand-dollar hi-fi set that's levitating in the middle of the room and about to crash to the floor."

Sharon Beckford had reacted on a more personal level. Why

was this violence, destruction, vulgarity, and hate permitted to go on? For their whole life, they'd worked to build a good home and raise a proper family. They and their children attended church every Sunday. With tears of anger, Sharon Beckford asked forceful questions to which there were no ready answers: "If this is the devil at work, then where is God? Is it *just* for our whole home to be destroyed because our daughter used a Ouija board?"

Father Daniel sympathized with Sharon Beckford. Her questions required a reply, however, and the priest was forced to answer her through the words in Chapter 18 of Deuteronomy: "Let there not be found among you anyone who immolates his son or daughter in the fire, nor a fortune-teller, soothsayer, charmer, diviner, or caster of spells, nor one who consults ghosts and spirits or seeks oracles from the dead. Anyone who does such things is an abomination to the Lord."

"People in oppression situations," says Ed, "often ask 'Why does God allow this to happen?' Well, God *does not* allow it to happen: *people* allow it to happen. The demonic spirit has to play by rules set down by the Creator. This is why its actions and behavior are so devious; the demonic cannot directly interfere in human affairs. But people have to play by the rules too! Therefore, when an individual violates the rules through his own free will, he is then on his own. Even so, the powers of the demonic are, theologically at least, limited to 'temptation.' In other words, the demonic spirit cannot *make* you do something against your will—but it *can* influence you to commit actions you mightn't ordinarily. Nor can the demonic oppress you beyond your ability to resist it. Cosmically, you see, the demonic spirit can come only so close, and no closer. But just as people break the rules, so does the demonic. In the Beckford case, the infesting spirits went *too far.* They broke God's law."

The effect of the horrendous disturbance on Eric was hard to determine. Being fifteen, the boy was sensitive and impressionable.

Before the episode, he'd been outgoing and gregarious. By the middle of April 1974, he was traumatized, quiet, and reclusive. For his own good, the boy might have to see a psychologist.

Vicky displayed a range of emotions from guilt to indifference. Often her behavior was defensive; on occasions she would become hostile and lash out at anyone around her. She was a definite candidate for possession, and the circumstances were ripe for that to happen.

All the while the phenomena kept up as usual. Before leaving, the Warrens had taken Father Daniel aside. "There are a number of entities in the home," Ed told him, "but judging by the intensity and power of the phenomena, we suspect the disturbance is being caused by more than demoniacal powers. There's the distinct possibility that a higher, diabolical entity is involved, possibly having been drawn from the retreat house, where it could have sought to victimize the monks. If so, you might observe some sign that would alert you to its presence." That sign occurred on Tuesday night, as Ed and Father Daniel spoke on the telephone.

One curious aspect to a diabolical siege is that rosary beads are a taboo item to the demonic spirit. Only the most menacing and blasphemous of entities would dare to move them. As Father Daniel was speaking on the phone, rosary beads floated out of the spare bedroom in which he was staying. He watched as they turned left, drifted down the hallway, turned left again into the kitchen, then finally wrapped themselves around a kitchen chair in a gesture of strangulation.

That was it! Ed told Father Daniel to get the family out of the house and stay away until he and Lorraine got back from New York on Thursday. With that, everyone packed up and left immediately.

Father Daniel returned to his rectory while the Beckfords went to stay with Pete's parents nearby. Once again, the phenomena traveled along with them. Pete Beckford never told his seventy-five-year-old parents what was happening to his family, sure the burden of such knowledge would be enough to petrify them. Yet that night, as everyone went to sleep at "grandma and grandpa's," the activity let go. Small objects levitated, pictures left the walls, and "did-you-hear-that?" knockings erupted all around the house. The problem was not enough to be troublesome on Tuesday night, but Wednesday night the whole house was resonating with merciless poundings. The next morning, bathroom faucets and plumbing fixtures were violently wrenched from the wall by some unimaginably strong force. Without trying to explain the situation, Pete called a plumber to repair the damage, packed up his family, and left.

Father Daniel was affected in a rather more sinister and ominous way. For the past two weeks he had witnessed the most incredible phenomena caused by the demonic. This theological devil had taken on real proportions, and he truly felt in danger. Indeed, a spirit from the Beckford house had followed him too. The first time, he saw a dark, black cylindrical form blocking his way in the narrow hall leading to his quarters. On the remaining nights, it posted itself in the hallway, keeping him a prisoner in his modest cell all night long. At the same time Pete's parents' house was experiencing damage, Father Daniel was shaving, when before his eyes, the bathroom light fixture went off and then disassembled itself from the ceiling. One by one, the parts floated down and landed in the sink.

On Thursday, April 25, the Warrens returned from upstate New York, having canceled other appointments and worked their schedule so they could fully concentrate on the Beckford case. They met Father Daniel at a nearby restaurant to discuss the latest developments. The Beckfords were nowhere to be found that morning, but Pete had given the priest a spare key to the house. Ed suggested it might be a good idea to go into the house without the family around to influence matters one way or another.

From the restaurant, Ed, Lorraine, and Father Daniel drove

directly to the Beckfords' house. Since no one knew what had gone on inside while the family was away, Ed decided it would be best if he first went inside the home alone.

Upon unlocking the front door, Ed discovered the whole place had been systematically vandalized. Lamps, tables, chairs, books, pictures, clothing, and furniture were strewn around the living room. The smell, too, was utterly repulsive. Anything that was fluid had been dumped and left to decompose. Walking through the house, Ed found beds turned over, drawers pulled out, and linens scattered everywhere. Indeed, anything movable seemed to have been ripped, torn, or turned upside down. In the kitchen, the contents of the pantry and refrigerator had been dumped in a pile on the floor, with dinner plates and silverware heaped on top of that. Sheer insanity.

Heading back down the hallway, Ed suddenly realized something was awry. A moment later, the house began to violently rumble and shake, as if an earthquake had just struck. Fearing the house might actually collapse on top of him, Ed tried to get to the front door, but he couldn't move!

At the same time, outside, Lorraine picked up on the fact that Ed was in jeopardy. When she and Father Daniel reached the front door, they saw Ed walking dazedly through the living room, his shirt covered with blood. Upon removing him outside, they discovered on his left arm two long, deep slashes forming the sign of the cross.

Refusing to see a doctor, Ed had them wash off the wound and then bandaged it tightly with gauze and tape from the first-aid kit in the car. Ed explained that "psychic slashes started to be thrown around the room, cutting into the walls and drapes." He was cut on the arm because he threw his arms up to cover his face, feeling that the forces in the home intended to mutilate him. Ed believed the attack was directed specifically at *him*, for it was he who originally challenged the forces in the home with religious provocation, and who threatened to end their rampage by alerting Church authorities to the case. However, it was also Ed's rationale that it was the Beckfords who were ultimately in danger.

"The spirits took over the Beckford house as a first step in a quest to take over the whole family," says Ed. "In cases of this sort, however, Lorraine and I have found that for the most part, people possess very strong willpower. Therefore, no alien spirit is just going to arrive and take over a person or family all that easily. That's why oppression phenomena tend to vary in intensity from one case to another. The spirit, or spirits, will methodically work on one emotion, or even a dozen, until you're vulnerable and irrational from the strain. Everyone has a breaking point, but a weak-willed person—say someone on the verge of suicide—can be taken over pretty easily. The spirit doesn't need to go off on a binge of activity. But with a strong-willed individual, the spirit will throw everything at him, *including* the kitchen sink. The oppressed may learn he can't *do* anything about the activity, so rather than fight it, he stops resisting and falls passive to the oppressing force. When the person's will is thrown open for domination, the oppressing spirit's next step is possession.

"On the other hand, if the person doesn't give up, the phenomena will go on or intensify until the stress becomes unbearable. A mental breakdown would be the next logical step, but at the point where a breakdown should happen, usually possession or some other catastrophe will occur instead. Violent inhuman spirits capable of causing fires could easily burn the house down with everyone in it." The worse the phenomena became, the closer the Beckfords came to either experiencing possession or death.

Thus now, more than ever, the case had transmuted into a confrontation, with the Beckfords pawns in a much bigger game. As a matter of survival Ed and Father Daniel *had* to stop these determined, maniacal forces. To back down would simply give the demonic a green light to kill, possess, or torment the Beckfords indefinitely, and also to torment Ed and Father Daniel for the rest of *their* lives. Consequently, they had no alternative but to persevere—and succeed.

Around noon that Thursday, April 25, the pale, drawn, and bedraggled Beckfords pulled into their driveway in a four-door sedan. When they went inside and saw their house torn asunder, the Beckfords plunged into despair. The Warrens and Father Daniel bolstered their confidence, though, and with everyone working, by nightfall the house was put back into a semblance of order.

On Friday, April 26, after a night of havoc, Ed and Lorraine assisted Father Daniel with the paperwork he had to submit to Father McKeegan. Under normal circumstances, verification could take a priest weeks to complete, but with the Warrens' help, Father Daniel left that same night with all the documentation he needed to request an exorcism for the family.

In the meantime, Ed and Lorraine stayed with the Beckfords. The oppressive siege had worn the family down physically and mentally, such that any one of them could now potentially come under possession. That had to be guarded against most of all, yet it took everyone's strength to withstand the barrage of activity that occurred the weekend of April 27 and 28.

Metal picture frames now smoldered and caught fire. Scarves, linens, dresses, and towels burst into flames and were flung directly at the people in the room, often causing painful burns. Night and day, without letup, the phenomena went on. Furniture from the living room was found in the master bedroom, while the bedroom furniture was now in the living room. Five minutes later, both rooms of furniture switched back to their proper place while the Warrens and the Beckfords watched in amazement.

Saturday night, April 27, Ed commented to the Beckfords how much he liked his car and how economical it was to run. The next morning, Ed unlocked the car door and found the directional signal had been snapped off the steering column and tossed on the seat. When the car wouldn't start, he released the hood-latch from inside, then checked the engine. Under the hood, the car's sparkplug wires had been tied up in knots, and the carburetor's vacuum hoses had been pulled loose and left dangling.

Sunday, at last, Father Daniel telephoned the besieged Beckford house with some very good news. Father McKeegan, with whom Father Daniel had been in constant contact, approved the need for exorcism to be performed on the premises. He would assign an exorcist who required three full days of prayer and fasting before the ritual could be performed. The exorcist assigned to the case would begin his Black Fast on Monday morning. The date of the exorcism, therefore, was set for three days later—Thursday, May 2.

With the final confrontation now imminent, the negative activity inside the house intensified in a strange new way. Movements now seemed to happen faster, like a movie being shown at twice its normal speed. That Sunday night, as a show of strength—or to indicate the arrival of new entities—two large metal radiator covers suddenly vanished into thin air. A few seconds later, a loud metallic crash was heard in the basement. Rushing to the cellar door, Eric found the radiator covers lying on the basement stairs.

Later on that night, there was an incredible commotion in Vicky's bedroom, but no evidence of activity could be seen. When Lorraine turned to leave the room, however, she tripped over a sixteen-foot aluminum extension ladder that had been leaning against the garage outside only hours before.

On Monday, April 29, while Lorraine was in Eric's bedroom, where the Warrens slept, she heard a metal object drop to the floor. It was a hinge pin. When she looked at the door, she saw the other hinge pin sliding up from its socket. It too fell to the floor, and a second later, the door vanished! Next, the hinge pins on the closet door rose out of their hinges and that door vanished as well. A few minutes later, both doors were found thrown atop one another in the basement. It was a show of force that did not intimidate Lorraine, however.

On Tuesday and Wednesday, with the exorcism soon to be performed, sleep at night was impossible. The ongoing activity was too dangerous for anyone to turn his back on. By May 1, the day before the exorcism, everyone was reduced to sleeping in shifts and taking turns patrolling the house to watch out for fires and other potential dangers.

About 10:30 Wednesday night, Lorraine was in the hall when the doorway to the living room began to brighten. A few moments later, the whole doorway was engulfed in a bright light so intense she could not look at it directly. 'Was this a positive sign?' she wondered. The demonic does not arrive in brilliant rays of glory.

Pete Beckford and Ed were in the living room at the same time, and they too saw the light. But in the middle of the light they also saw a figure slowly begin to emerge.

Lorraine entered the living room through a different door and with the men she watched the materialization become ever more distinct. Within a minute, the form of an older woman was visible, though complete only from the waist up. What did this mean? Was this entity claiming to be responsible for all the calamity that had occurred?

"Speak to us," Ed called out. But the eerie specter simply looked them over individually without replying. It appeared to be a ghost but Lorraine, who had been concentrating on the semi-materialized figure in the doorway, now realized the whole scene was a deception.

Ghosts are often called "angels of the devil," and at least half the time what comes across as a ghost is really an inhuman spirit projecting itself in human guise. "Ed," Lorraine told him, "back away. *It's not human!*"

At that instant, two velvet fireside chairs fell over on their side. They tumbled toward Ed, rose into the air, legs pointing toward him, and effectively pinned him against the wall. The figure in the doorway watched with a sardonic grin, then disappeared. Ed made a sign of the cross over the chairs, which dropped immediately to the floor. A moment later, a bottle of nail polish levitated and flew across the room, barely missing Ed's forehead.

With only twelve hours to go before the exorcism, Ed, Lorraine, and the Beckfords were not about to close their eyes. Though fatigued and weary, they kept an all-night vigil. Lights were left on and pot after pot of coffee was brewed.

Two, three, four o'clock in the morning went by with no major incident. By five, night finally began to yield to day. Outside, birds started chirping as the sun rose slowly through the newly budding trees.

The morning of the day had come. In their own gesture of preparation, the Beckford family along with the Warrens drove to a nearby church and attended an eight A.M. Mass. They then returned to the house at nine and waited for the exorcist's arrival.

At 9:30 he arrived. Though balding and middle-aged, Father Roark was powerfully built and looked more like a stevedore than a man of the Church. An intense, unsmiling priest dressed in a black, short-sleeved shirt and white clerical collar, his attitude was all business. Yet he, along with many other priests, had prayed long and hard for the effectiveness of the exorcism he was about to perform.

Father Roark and Ed Warren had worked together once before, and each man had confidence in the other. Now they walked into the kitchen to confer. Did Ed think the spirits involved in the case were more than demonic?

Ed felt fairly certain that along with lesser inhuman spirits, an Incubus entity was present, having been attracted by the girl. But because of the unusual power of the assault and its proximity to the retreat house next door, he believed that a higher diabolical intelligence—a devil—was actually directing the attack.

Looking down at Ed's bandaged arm, the priest asked, "Did that happen here?"

"Yes," Ed was obliged to say.

Ed and Father Roark returned to the living room where Lorraine and the Beckfords sat waiting. From his black bag, Father Roark removed a purple stole, kissed it, and then placed the garb over his neck. Before beginning the ritual, the exorcist individually blessed all those present in the house so that no harm would befall them during the reading of the exorcism.

Since his arrival, the priest had spoken very little to anyone other than Ed. When he came to the daughter of the house, however, he sternly asked, "Are you Vicky?"

"Yes, Father," the girl replied.

"Father Daniel Mills told me what you've done here," he said flatly. Suddenly frightened by the priest's intimidating tone, Vicky Beckford tried to fight back tears of guilt and shame.

Unyielding, the priest asked, "Vicky, did you *will* this terrible thing to happen to your family?"

"No, I didn't!" Vicky shot back in anger. Then she lowered her voice. "No, Father. I did not will this to happen. It was an accident."

"The Church considers what you have done to be a sin. Do you know that? Have you asked the Lord for forgiveness?"

"Yes, Father."

"Good," he said, blessing the girl. "It's necessary we understand each other." Having blessed all those who stood present as witnesses, the exorcist then began reading the rite of exorcism.

Spoken partly in English and partly in Latin, the rite consists of prayers, psalms, and pronouncements commanding the invading spirits to leave the premises. It took the exorcist more than an hour to read the entire ritual. During that time there was not a sound in the house other than the priest's voice. Save for the obvious destruction visible all around, it was as though nothing had ever happened there.

The concluding act of the exorcism is an outright command for the spirit to reveal its identity. With everyone standing in a wide circle in the middle of the living room, Father Roark read in a deep, somber voice:

"I command thee, thou unclean spirit, O Serpent of Old. By the Judge of the living and the dead. By the Creator of the World who hath the power to cast into Hell, tell me thy name or give some sign, and depart forthwith from this house!"

The priest waited for a full minute, but nothing happened. Obviously displeased that his words had been ignored, Father Roark read the command once again in a loud, booming voice, adding even more threatening phrases:

"I enjoin you under penalty, every unclean spirit, each devil, each part of Satan: begone in the Name of God.

"Yield to God!

"It is not men you are disobeying. God the Father commands you! God the Son commands you! God the Holy Spirit commands you!

"Hear, therefore, and fear, Satan! Enemy of the human race! Source of death! Root of evil! Seducer of men! Cause of discord! Creator of agony! Behold the Cross of the Most High God! I command thee: obey and begone! Tell me thy name or give some sign and depart from this dwelling!"

Suddenly Sharon Beckford cried out: "There! By the fireplace!"

As its manifesting visage slowly became clear, it was evident to all who witnessed the thing that its head was horned. It stood on cloven feet and it had a tail! At the same time the temperature in the room dropped to near freezing while the stomach-turning smell of rotting flesh filled the air.

Casting holy water on the brazen seven-foot-tall image, Father Roark commanded, "Begone in the Name of God."

The spirit instantly vanished. Yet no sooner did the figure disappear, than the blood-red face of a devil, with a head as big as a basketball, developed on the soiled, beige carpet. Again the menacing head had horns protruding from the side.

Father Roark swung the aspergillum filled with holy water at the two-dimensional figure looking up from the floor, projecting a look of enraged hate. Then it slowly faded away. A minute later, all that was left was a pink outline on the rug.

The sign had been given. Accordingly, the exorcist then read a concluding prayer of thanksgiving, finally ending with the statement: "The sign of departure having been shown to us, I commend the safety of these people, the Beckfords, and their dwelling into your hands, Lord. Hear us, and hear their prayers; deign them to live in peace and contentment from this day forward. In the name of the Father, the Son, and the Holy Spirit Amen."

What occurred in the home of Pete and Sharon Beckford between March 3 and May 2, 1974, is classified as a true diabolical attack. The terrible assault that lasted for sixty consecutive days came to an abrupt halt with the exorcism conducted in the house on May 2, 1974.

The case, and all its particulars, is now a matter of record In his own files, Ed Warren retains a statement written by Pete Beckford's brother who himself was an involuntary witness to the phenomena in the home.

I, nor anyone else in my family, have ever before witnessed or actually experienced anything so weird and terrifying. I am sure the impact of that obscure experience shall remain with my frightened children and wife indefinitely. The incomprehensible predicament that we have witnessed leaves our frightened family group in complete bewilderment. At least for the present time, it defies all rational and logical explanations. All the tangible evidence and facts related to the preternatural mysteriousness of those events witnessed by our family group should be laid bare and then rationally reviewed by competent people who are experienced in these weird and perplexing matters, When and if a review is completed, I firmly believe that the ultimate conclusions will eventually suggest that unearthly powers or influences were at work.

—Terence Beckford

After the exorcism of their home, the Beckfords' life slowly returned to normal. However, the damage sustained to the furniture, walls, rugs, mattresses, bedding, plumbing, roof, and cars amounted to well over $5,000. (Their insurance, ironically, did not cover "Acts of God.") Today, the Beckfords live contentedly in the same small suburban house. Eric is away, a college student now. And of course Vicky, now married, is always busy—as one might expect—what with three small children to raise.

II.
A Servant of Lucifer

What happened to the Beckford family is not an ordinary event by any stretch of the imagination. Yet attracting negative spirits to one's side is not all that *un*common either. Every year, Ed and Lorraine Warren deal with at least a dozen serious cases of demoniacal oppression and possession; there is no telling how many other cases the specialist clergy are called upon to resolve at the same time.

What sets the Beckford case apart is that it was a *diabolical* attack. "Infestation and oppression phenomena are one thing," says Ed, "but when you have a diabolical attack, you're dealing with something far more powerful than the demonic spirit. The demonic spirit has only so much knowledge and its intellect can go only so far. This case, on the other hand, got out of hand through the intervention of the satanic hierarchy. To use an analogy, it's one thing to be a bombardier and drop an atom bomb; it's something else to *invent* the thing. This is the same distinction with devils and demons. Although both are of the so-called Kingdom, the demonic spirit is a debased, bestial entity when compared to the deeper intelligence of the diabolical hierarchy. Make no mistake, though, they're both after the same thing: the demonic spirit just does the dirty work. Yet, when you have a case involving fire; the teleportation of anvils, doors, and radiator covers; the levitation of extremely heavy objects; the sacrilegious movement of rosary beads and blessed statues; plus, irrational, almost berserk instances of blasphemy—then it's certain there's a true maniac in the wings orchestrating the pandemonium."

Why did this diabolic power show itself during the exorcism as a classical devil, with horns and a tail? That detail is hard to believe.

"Well, of course it is," Ed replies. "That's precisely why it manifested in such a way. It took the form of an archetypal devil, first, to preserve its anonymity—always a priority with the demonic. And second, to make the exorcist possibly look the fool. When he had to report what appearance the spirit took when commanded to leave, it might cast doubts on the credibility of the exorcist, or on the case in general. This kind of behavior is standard procedure where the demonic is concerned. But regardless of what form it took, the important thing for the Beckfords is that the forces *were* expelled from the home."

What about the people? What is the effect on human beings who have been through an episode with the demonic?

"Given the severely traumatic nature of most cases involving demoniacal phenomena," Lorraine replies, "we recommend that the principals participate in a six-month follow-up program so they can come to grips with what has happened in their lives. Regaining a stable psychology is a very private thing: it literally takes a lot of soul-searching. Ordinarily, the follow-up is conducted by a clergyman of the family's faith, sometimes even their own minister. When that's not possible, Ed and I will help these people over the difficult months. Sometimes, of course, the shock is just too much, and certain individuals will require psychotherapy. Still, no one is ever left *un*moved after an experience with the phenomenon. Some choose to see it for what it is; others go further and take it as 'revelation'; still others require long-term therapy, even hospitalization for extended periods. And others, for psychological reasons, will just plain deny that the negative events ever happened at all.

"As a rule, those who can come to grips with the problem will take the necessary precautions against it ever happening to them again; those who fail to understand, or don't care, leave themselves open for even more serious problems later on. The majority, though, do take seriously what has happened, and therefore undergo major, often radical changes in lifestyle.

"They'll begin by physically distancing themselves from the scene," Lorraine continues. "The person or family will move from one coast to the other, leave the country, or return to the state or town where they grew up. Their attitude is often 'Anything to get away from here!' Although people can't physically distance themselves from spirits, the *sincerity* of their action is what's significant—and that's the true distancing mechanism. Beyond that, such a heavy dose of reality will prompt other individuals to reevaluate the course of their lives. Many times, adults will quit an unsatisfying job and take up creative or socially-minded employment. Invariably, if the principals weren't religiously oriented beforehand, they'll quickly 'get religion.' Their overall emphasis is on security, reduction of fear, and preventing any recurrence of the negative episode.

"These are the outward changes," says Lorraine. "But emotionally and psychologically, people who've been the target of a negative spirit assault have a lot of mental repair work to do. Children, sadly enough, are often the worst affected. The terror they've witnessed is permanent. Being exposed to such violence, vulgarity, indecency, and gnawing fear leaves a child with a perception of the world few of us ever know.

"For grownups, counseling is often required. Even though the pandemonium or possession has been personally witnessed, people often can't accept the fact that invisible forces of a supernatural nature were the true authors of the havoc. Society is partly responsible for the problem, of course. People have been methodically taught *not* to believe in ghosts, spirits, and nonmaterial forces because such things are supposedly 'irrational.' In my estimation, shutting your mind to knowledge is irrational. Through counseling, people often have to *unlearn* the narrow perception of life they've had drummed into their head, and then be exposed to the fact that the world is a far more complex and serious place than they've ever been taught to believe."

Why does Ed think some people have called *The Amityville Horror* a "hoax"?

"This is part of a pattern of denial that goes hand in hand with this business of spirits," says Ed. "When something is threatening, the mind tries to deny it. In psychology, this is called repression. Personally, I am not surprised about this outcry of hoax; it's an expectable part of the overall reaction to demoniacal phenomena. Years later, when you talk to people who have personally undergone possession or were on the receiving end of a diabolical siege, these same individuals often deny the event ever happened. Are they liars? No, they're reacting to trauma. What has happened to them is so incompatible to their reason that as a psychological defense mechanism, they deny the event ever occurred at all. To a lesser degree, the same thing happens when a book like *The Amityville Horror* appears. The subject matter is threatening, even traumatic to some readers. Plus, the word 'hoax' is a guaranteed profit-maker when used in a banner headline."

One rarely reads about the first two stages of demoniacal phenomena—infestation and oppression—in newspapers, except in terms of so-called "poltergeist" activity. However, cases of diabolical possession do get reported, but no one is ever told *how* the possession occurred. Yet if physical or psychological oppression is not resisted or the appropriate help is not brought in, then the oppressing spirit is capable of possession. And when that happens, things become far more complicated and sinister. For all the violence and terror that is liable to occur during the infestation and oppression stages is dedicated to nothing less than the diabolical possession of a human being. If oppression succeeds, the door to the will is simply torn away. The individual is then invaded by one, or even a multitude, of possessing entities.

"You have to draw a thick black line between oppression and possession," says Ed, marking a line on the table with his finger. "During oppression, the demonic spirit tries to manipulate the human will through temptation, intimidation, and other nasty influences that the individual can usually stave off or resist. But when possession occurs, the inhuman spirit no longer attacks you, it *becomes* you, so to speak. Seizing the body of the person and imposing its will over that of the human spirit is the ultimate goal of the demonic spirit. As incredible as it may seem, the body is host to a whole other being. What possesses the body is an alien, inhuman spirit of a distinctly diabolical nature that bears no relation to the possessed individual. An independent spirit, with a will and intelligence of its own, forcibly takes over the human body and, in its own voice, *defies* anyone to make it leave."

Expanding the point, Lorraine says, "Theologians have often called the human body the 'mansion of the soul'; the dwelling where the spirit resides. The demonic spirit crudely calls the body a *house* to inhabit. People who leave the 'front door' unlocked, by inviting or attracting spirit forces, court the real possibility of possession. 'One man's trash is another's treasure.' Those who don't appreciate the gift of life stand in jeopardy of having it snatched away from them in a very real, very physical way."

When possession does occur, is there anything noticeably apparent about the afflicted individual?

"Many times, the possessed looks just like you or me," Ed replies. "Except for one thing: *the eyes*. They say the eyes are the window of the soul. I believe that's true, because the look in the eyes of the severely oppressed or possessed is like nothing you've ever seen. The eyes aren't drooping or half-asleep; they're wide open and alert. Yet the look in those eyes is not human; it is wild, bestial, and full of hate. I have seen this crazed, otherworldly look many times in my life, and every time, I seem to lose a small part of myself in the process. I'm convinced it is a look people are *not* supposed to see, because it is truly the spirit of evil looking out the window of a human being.

"Only a few months ago, Lorraine and I had just been on a television show uptown in New York City. Afterwards, we took a taxi down to Chinatown for lunch. As we were walking along the street we saw there was some trouble at the corner, with police cars all around. So I suggested we cut through a walkway or alley on our left-hand side which led to Mott Street.

"Well, we took the alley, which was full of beat-up trash cans overflowing with garbage. Flies, maggots, and vermin were everywhere. The combination of the heat and the stink of decomposing garbage quickly began to sour our stomachs. Nevertheless, we kept going. Further back, the alley crooked slightly, so that beyond the middle you could no longer see the street.

"We walked quickly, but as we got to the middle of the alleyway, at the end of this long row of trash cans, we saw two feet sticking out. I told Lorraine to stand still while I walked up ahead. When I got closer, I saw it was a man, a derelict. He was a Caucasian, between thirty-five and sixty-five—you couldn't tell. The man was just barely alive, sitting up against the wall with his legs stretched out into the path. He was filthier than anyone I have ever seen: covered with sores and scabs, and obviously riddled with disease.

"But that just begins to tell the story. Because piled on top of him—as though he were sitting in bed with a quilt over him—were heaps of runny, putrefying garbage. This foul mess covered the man all the way up to his chest and down to his knees. His arms were plopped in the middle of this rotting slop, and flies were landing all over his face and body. Rats had apparently been gnawing on his feet and toes. It was evident the man hadn't moved in days.

"Ironically, his shoes were neatly placed beside him, shined up and ready to go. Now, I have been in war and I have seen spiritual abominations in haunted houses, but I doubt if I've ever seen anything so repulsive or disgusting in my life. How could this happen? *How* could a human being be reduced to such a state?

"I looked at this poor, wretched soul from the feet up, and was overtaken with compassion and grief. When I finally came to look upon his face, I was stunned, and instinctively took a step back. His face was twisted into a perverse sneer—and there was that ugly, inhuman look of delirium in his eyes. Then I knew what had happened to him. And what was possessing that man, in turn, knew me too.

"'You bastard!' I said to it, so sickened was I by this scene.

"It laughed, mockingly. 'I am killing him!' it said to me. 'In a few days, he will be dead. And do you know, there is nothing you can do about it. *Because it is already done!*'"

"Demoniacal influence can be sickeningly ugly," Lorraine emphasizes. "When a person succumbs to the impulses thrown out by the demonic—and those impulses are usually the most negative and bestial—the spirit can have the person wallowing around the floor like an animal. Why? Because the demonic is inhuman. When it oppresses people it *de*humanizes them, just like it did to that possessed man in the alleyway. Before becoming possessed, he would have been severely oppressed. When his emotions equaled the destructive temperament of the oppressing spirit, then possession occurred. This is why 'successful' demoniacal oppression can turn a human being into something *lower* than a beast."

What is Ed's response to criticism, or allegations that the demonic is nothing more than an extremely vivid figment of the imagination, or simply a psychological matter of dual personality?

"The phenomenon is imaginary only to those who have never witnessed it," Ed retorts. "So the answer I give to that question is no, these are not psychological demons. These are *entities.*"

But how can you tell? When possession occurs, does anything specifically physical happen to distinguish it from a purely mental change?

"My God, yes," Ed replies. "Specifically, when possession occurs, an inhuman possessing entity moves *into* the body of the person, sometimes through the solar plexus, but more often from the individual's left-hand side, entering at the base of the neck where the brain meets the spine.* Meanwhile, the astral body—the spirit of the person—is usually displaced and moves out of the physical body from the right. The human spirit looks cloudlike and white; the inhuman spirit looks cloudlike and black. Beyond that, in my experience, nine out of ten times when possession occurs, the person's facial characteristics change into a bony, distorted appearance totally unlike the appearance of the possessed person. The voice that comes through is often gross and manlike, although you can't generalize: many spirits usually partake in the possession of a body, each with its own bizarre way of vocalizing. As for changes to the body, the strength of the possessed is completely overwhelming. I have seen a possessed child throw grown adults around the room like a sumo wrestler. And a possessed adult is completely unmanageable. I know—I have been attacked by the possessed on more than one occasion, and big as I am, at two-hundred-and-twenty pounds, I can report to you that no human being could ever single-handedly

---

* At the Medulla oblongata. For a fuller explanation, see *Autobiography of a Yogi*, by Paramahansa Yogananda. Los Angeles: Self-Realization Fellowship, 1946.

fight off a possessed individual. You're dealing with something that has the strength of six men.

"That's the physical side," says Ed. "Once possession takes place, the spirit will then either seek to mutilate the body it inhabits—as was portrayed in *The Exorcist*—or take off on a spree of wild physical mayhem. The demonic spirit isn't content simply to possess the body: its mind is fixed on death. The basic motive behind possession is that 'One can kill many.' It doesn't matter whether the diabolically-possessed is a tyrannical world leader or a street killer, the objective is the same: one can kill many. When you understand this, then the demonic spirit's whole strategy starts to make sense. Until exorcism takes place, the body will be a 'house' for one or more entities. The bottom line is, there's nothing psychological about true cases of possession. In one major case of possession, the exorcist called as many as ninety-eight different entities out of the body of the possessed—each and every one of which answered to a name! Although psychologists often mistake the phenomenon for multiple personality, the only multiplicity involved is the multitude of spirits possessing the victim's body."

Anyone who asks Ed and Lorraine Warren for proof of "true cases of possession," had better stoke up enough courage to sit through their reply. After a lifetime in the study of the supernatural the Warrens have collected a unique, unduplicated treasury of data covering all aspects of spirit phenomena—evidence that functions to substantiate everything they say a dozen times over. Much of this evidence is located in what the Warrens call the Occult Museum.

The museum—its contents to be bequeathed to a British university—adjoins Ed Warren's office. It contains an extraordinary tape library of interviews with uncounted thousands of people who have called on the Warrens over the years because they—or their families—were experiencing spirit-related problems. The factual, detailed interviews are true stories of horror, tragedy, and death wreaked on ordinary people by hostile spirit forces. There is also a sub-library of tapes upon which are recorded the voices of spirits that spoke openly in a room, through the body of the possessed, or through the agency of a trance medium—very sobering material indeed. The Warrens' evidence continues with some one thousand slides and photographs showing the whole range of supernatural activity they've witnessed in their work, including a remarkable array of spirits in various stages of manifestation. The museum also contains files of affidavits, testimonials, corroborating evidence, and newspaper accounts of the Warrens' work over the years. Yet what strikes the visitor most of all are the strange, sinister-looking objects that surround one in the Occult Museum.

Every object in the museum was removed from a home or situation where demoniacal phenomena once occurred. Some of the objects and amulets stored there are so negatively "charged" that just by holding one of the items it is possible to provoke the original spirit to manifest or cause possession to occur instantly. The Warrens do not keep these dangerous objects as fond mementos of past exploits—they keep them because they *have* to. For if a diabolically-charged object is destroyed, say the Warrens, reciprocal harm could be visited upon the person or family who once owned it. "It's the demonic version of the Biblical eye for an eye, tooth for a tooth," says Lorraine. If destruction of a negative object doesn't result in physical harm, then the spirit may instead return to the premises from which it was exorcised. Rather than put anyone in physical jeopardy, the Warrens respect the power in these negative objects and allow them to stand as hard physical evidence that evil exists in the world as a real, moving force.

There are about a hundred items in the collection so far, and almost every item has a story attached to it. There's a string of pearls that when worn around the neck, strangles the wearer. There's the long black spike a satanic witch used long ago to murder her newborn infant as a sacrifice to the devil. There is the large plaster doll dressed in Victorian clothing that not only took on the features of the old lady who once owned it, but became animated and behaved like a human being for over twenty years. There are the crania of human skulls that have been used as "chalices of ecstasy" for drinking human blood during witchcraft rituals. There's the coffin in which a possessed man slept each night for his whole adult life. There are stones—some quite sizeable—that fell out of the sky onto homes under diabolical siege. There are crucifixes that have actually been *exploded* by demonic spirits and still others that Satanists have defiled with urine and excrement. There are written pacts with the devil, crystal balls, ceremonial swords, and sacrificial daggers. There are the black candles and conjuring book from the Foster case, and by the door to Ed's office is hung the conjuring mirror taken from Steven Zellner's house in New Jersey. The planchette and burned picture frames from the Beckford case are displayed on a table not far from a wooden cabinet in which Annabelle, the Raggedy Ann doll, now sits holding a plain wood crucifix in her little cloth hands.

And finally, there is the black lace veil.

The veil figured in a case of possession where an inhuman spirit delivered a pointed message to Ed Warren. The possessing entity's voice was clearly recorded on tape. The Warrens, sitting together on an overstuffed sofa in the Occult Museum, now explain the strange case of the young woman—bizarre in her own right—who had one day been brought to Ed's office with other spirit-related problems.

"Ed and I had been lecturing to a college audience," Lorraine begins. "It was an otherwise normal lecture, except that I could sense there was a negative presence in the auditorium, and for the life of me I couldn't pick it out. When we speak to groups of people, I can usually tell who's there. Clergymen, for instance, often come wearing turtlenecks or sport shirts, but I can see they're clergy by the light-beige aura that surrounds the ordained. Satanists and black witchcraft groups often show up at our lectures dressed like everyone else, but their auras stand out too. On this occasion, however, I just couldn't localize the source of the negative vibrations.

"When the question session was over, people from the audience came forward as usual; a dozen people surrounded Ed, and a dozen people surrounded me. After about fifteen minutes, I looked over and saw that Ed was speaking with a young male student. Next to the boy stood a girl who, for some reason, was seething with rage. I promptly excused myself from the group around me and went over to be with Ed."

"Jimmy, the boy who'd been talking to me," says Ed, "brought his girlfriend, Kendra, to our lecture because he suspected that she'd been overtaken by some occult influence. He told me that when his girlfriend became angry, she would fill up with intense hate and rage; her features would change into something resembling a 'wolf'; and then the voice of a different 'person' would speak from inside her.

"When Lorraine came over to me, the girl experienced an episode of instantaneous possession right there on the stage. She lurched out and actually tried to *kill* Lorraine. The incident not only scared Lorraine, it also scared the wits out of everyone else around us, who quickly moved away. We ended the audience chat session right there. I took Kendra and her boyfriend to an offstage room. In the meantime, Lorraine waited out in the hall while I spoke with these two.

"In the backstage room, the girl was fully under possession. She was breathing heavily, while the entity possessing her was completely overtaken with an intense violent hatred. Her facial features were also somewhat transformed into the wolflike appearance the boy had talked about The off-pitch voice projected by the entity later proved to be dissimilar to that of the girl. I didn't have a tape recorder with me at the time, but it hardly mattered, because the thing possessing the girl was simply caught up in a snarling, accusatory rage.

"After about ten minutes, the possession passed. Then the girl seemed to be all right—at least if I didn't crowd her, which seemed to reinstigate possession. So to avoid trouble, I sat on the opposite side of the room. When I felt she could be spoken to, I told her about the incident I had just witnessed. She told me she had some slight awareness of her condition, though what she complained about was a loss of memory that made her think she was losing her mind. She couldn't account for hours, and even whole days, in her life. Over the course of the previous three months, she explained, this had been getting worse. I told her that loss of memory went hand in hand with possession, because there was nothing *for* her to remember. The gaps in time represented episodes of possession—where life was being experienced not by her, but by the possessing entity. Yet before anything could be done for the girl, the real question that had to be answered was why had she been experiencing possession at all?

"Kendra, I found out, was a well-to-do—perhaps even spoiled— young lady who was wealthy enough to buy anything she wanted. About a year earlier, however, there came a point in her life when she encountered something money couldn't buy. That 'something' was the young man sitting next to her. Jimmy was a Nordic type, enrolled at an Ivy League school in a nearby state. Kendra had met him in her home town the summer before, and apparently they went out on a few dates. By the end of the summer, though, the boy had no feelings for Kendra and ignored her subsequent approaches.

"She, on the other hand, had seized on this guy passionately and couldn't rest until she made him her own. In essence, she saw Jimmy as a desirable commodity, not as a human being. This *de*humanization of a person got noticed. I say this because the girl tried every possible method to gain the boy's affection—from writing him enticing letters, to sending him money for travel tickets so he could visit her at school. But none of the tactics worked. At least, not until she hit upon ritual witchcraft, which is where the black lace veil comes in. To get Jimmy in her clutches, she turned to the occult. Kendra went out to a store and found herself a book on the black arts, the title of which I won't mention. Kendra took the book home and later that week, privately performed a ritual for acquiring lovers—an old ritual that has gotten people in trouble for ages."

The Warrens are often reluctant to give precise details, such as the names of conjuring books, the specific ritual of witchcraft an individual used, or the name of spirits responsible for particular demonic attacks. Why?

"I don't mention the names of spirits," says Ed, "because knowing a particular demonic name is to give recognition to that entity; if you give it recognition, no matter how small, you're giving it fuel to manifest. As for specifics, let me put it this way. If you give someone a loaded gun, they'd be liable to fire it. If you give them a loaded gun with the firing pin taken out, then there is no danger of it going off. That's what I do: I take the firing pin out of my statements. That's what has to be done with such material. People who really want to know how to perform satanic rituals can walk down to the local library and find out. But *I'm* not going to be the one who told these people how to travel down the road of no return. My job is just the opposite: to help people who have already gone too far; and to tell those who may want to dabble in the occult: *don't!*"

Ed then resumes. "The essence of black witchcraft is a pact with the devil, and women who make such pacts become, in effect, brides of the devil on earth. Now insofar as the devil is called the Prince of the Earth, the devil's bride need only ask her 'husband' for earthly pleasures, and supposedly they are hers. The only hitch is that before any of these benefits come to the witch, she's got to give her soul willingly to the devil. Kendra was mercenary enough to go through with such a pact. Part of the paraphernalia was the black lace mantilla, which she wore as a perverse 'wedding veil,' on top of which she placed a crown of goat horns. Next, she married herself into evil by renouncing God and her baptism and swearing allegiance to Satan. She finalized the ritual by washing down the vow with a cup of animal blood. The cup," says Ed, pointing to the oak table in the middle of the Occult Museum, "is there by the veil and goat horns.

"About a month after Kendra performed the ritual, the girl explained that Jimmy started to take an interest in her. He began calling on the phone and eventually started visiting her on weekends. For Kendra, things were hunky-dory. What she hadn't counted on, however, was that she was in debt to the demonic. By performing the witchcraft ritual, Kendra had given permission for the demonic to enter her life. Ordinarily, the witchcraft formula she used would have attracted either Incubus, the sexual oppressor of women, or Succubus, the sexual oppressor of men; but in her case it drew a lesser demonic spirit. Nevertheless, this entity went forward and oppressed her sexually just the same, apparently because this was her point of greatest vulnerability. The spirit inflamed her passions again and again until she was reduced to being a servant of impulse. At that juncture, the oppressing spirit was able to possess Kendra at will, which was when she began to experience memory gaps.

"Having spent well over an hour interviewing this couple—and I should mention the boyfriend wasn't too pleased with what he'd heard—I knew that for the girl's own safety, I had to arrange for an immediate exorcism. Otherwise the entity, knowing that *I* knew it was possessing the girl, might take her over one last time and bring about a suicide situation.

"With that in mind, I went out in the hall and explained the problem to Lorraine, and told her to take the rented car back to the hotel for the night. The three of us then drove in Jimmy's car to Kendra's apartment. I spent the night watching old movies on television with Jimmy, while she slept in her bedroom with the door open and a light on.

"The next morning I put a call through to a local Protestant exorcist in whom I had great faith. I couldn't call on a Catholic exorcist at the time, because their clergy has to follow Vatican policy and undergo a three-day period of prayer and fasting before conducting *any* exorcism of the possessed.

"The exorcist and his assistant, both Protestant clergymen, arrived about an hour later. Both were capable men, and I explained the background of the case to them. Of course, they'd heard it all before. Then Kendra was brought into the room. Up to this point, the clergymen had not witnessed the possession, nor had the girl been possessed since the night before. What I had to do first, therefore, was to prove to them that possession was in fact taking place.

"One of the many tests for possession is to discreetly place a crucifix behind the head of the possessed. So in this case, the exorcist instructed the girl to close her eyes and slowly count to twenty. His assistant, already standing behind the girl, then placed a cross six inches behind her head. The entity possessing the girl suddenly let go with wild, violent screaming: 'Take it away! It burns! Take it away!'

"Using the cross provoked the possessing entity to reveal itself, at which time we were able to intellectually confront the entity that had taken over the girl. The spirit, the same one that had possessed her the night before, admitted it was alone in the seizure of the girl's body. When the exorcist told it to identify itself, it responded by declaring: 'I am a servant of Diane.' Diane is a sexual-oppressing spirit, by the way, known as 'the goddess of the hunt' in mythology. We got very little else out of the spirit. For the most part, it went off on binges of screaming, cursing, and howling.

"Ordinarily, before an exorcism is allowed to take place, a formal investigation is conducted to prove possession has occurred in an individual. At the time, though, it was incontrovertible that the girl was possessed. Therefore, the exorcist decided it would be best to perform the deliverance ritual right then and there.

"In this case, the exorcist had the upper hand right from the beginning because the thing was so fearful of any mention of God or of being in the presence of a cross or holy water. Still, the possessing entity was quite resistant during the reading of the ritual, which took about one hour to perform. During the ritual it kept screaming, 'She's mine, she's mine. Her soul is mine,' in reference to Kendra. In time, the spirit was exorcised from the girl that day, but just before it departed, the thing vowed it would 'return to another.'

"None of us present had any idea what the spirit had in mind. Later, I would be the one to find out."

12.

The Entity Returns

"**A**fter the exorcism was over and Kendra was freed from bondage to this spirit," Ed continues, "the girl turned the black lace veil, the goat horns, the cup, and the conjuring book over to me, lest she be tempted, or oppressed, to use them again. Lorraine then picked me up at the girl's apartment, and later that day, as is my custom, I brought these articles home with me for safekeeping.

"Right from the very beginning, the witchcraft paraphernalia caused me trouble," recalls Ed. "A presence followed me everywhere. Then, the following night, after sunset, a psychic cold filled the office and Occult Museum where I'd put the objects. Sensing the change in temperature, I got up from my desk and looked out into the museum. There, by the veil and horns, I saw a dark gray cloudlike mass about the size of a man building into a dense black form. To prevent the thing from manifesting, I used holy water to drive it back into invisibility. Still, it was evident that the entity which possessed Kendra had traveled along with the profane objects.

"As fate would have it, I received a phone call the next day from a fellow named Robert Goldstrom, who wanted to make an appointment to come to my office with his daughter Denise. 'Why do you need to see me?' I asked him.

"Frustrated and upset, he explained that his daughter possessed a natural knowledge of what he took to be witchcraft. He said, giving me a quick run-through of the girl's life, that instead of playing like an ordinary child, Denise was often found off on her own, performing complicated rituals involving pentagrams, animal blood, and so forth—things a six-year-old would have no familiarity with. As the girl got older, she displayed an aversion to church and withdrew in the presence of clergymen. Meanwhile, neighborhood kids were instinctively frightened of Denise; even her own mother was afraid to be left alone in the same room with her.

"As a teenager, Denise got even worse. When she stared at people, even when they weren't aware of it, she'd fill their mind with inhuman terror. The girl's gaze was so intense she could actually stop machinery! I know this is true, because I later saw her do it. She brought a car moving along a highway to a stone-cold stop. Yet, this activity was not the reason why Goldstrom had called me. Rather, Denise was now manifesting different personalities: some male, some female, and some that couldn't even be called human. Moreover, the statements these 'personalities' made were extremely threatening to Robert Goldstrom and his wife.

"In response, he brought the girl to psychiatrists, who recognized her problem as being something more than psychological. The doctors told him to bring his daughter to a clergyman, but the minister whom Goldstrom consulted wouldn't see the girl unless he brought her to see me first. After listening to the man's problem, I made an appointment to see them both the following Saturday at eleven A.M.

"That night, the spirit again attempted to manifest in the Occult Museum; and again I did my thing with the holy water. The next day, Monday, Lorraine and I left for speaking engagements in Pennsylvania and Ohio. We didn't return home again until late Friday. The following day, Saturday, at eleven in the morning, Robert Goldstrom arrived with his daughter for their scheduled appointment. Denise was about nineteen. She was a tall, thin brunette with blue eyes that put out a fierce, penetrating gaze. When I attempted to shake hands with the girl, she backed away and stared distrustfully at me, keeping track of every move I made.

"Bringing these two people out to my office, I asked Denise to take the chair beside my desk, while her father sat in an easy chair close by. I then switched on the tape recorder and asked Mr. Goldstrom to state the problem again. He repeated that whenever he or his wife spoke to their daughter, they could never be sure if they were talking to Denise—or to some alien personality. The girl all the while never took her eyes off me.

"When the father was done, I attempted to question the girl. 'Who are you?' I asked.

"'Denise Goldstrom,' she answered me contemptuously.

"How old are you?

"'Older than you think,' she said.

"How about what your father told me? Is it true you've been manifesting different personalities?

"'He's paranoid,' she answered. 'I'm myself. I'm whoever I want to be.'

"'Are any of your personalities inhuman?' I pressed her.

"'I don't have to answer any of your goddamn questions,' she shot back.

"When I looked up to ask Denise another question, she was directing one of her piercing gazes at me. 'You picked the wrong guy to try that on,' I told her. 'Don't you ever, *ever* do that to me again!'

"For the first time since she entered our house, the girl looked away from me. She seemed dazed and disoriented, as though she'd just been clunked on the head with a baseball bat. Her eyes wandered over the articles on my desk, then came to rest on the black lace veil that I'd put in the far corner to stop the spirit from manifesting. Suddenly, before I could block her, Denise jumped up, grabbed the veil, and drew it to her breast. Her features immediately began to transform into those of a wild, sneering creature distinct from this otherwise attractive girl. I drew two vials of water to myself, one unblessed, the other blessed by a very pious exorcist, and moved away from what was no longer Denise, but an inhuman spirit: a lesser devil of hell. This," says Ed, pushing the Play button of the tape recorder, "is what I heard."

Raucous, diabolical laughter suddenly erupts from the twin bookshelf speakers.

"You're laughing at me," Ed's voice says, "but who am I talking to?" And the spirit that possessed Denise begins to speak.

Voice: I know who *you* are! Ha,ha, ha, ha, heee . . . *(laughter)*.

Ed: Who are you?

V: Ho, hoo . . .

Ed: Who are you?

V: Don't you know *me*? Ha! Don't you know me? Oh, come on, you know who *I* am. Don't you know who *I am*? I'm suffering. I'm suffering *(because the spirit has recently been exorcised)*.

Ed: Why are you suffering?

V: Ho, ho, heee . . . Black is my color. It's the color of death, the color of *death! The color of DEATH!!*

Ed: Who sent you here?

V: I worship Diane, *and Lucifer!* . . . And light, light, light: everything holy is damned!

Ed: I have something for you.

V: *(Defiantly)* What have you got for *me* that I don't already possess? I can possess anybody that I want, you *(expletive deleted)*.

Ed: I'll put it on your hand, and you tell me what it is. *(Testing the entity, Ed puts unblessed water on Denise's hand.)*

V: Oooooh. It's wet!

Ed: That's right.

V: It's wet, and I don't like it. I like putting *fats* of people's body over my body. And I like blood. And I like to see blood. And I like to drink blood.

Ed: I have something else for you. I have holy water for you.

V: Holy water? Holy what? You? . . . .you're no man of God!

Ed: No, I'm not.

V: You're in between, *aren't* you?

Ed: That's right, in between.

V: You don't know! He stands in hell or heaven. And there's not a hell, and there's not a heaven. No, there's not a hell, and there's not a heaven. There's just a place, and I won't tell you of that place now, will I? You know, don't you? You know. You're standing between heaven and hell. And there's no heaven *or* hell. But you're gonna get it!

Ed: No, you're the one that's going to get it.

V: *(Diabolical laughter rings out for ten seconds.)* I like this. Do you know that? It gives me peace. *(Spirit now crying.)* It gives me peace, and I like peace. I like peace, and to be quiet. *But I don't like you! (Screaming.)*

Ed: And I know why you don't like me.

V: *(Screaming, enraged)* Why?

Ed: You don't have Kendra to possess anymore, do you?

V: *(Cackling)* I have anyone I want to have. I am stronger than you and your man of God *(the exorcist)*!

Ed: We'll see. We'll see who's the strongest. What is your name? What do you call yourself?

V: Let me put it this way, man . . . *(vulgarity)* I'm a favorite of Lucifer. Do you know who Lucifer is?

Ed: You tell me, who is Lucifer?

V: Ha, ha, ha, ha. He's the one god who's right! Do you know, when I want something *I can have it? (Proclaiming) I can have what I want!*

Ed: You wanted Kendra, but you couldn't keep her.

V: Ho, ho, ho. Kendra doesn't know! Kendra doesn't know!

Ed: *What doesn't she know?*

V: She will drink the blood! She will drink the blood! And she'll see me! I'll possess her again!

Ed: Again?

V: *(Adamantly) Again!*

Ed: No, she won't.

V: *(Shouting) And by what means are you going to protect that girl? She's mine! Her soul is mine!*

Ed: *Nothing* of her belongs to you.

V: I will suck the blood out of her!

Ed: You'll do nothing to her!

V: Ha, ha! I like her. She's my toy *(cooing)*.

Ed: She *was* your toy, until she came to me. But you'd like to get even with me, wouldn't you?

V: *(Cackling and laughing)* I can do *anything* I want to do!

Ed: You'll do nothing! I have something *(holy water)* that is stronger than you'll ever be. You know that too, don't you?

V: Oh, ho! Yes. *(Shouting)* You believe in such false things! Ah! What's that?

Ed: You tried to come to me the other night. What did you intend to do? I drove you off, didn't I?

V: I wanted to kill you, and I really meant it. *(Unintelligible screeching)* . . . Are you going to stick something in my heart? I don't have a heart!

Ed: That's right, you don't have a heart.

V: No.

Ed: But, I'll give you something else. *(Ed casts holy water on the possessed.)* You don't like that very much do you?

V: *(Enraged, screaming)* No!!!

Ed: Do you like the sign of the cross?

V: No!

Ed: All right, now I'm going to tell you something . . .

V: *(Violent screaming.)*

Ed: . . . I want you to leave. And I don't want you to ever come back here again!

V: Stop it!

Ed: No, I won't stop it. In the name of God, you're going to leave . . . .

V: *(Screaming violently)* In the name of Jesus Christ, shut up!

Ed: It will be in the name of Jesus Christ! And you'll leave! And you won't come back again!

V: *(Declaring) I shall return! Or, if I do not return, one stronger will! I am weak, but there are others stronger!!*

Ed: You're weak, and you'll go, and I'll drive you off. In the name of God, I'll drive you off.

V: Ha, ha, ha, ha, ha, heeee . . .

Ed: Here's something else for you to think about *(Ed anoints the body with holy water in the sign of the cross.)*

V: *(Agonized screeching)* Oh, my God, fire! Fire, fire, fire!

Ed: *(Above the screeching and wailing)* I don't want you to come back to this house again! Do you understand me?

V: Oh, my God. Oh, my God. Oh, my God. Oh . . .

Ed: I don't want you to ever come back to this house again! Now leave. Leave!

Baleful moaning, caterwauling, and various animal sounds are then heard receding into the distance as the possessing entity withdraws from the body of the girl.

Ed puts an end to the moaning by hitting the Stop button on the tape recorder, leaving the Occult Museum as silent as a dungeon.

After a long minute of reflection, Ed finally breaks the silence: "That's what's out there. That's what's possessing these kids . . . *in*human, demonic spirits. *Inhuman*, because they're not man and have no positive virtues; *demonic*, because they're an order of angel that call themselves devils; and *spirits*, because they do not exist on the physical but on the metaphysical plane. They're invisible, they're intangible . . . but they're there!"

Did the spirit actually return to possess Kendra?

"Oh, my God, yes!" Ed replies immediately. "No more than a week later, her boyfriend called on the phone and told me what had happened. The girl drank the blood offering once again—just like the spirit said would happen—and she came right back under possession by the same entity. I had to go all the way back to the college, confront the entity, and again arrange for Kendra to be freed through exorcism."

Why didn't the first exorcism on Kendra work?

"It *did*," says Ed. "But it takes the person's cooperation for an exorcism to be totally effective. 'God helps those who help themselves!' The exorcist restored the girl's free will, but the spirit oppressed her will *again*. Rather than fighting the temptation, she went ahead and drank the blood offering a week later. This opened her will back up, and gave the spirit the permission it needed to return and possess her body once more."

Did the spirit possess Kendra a third time?

"No, she's free today."

What about Denise? What became of her? And what *was* her problem, anyway?

"After the incident of possession," Ed answers, "her features returned to normal, at which point I continued with the interview. The incident you heard on the tape showed me that the girl was an open vessel for possession, which accounted for why she was manifesting different personalities—at least inhuman ones. In fact, it turned out that Denise was a *medium* for communication between the demonic and the human realm. What I tried to find out was *how* she got this ability.

"The holy water that I'd cast on her managed to tone the girl down enough for me to be able to converse on a semirational level. During that time, Denise unraveled a long, complex involvement with sorcery and negative practices that went back beyond the bounds of her present lifetime. She's what we call a natural sorceress: no one told her what to do, nor did she read about it in a book. She was *born* with negative knowledge and power. Her knowledge came from experience gained in past lifetimes—and one never forgets knowledge, especially negative knowledge, that is gained in past lifetimes. This case, you see, gets into the really hard-core stuff, back into the dimension of true evil that most people know nothing about.

"Denise was an instrument of the demonic, in other words; she existed as a virtual mouthpiece for demonic spirits. She as not a witch, however; the power of witchcraft comes from a vow to serve the devil. Instead, Denise was a sorceress. Similar to witchcraft but not the same, sorcery is the ability to manipulate the physical world through an arrangement with spirit forces. This girl was in league with negative inhuman spirits, an arrangement made in a previous incarnation—about which she spoke knowingly and in great detail.

"However, this girl didn't totally know *how* to get the demonic to do her bidding for her. Though it used her at will, she couldn't do the same with it. That's the reason why she allowed herself to be brought to me. She knew who I was, by the grapevine, and came to my office under the mistaken assumption that she could coerce or intimidate me to reveal certain pivotal secrets of demonology that she hadn't yet learned on her own. Of course, I wouldn't tell her anything. Giving this girl mystical knowledge would have been like giving a hand grenade to a small child.

"During the next month, I met with Denise and her father about three times, but there was just nothing I could do to correct the situation. All I could do was give the father a referral letter to present to the clergyman, affirming that Denise required religious counseling: her life, unless she saw fit to change it, was dedicated to the negative. In fact, unless she does see the light, she'll live and die under its influence."

Does Ed believe in reincarnation?

"Let me put it this way," Ed answers. "I cannot straightforwardly tell you that reincarnation is a principle or process that all people naturally undergo. I can tell you I do have cases on file that prove certain individuals have lived more than one life. On the other hand, I do not have information to prove that *all* people experience the phenomenon. Furthermore, when the demonic is involved in any situation, you're dealing with a disruption of the natural order. Consequently, an individual who makes a deal with the demonic and then actually experiences rebirth into another lifetime has done so under questionable circumstances. That additional lifetime would—to some degree—have to be considered a 'bogus incarnation.'"

Had Kendra and Denise known one another before Ed got involved in the case?

"No," he answers. "They have never met, and they do not know each other now. The only reason Denise came to my office was because the exorcised spirit arranged for it to happen."

Psychometry is to "know by touching." Isn't it possible that Denise, when she took hold of the black lace veil, made a link with Kendra and therefore psychometrized the whole event?

"In this case," Ed replies, "that's stretching psychometry a bit too far. ESP *could* have occurred, I grant you, but that wasn't the situation here. An external entity, independent of both of them, was involved. When the spirit wasn't possessing either of the two girls, it was present in this office. When it did possess Denise, the very first thing it said to me was, 'I know who *you* are.' I didn't know who or what *it* was, of course, but I've been told the exact same thing many times before, by other inhuman spirits possessing other people. After that, it began telling me it was 'suffering.' This didn't pertain to either Kendra or Denise, but to the emotional predicament of a spirit that has been exorcised. You'll also notice it's an independent entity because it referred to Kendra *by name*, indicating a separation of identity.

"Later on, bypassing all else it said, the entity gave precognitive information about repossessing the college girl, Kendra. This second possession occurred; the second exorcism is on record as having been performed. Finally, add to this the symbolic fact that the entity could distinguish between blessed and unblessed *water*: unblessed water felt 'wet,' blessed water felt like 'fire.' Have you ever seen a *person* carry on that way when touched with holy water?"

Why did the spirit have such a violent reaction to holy water?

"Water is water, but holy water is charged with the spirit of the positive—with the spirit of what we call God. On people, holy water can have a positive effect, and in some cases, it can even be used for healing. For the demonic, though, holy water has just the opposite effect: if feels like acid or fire to the entity."

What did it mean about "I like peace and to be quiet"?

"The spirit finds peace only through possession of a human body. Otherwise, it is in a state of suffering."

Was the spirit really suffering, as it claimed it was? And if so, why?

"Yes, it was suffering, for the reason that it had been exorcised; but the answer is more complicated than that. The demonic spirit is *driven* to possession for two reasons. First, their realm—call it hell, call it whatever you want—is so intolerable that these spirits will do anything to escape it. The place, you see, is unlivable—it's hell!

These spirits not only torment people—they torment one another. Their only way out is to possess a human body. And when a person can be possessed by one entity, he can be possessed by many. In fact, possession by many entities isn't the exception, it's the rule. In major cases of possession six or more spirits often inhabit the body of the victim. Through possession, these spirits find 'peace' from the ongoing torments they experience. Exorcism, therefore, is the worst thing that could befall them.

"The other, grander motivation for possession is based on the Antichrist concept. The whole effort of the inhuman spirit is dedicated to this end: to seize the earth and destroy mankind *in front of* the eyes of God. So, through possession, the inhuman spirit kills two birds with one stone: it hides out from hell; plus it does its work of ruining man. The inhuman demonic spirit is a true enemy of mankind. I don't know how else to put it."

Do you believe in hell as a place of fire and brimstone?

"No," he answers. "I don't believe in a fiery hell. Although, through the possessed, I've heard the demonic spirit wail about 'hell-fire,' I can't for a moment believe that an all-loving God would create such an incomprehensible horror as hell. However, through their perverse approach to existence, these spirits *may* have created their own fiery hell; insofar as their existence is the antithesis of the positive, such torment would be their own doing.

"Ultimately, though, the demonic spirit has a far more poignant sense of hell than physical punishment. These spirits know they are doomed to eternal punishment, meaning the demonic spirit— the carrier of the plague of evil—will be deducted away from the natural universe. Or, as the Bible puts it: 'the wicked shall perish.' Yet rather than change, it elects to be what it is: wicked and pernicious. Consequently, on an intellectual level, hell makes more sense when seen as eternal *separation* from God: that is, separation from the source of being altogether."

Then what did the spirit mean when it said, "There is no heaven and there is no hell, there's just a place"?

"I can't say, because I don't know," Ed replies. "Don't forget, the demonic spirit is a master liar. The exorcist, for example, is taught *never* to engage in conversation with the demonic. So, you can't take everything it says as true. In this case, though, possibly it was referring to the idea of being—and nothingness. That is, in the end, when it's all totted up, the *only* place where there will be life is where there is being. Beyond that, I really don't know. I'm a practicing demonologist, not a theologian."

What about the spirit's statement about smearing fats on its body?

"This goes way, way back into history. In black witchcraft, the killing of a child was a traditional gift to Lucifer. The body would be boiled down and its fat would be rendered into a grease that could then be mixed with belladonna and other herbs and smeared on the body of the witch. This shows you that this spirit has possessed others in the past, because of its familiarity with the practice."

What about the emphasis on blood?

"Blood is the other half," Ed answers. "The entity seeks to desecrate the body *and* the blood. Blood is the gift of life from the Creator. These entities may mock or simulate life by drinking blood or smearing human fats, but they are nevertheless jealous of the incarnate body and its life-giving substance, the blood."

The possessing entity said it worships Diane, the goddess of witchcraft. Is Diane female?

"No, Diane is a devil. It is people—mythologists—who give these entities a gender. If there are two sexes to the demonic, it would be hate and jealousy. You have to remember the demonic spirit is actually an angel, though an angel of perdition."

As is evident in this black veil case, possession is not a matter of mistaking a psychological problem for a religious one. Instead, it is the actual seizure of a human body by an entity that forthrightly identifies itself as being a servant of the devil (in this case "Lucifer"), and thereupon backs up its claim with preternatural knowledge and power. Moreover, the spirit is not timid to make its motives known. Probably the possessing entity's most significant statement in Ed's office was spoken in reference to Kendra: In absolute vehemence, the spirit declared: "She's mine. Her *soul* is mine!" This taking of the human soul is the very essence of possession. And the only way to get the soul back is through the process of exorcism.

In this particular case, exorcism was twice performed on Kendra to expel the invading spirit. As the possessing entity itself admitted, it was "weak," but it also declared "there are others stronger," referring to the diabolical hierarchy. "Though devils *order* the possession of a particular human being," Ed says, "a devil will almost never participate in the possession itself. Instead, the demonic spirit possesses people. There are exceptions, of course. We know that Lucifer himself was involved in the possession of a woman in Iowa in 1928 named Anna Ecklund because witnesses at the time reported that he showed himself and remained present during the latter part of the exorcism standing in a circle of fire wearing a crown."

According to Ed Warren, diabolical possession is *meant* as a challenge to the authority of God, because in such cases, "the devil, in violation of cosmic law, has actually done the forbidden and taken on incarnate form. When this happens, there is no alternative *but* to perform major exorcism."

And regrettably, there is no proof so clear of the Devil's existence than that which is gained during a major exorcism of the possessed.

13

A Soul in Hostage

On July 1, 1976, just six months after the Amityville case occurred in Long Island, a twenty-two-year-old student at the University of Wurzburg, West Germany, died during an exorcism that was recorded on some forty-three hours of tape. Portions of that terrible, grueling exorcism were broadcast on German television. The girl's death, coupled with the fact that exorcism was still performed in this modern day and age, shocked the West German public. As *The New York Times* reported on August 8 of that year:

> After an agonizing ritual that might have come from the movie *The Exorcist,* a 22-year-old West German woman—possessed by demons, according to her priests—died of undernourishment on July 1. . . . That exorcism even existed in West Germany was unknown until the death of Anneliese Michel, a student-teacher. But according to some reports after this case, exorcism may be almost commonplace.

In response to the death of Ms. Michel, the German authorities pressed charges of negligence against the Catholic exorcists. The local district attorney claimed the girl had been denied sustenance, and therefore died as a result of "undernourishment and dehydration."

The charges were just a bit simplistic, though, because it made it seem as if the Jesuit exorcists were responsible for the girl's death, which was hardly the case. Ms. Michel died not because exorcism had been attempted on her, but because she could no longer withstand the ordeal of possession. Furthermore, contrary to the legal charges, the exorcists did not deny the girl sustenance; there would have been no point in that. A medical doctor attended the girl throughout the whole ordeal. According to Ed, "The fact was that for six months, during the entire process of exorcism, Anneliese Michel existed entirely *without* food or water."

Moreover, Ms. Michel had been under varying degrees of possession for three years before exorcism was attempted; during that time, medical doctors and psychiatrists had every opportunity to cure her of any mental or physical malady. But despite the medical profession's best efforts, the girl's health degenerated significantly between 1973 (when the possession began) and 1976. Anneliese Michel was involved in a supernatural battle that concerned not her body, but her soul; exorcism was performed only as a last resort in an effort to *prevent* her death.

Still, the question that persists is not legal, but religious: why did Anneliese die?

"People have asked me this question many times," Ed replies, "but they usually aren't prepared for the real answer. I end up sidestepping the issue by explaining that not all exorcisms have a happy ending. But the reason this German girl died is because she had to. The case is complicated but it amounts to murder on the part of the demonic.

"The girl was a 'soul victim,' as the Church calls it. She came under possession not because she had done anything wrong—but because she was so good. This happens about once every ten years: the religious term for it is 'iniquity'—meaning gross moral crime. The demonic seized on this girl *because* she was a devout, kindly human being. It possessed her body in a deliberate effort to impurify her *and* to provoke a confrontation with the Almighty. So the act of possession had both physical and metaphysical significances. Demonic spirits first entered the girl's body in 1973. Then, as I understand it, devils joined the possession in 1975. Their presence in this realm is rare, as I've said, except in significant cases of possession.

"These devils called themselves 'Hitler' and 'Nero,' by the way, but the names were only symbolic to keep them from being identified. Yet reviewing the data I have on that exorcism, it is recorded that the high devil Beelzebub *was* present in the possessed, and responsible for the seizure.

"Now, desperate to help their daughter, the girl's parents—being practicing Roman Catholics—sought the help of the Jesuit clergy. During the early period of possession, the girl had lucid moments and gave instructions to the Jesuits not to compromise with the entities that had taken her over. In turn, these priests did everything that could possibly have been done for the girl, short of exorcism. They prayed for her continuously. They put themselves in physical and psychological danger by confronting the entities and trying to talk them out of the possession. But exorcism was purposely held off as the last resort. Exorcism was not considered, you see, because all those involved were working under an impossible proposition put out by the possessing entities—the classic one in cases of this sort: *Believe in me, and the girl will live; believe in God, and the girl will die!*

"For the family and the exorcists, the whole idea was completely unthinkable: they would not trade her body for her soul! Consequently, the situation evolved into a matter of faith. The issue was not food and water: like Teresa Neumann, a twentieth-century stigmatic, this girl lived with no food or water at all. Instead, the issue was whether the devil was going to be permitted to take on incarnate form in the year 1975, anno Domini. And the reply from these people was *No!* Though the girl's family lived in anguish every minute of every day for the three years she was possessed, they understood what was happening, and their faith never faltered.

"Eventually, because of this unflinching resistance, the diabolical entities subjected the girl to terrible mental and physical torment, such that the only remaining alternative was to resort to exorcism before these things destroyed her completely. As a result, early in 1976, the Jesuit exorcists began reading the Roman Ritual of exorcism over the girl. After six arduous months, the exorcists had read the ritual a total of sixty-six times—notice the number—at which point she succumbed to death. Death was a release for the girl: like a martyr, it was her only access to freedom."

Why didn't the entities obey the commands of the exorcist, as they're supposed to do?

"The demonic entities *did* leave. The devils, on the other hand, defied not only the exorcist's commands but the laws of God, for which they will experience rebuke beyond all our reasoning. Rather than give up the possession, these diabolical entities used it instead to *affirm* their hate for God. Like Christ, the girl's life was unfairly taken away from her by others. And though she died in a physical sense, she survived with her soul intact and her spirit unblemished. It wasn't the priests who killed her. Nor did the ritual of exorcism have anything remotely to do with it. The girl was killed by the devil, and that's a fact documented on tape."

Some cling to the belief that diabolical possession is a purely psychological event—that there's no such thing as "external entities," and talk of spirits is hogwash. Considering that so much of the activity of the demonic does have a psychological interlink, it is only fair to ask where psychology stands on the subject of demoniacal oppression and possession.

Until roughly a century ago, *all* mental illness was treated as a sign of possession. Today, all oppression and possession is treated as a sign of mental illness. This drastic change from one absolute interpretation to another has done nothing to solve the ongoing problem of demoniacal influence: it has only resulted in a change of labels. Thus, in the past, an individual who displayed unseemly behavior was branded as "possessed" and locked away in an institution. Today, the oppressed or possessed individual (who also displays unseemly behavior) is diagnosed as being "mentally ill" and once again locked away in an institution.

"The majority of people who complain about being oppressed or possessed by spirits *are* mentally ill," Ed notes, "but this isn't always the case, as I've learned by experience.

"Back in 1971, I was approached by a family who calmly and reasonably told me they believed their son was under possession by a demonic spirit. I let them talk, then said, 'Okay, where's your son so I can take a look at him?' They told me he was in a New York state mental hospital, where he'd been committed eight years before as a schizophrenic.

"As a patient, the young man complained about something else *in* him, while making occasional murmurings about the devil. No one took him seriously except his parents, who read about the subject of possession and found enough data to convince themselves that their son just might be possessed.

"A few weeks later, I accompanied the family to the hospital to see the son. Well, he was a dribbling, mental wreck; he hardly moved, and recognized no one. I'd brought a cross with me at the time and started to walk up behind him. I was about to put it behind the boy's head when he suddenly swung around, his eyes wide open like saucers, and stared at me with that look of furious hate so characteristic in the possessed. What we all saw was not the boy who had been brought into the room in a wheelchair. We saw another being emerge: this one alert and vicious, which had been provoked by a religious object that the boy never saw.

"The son's previously healthy background, coupled with his reaction to the cross, gave me reason to believe that he just might be possessed. To make a long story short, I went ahead and assembled all the facts available on the case, which kept tilting toward the possibility of possession. I then went through a lot of effort, even putting my reputation on the line, to get an exorcist assigned to the case. Well, I succeeded, and a few months later the Catholic Church assigned an exorcist to conduct the ritual.

"When the priest flew into New York from abroad, I had everything arranged. With the permission of the hospital authorities, the parents picked up the boy and brought him home. He was limp and lifeless and had to be helped around like a child. The boy was laid down on a bed. The exorcist then read the ritual of exorcism over him. During the reading, nothing unusual happened. The boy just lay there, inert and barely conscious. There was absolutely no indication of possession until the very, very end, when the exorcist commanded the spirits to vacate the boy's body. Suddenly he convulsed and thrashed around and moaned and panted and sweated and hollered and yelled.

"A minute later, he collapsed back into bed. A look of serenity and peace swept over his face. The boy opened his eyes, now clear and devoid of any negative influence, and articulately said, 'It's over: the spirit is gone.' Well! Twenty minutes later, that young man stood up and was just as sane and well-spoken as anyone in the room. A few days later, he was discharged from the hospital, and he's never had a problem since. Whether that boy's condition was mental illness—or possession, as I contend—the fact remains that exorcism cured his problem."

Psychology tends to see all cases of oppression and possession as being the manifestation of one or another type of mental disorder.

The prevailing tendency is to diagnose such cases as paranoia, hysteria, or schizophrenia because the outward symptoms of spirit oppression or possession (stress, anxiety, disorientation, fantasy images) *are* similar to textbook symptoms of neurosis and psychosis. Yet no matter how similar the overt symptoms, the etiology or cause of the problem is not the same. Rather, closer scrutiny of the oppressed or possessed individual's complaints should reveal that, although his behavior may *appear* abnormal, he is functionally sane. All he's really doing is reporting exactly what's happening to him—namely, that he is being harassed by external forces. However, because these "external forces" have long ago been exorcised from scientific literature, closer scrutiny is rare. And so the spiritually-afflicted individual gets put away in an institution instead.

Dr. Jean Lhermitte is a French neurologist and medical examiner for the Catholic Church to whom many potentially possessed individuals have been referred for diagnosis. In *True and False Possession ,** Dr. Lhermitte notes:

> Whatever sceptics[sic], unbelievers and the ill-informed may think, demonopathic manifestations are not extinct; we still observe the phenomena which startled and alarmed our forefathers, but with a critical sense and knowledge they did not possess. But I must make clear that while the neurologist and the psychiatrist are qualified to discern and define an abnormal structure of the mind or some bodily disorder, they should remain physicians and not exceed their powers, so that in cases where mental illness is not clearly present, the neuro-psychiatrist ought to call in the help and cooperation of the theologian.

---

* *Vrais et Faux Possédés*, 1956.

Given such concepts, it is no wonder priests and psychologists have been called "half brothers" in the study of man. But how can true cases of diabolical possession be differentiated from mental illness?

The first, and probably most significant distinction would be *loss of self*. Nowhere in psychology is loss of self considered to be a real factor in mental illness. Indeed, Freud notes in his *Outline of Psychoanalysis* that loss of self *is not* a medical condition, no matter how complete the degeneration of mind might appear to be.

> Even in a state so far removed from the reality of the external world as one of hallucinatory confusion, one learns from patients after their recovery that at the time in some corner of their mind (as they put it) there was a normal person hidden who, like a detached spectator, watched the hubbub of illness go past him.

Yet, in true cases of possession the individual *does* experience the phenomenon of loss of self. What replaces the self, or spirit, of the human being is an entity totally independent of the person. As Ed explains: "The demonic spirit may either dislodge the human spirit *or* cohabit the body with the human spirit. When this happens, both the possessing entity and the person may speak from the body *at the very same time*. In cases where more than one entity is possessing a human body, as often occurs, the problem is determining *how many* possessing entities are in the group. In those rare cases where more than one person in the family is under possession, the possessing entities tend to reveal their identity inadvertently by speaking from *either* of the two bodies.

"As for distinguishing characteristics, possessing entities usually talk in the gruff, manlike voice I mentioned earlier, even when speaking out of the body of a woman or young child. When speaking through a woman, though, the demonic will occasionally use a high-pitched falsetto. Utterances may emanate from the voice box—although the possessed individual may be inert and unconscious at the time—or else simply resonate from somewhere out of the body. If it so desires, the demonic *may* identify itself by name: It will tend to say, for instance, 'I am Hate; I am Sloth; I am Lust'; or else go further and give its demonic name, usually one of ancient origin that is already on the books. The possessing entity or entities may use familiar language, but it isn't uncommon for them to lapse off into foreign or dead languages of which the possessed individual has no knowledge whatsoever."

Not only does the truly possessed individual experience a loss or displacement of self; there are additional symptoms that bear no relation whatever to classic psychological disorders. One factor is "metamorphosis," for want of a better term. In other words, physical transformation of the face and body may occur. Again, this phenomenon *is not a medical condition*. People cannot and do not grossly transform from one appearance to another—unless possession is a factor. Yet, as Ed states, "I, along with other witnesses, have seen the appearance of the possessed change into that of a wolf, a pig, and most often, a gorilla. I have seen the possessed take on the features of the dead, as well as transform into things that could only be described as macabre grotesqueries. And all these changes are *physical*. The skin and bones actually change their form, then recede back to normal once possession has passed."

Besides loss of self and "metamorphosis," a third factor unseen in cases of mental illness is the occurrence of distinctly supernatural phenomena in the vicinity of the possessed individual. "In cases of possession, external, observable phenomena occur about fifty percent of the time," Ed notes. "The activity tends to be of the order of levitation, teleportation, materialization, and dematerialization of physical objects. The demonic spirit brings about unnatural activity to *prove* to witnesses that inhuman powers are in effect. In a nutshell, the distinction between mental illness and true diabolical possession is often as different as night and day."

When a person has truly come under possession by the demonic, only exorcism will reverse this humiliating seizure of a human being. But it is not simply the body that the demonic takes into bondage, but ultimately, the soul—the metaphysical essence of the human being. "If you want to understand why exorcism is necessary," says Ed, "then you've got to understand what man's got going for himself. He's got life, he's got free will, and he's got that *touch of grace* called soul. The life and free will part belong to man, but, theoretically, the soul belongs to God. So to use an analogy, the soul is like a relic of God that man's been given and told not to lose. But along comes the demonic spirit that sees man as the hateful image of God, and so it attacks the soul, for no other reason than spite—to withhold it from God as a show of force. In *The Exorcist* case, the letters *S-P-I-T-E* actually showed up in red welts on the possessed boy's chest.

"Nevertheless, the demonic spirit can't just possess a body and take the soul—because if it could, it would! Instead, it's got to find a way to get it from you. This it does either by breaking down the will, or by influencing the will away from the positive and toward the negative. In time, if permission is granted or if the influence has been successful, there comes a point when possession must almost inevitably take place. And in most cases of possession, the spirit claims it has *earned* the soul because it was able to effectively dominate the person's will. Even if the person has been tricked, this is basically true; so the only thing that can be done is to exorcise the spirit, then reeducate the person to the black facts of life."

Exorcism literally means "to cast out evil spirits in the name of God." All major religions have some form of exorcism ritual as part of their liturgy. The ritual with which most people are familiar is the *Rituale Romanum* which was developed by the Church of Rome for the express purpose of exorcising diabolical spirits from the body of man. Not all exorcisms are of a major order, however. As a religious procedure, exorcisms vary in type and function.

"There are minor and major exorcisms," Ed Warren explains. "Minor exorcisms take the form of a blessing. In fact, it's a rare person who hasn't undergone the most basic rite of exorcism. Although it's not generally known, baptism is actually an exorcism ritual, and one of the chief reasons why so few people come under spontaneous possession during the course of their lives.

"Beyond that, minor exorcisms are intended to clear a house of demonic spirits, or rid a person of negative spirits that may be bringing about oppression. The point is, a negative influence can dominate a person or dwelling simply because there isn't any positive influence to counteract it. When a blessing is performed, positive supernatural power is deliberately and methodically brought to bear to counteract the negative. The clergyman conducts the ritual in the name of God. As a result, if the demonic violates the exorcism, it doesn't have to contend with the clergyman, but with the wrath of God."

Even though minor exorcism may clear a dwelling of negative spirits, in reality, the demonic does not possess homes or objects. Reverend Christopher Neil-Smith, an Anglican clergyman and one of the better-known exorcists in the world, explains it this way in his book *The Exorcist and the Possessed:*

> Exorcism is not intended essentially to deal with ghosts or even houses, but with states of soul of living people molested by evil spirits. . . . Evil comes through people and [exorcism] only has a secondary or residual effect on places or houses. Places are affected because the people who lived there enacted evil deeds.

Thus a home has no soul; the devil has no soul. Only a person has a soul; and it is that unique commodity, that key to immortality that the demonic seeks to possess—if only to destroy it. For this reason, major exorcism of the possessed is not a passive blessing, but an active expulsion of spirit entities that will not leave unless properly commanded to do so. In contemporary terms, demonic spirits are inhuman terrorists that possess an individual's body and hold the soul as hostage; major exorcism is therefore a prayerful procedure for freeing the soul from such tyranny. "When a major exorcism must be conducted, it means that an inhuman spirit has possessed a person's body and soul, and that soul has *got* to be saved," Ed declares.

In the West German case, the ritual of exorcism performed over Anneliese Michel was the *Rituale Romanum,* the *major* ritual of exorcism. It is a black day indeed when this ritual must be performed. Because if it has been determined necessary to perform a major exorcism, church authorities will have so judged after long and diligent deliberation that a human being has been possessed by that which calls itself Legion. And this is no frivolous decision; in fact, before church authorities will even contemplate a major exorcism, the evidence for possession must be unchallengeable and overwhelming. All natural explanations must be eliminated, while all supernatural claims must be proven and verified.

The individual under possession will have to be thoroughly examined by a medical doctor. Brain tumors, hormonal imbalances and narcosis, for example, are just three of many routine factors that can alter an individual, physically or mentally. Even if examinations, X-rays, and medical tests show the person to be physically sound, a psychiatric examination will be called for next. Abnormal psychology is tricky and complex, and the consulting psychiatrist is charged with determining whether or not the person is possessed or experiencing delusion, hallucination, multiple personality, or any of a variety of mental disorders that seem like possession.

While the individual's physical and psychological health are being checked out, church authorities will assign a demonologist to the case.

"The demonologist is responsible for conducting an onsite investigation to determine the validity of any alleged case of possession," Ed explains. "This investigation involves interviewing all persons related to the case, including the individual purported to be under possession, to learn if factors were present, or actions were committed, that could have permitted an inhuman spirit to inflict possession. If external phenomena have been reported in association with the case, the demonologist must personally witness the occurrence of any such activity; then determine whether that activity was caused by natural or supernatural agencies. Lastly, the demonologist must witness the possession in order to assess the nature, power, and number of spirits involved, and if at all possible, attempt to learn the identity of the possessing entities.

"Yet the demonic spirit is hardly eager to reveal itself to someone in authority who would be able to bring about its expulsion," Ed goes on. "So in cases where possession is not readily apparent, which happens about half the time, the demonologist is forced to use religious provocation—kind of like using tear gas—to bring the entity forward."

When asked for a specific example, Ed rattles off at least a dozen cases where he's had to use provocation to test for possession, and then expands on one particular case that certainly illustrates the process.

"In this case, I was dealing with a very refined, very beautiful Hispanic woman, about twenty-five years of age, who drew a demonic spirit into her home by fooling around with an automatic writing device," Ed relates. "As is often the case, the possession was noticed not by the victim but by members of the immediate family. These folks became aware of the problem when they heard crude, coarse men's voices talking out loud in this young woman's bedroom. When family members, concerned for her safety, actually went into the bedroom, they were astonished to find that the voices were *coming out of the woman,* although she was sound asleep at the time. When they tried to rouse her, she would raise up out of bed and come at them snarling, with her teeth bared, and her fingers curled up like claws.

"Before I became involved in the case, the family had already gone the whole route with doctors and psychiatrists who gave these people no help whatsoever. Having reached an impasse, they consulted their own Baptist minister, who was then instrumental in putting the family in touch with me.

"Upon interrogating the family about the young woman's unnatural behavior, I made an afternoon appointment to interview her during the daylight hours when she was home. Now when you're dealing with the demonic, you're dealing with something that's dangerous. For this reason, when I went to the family's home, I arrived with three big football players who attended a nearby college. Also present in the house that afternoon was the woman's father and the Baptist minister, both of them as big and burly as the football players.

"Before I went into the house, I told these young fellows I was going to have the young lady sit in the middle of the living room couch, and then I picked the two biggest guys and told them they were to sit on either side of her. I gave one of them a small silver crucifix to put in his pocket. I explained that when I nodded, the young fellow was to reach into his pocket, cup the crucifix in the palm of his hand, discreetly place his arm up on the back of the couch, and then move the crucifix up behind the nape of her neck.

"The usual test for possession is accomplished by the recitation of prayers, readings from the Bible, or by exposing the possessed to a crucifix or some other *blessed* holy object. The object or method of provocation naturally depends upon the demonologist's religious persuasion. I'm Catholic, so I use Christian methods. But it's not my style to stand around reading prayers and whatnot, so when I have to provoke—as you may have noticed—I use a blessed crucifix because I find it to be the quickest and most certain test.

"When we went inside, the father and Baptist minister were waiting with the young woman. I asked her to take a seat in the middle of the couch. The two football players then sat next to her, as I'd instructed them to do. I asked the third young fellow to stand nonchalantly beside me, yet be ready to grab the girl if necessary. With that, I began asking the young woman a run of ordinary questions: 'How do you feel?' 'What do you do for a living?' and so forth. After about five minutes, I nodded to the fellow with the cross, who casually put his arm up on the sofa behind the woman's neck.

"The moment he brought that crucifix up to the nape of her neck, a big studio chair on the far side of the room tumbled over on its own. A few seconds later, a table turned over and crashed to the floor. Knockings and rappings started up in the walls, followed by concussive poundings on the roof that sounded like a giant was walking on top of the house. Next, a big table lamp lifted up in the air, flew across the living room, and smashed against a wall.

"Seeing and hearing all this, the father was utterly terrified," Ed says compassionately, "and I thought the poor Baptist minister was going to go out of his skull right then and there. As this was happening, the beautiful young woman's features transformed into that of a gross, subhuman beast. Growling animal sounds began emanating from her body, and at the same time she clawed up her fingers and tried to come at me and tear my face apart. All five of those men, the three football players, the father, and the minister— weighing well over a thousand pounds—were just barely able to restrain her. In that case I subdued the spirit by holding a second crucifix right between the woman's eyes, and then commanded the possessing entity to leave, which it did after about five minutes."

Having related this provocation incident, Ed then plays the original tape recording of the episode in the young woman's house.

It proved to be an awesome, ugly demonstration of inhuman hate, rage, and violence.

"Briefly, therefore, as a demonologist, I interviewed the family, witnessed external phenomena occur in the room with the possessed, and confronted the entity in the presence of witnesses. Having gained this information, I recommended that exorcism be carried out in her case, which was then performed some two weeks later. As a consequence, that woman is free today and lives a respectable life in the New York City area."

Although reports and recommendations submitted by medical examiners and the officiating demonologist may often be enough to convince church authorities of the need for exorcism, usually additional evidence must be brought forward to ratify that need overwhelmingly—especially where the *Rituale Romanum* is concerned. For example, tape recordings, photographs, test instrument readings, materialized substances or objects have to be submitted as hard physical evidence that distinctly "preternatural" phenomena have occurred. Also, credible witnesses will be required to testify to changes in the possessed's character and demeanor, and when applicable, confirm that unnatural activity has gone on in their presence. The criteria for judging possession, particularly for Catholic exorcisms, are strict. Because in addition to all the above, no judgment of exorcism will be given unless there is at least one *yes* answer to these four critical questions:

- Has the individual divulged hidden or future knowledge?
- Has the possessed individual spoken in "tongues" or languages previously unknown to him?
- Has the individual demonstrated inhuman powers, or brought about activity distinctly beyond the bounds of human ability?
- Has the possessing entity identified itself by name or given some indisputable sign of a diabolical presence?

Once these questions have been answered and all the other information is gathered together, it is then submitted to church authorities. If, after studious contemplation of all the data, a judgment is returned that major exorcism is called for, then an exorcist will be assigned to the case.

"Every major religion has its own ritual of exorcism," Ed comments, "not as a vestige from the past, but as an everyday necessity. It's a popular misconception that exorcism is an obsolete medieval ritual that is no longer performed. Exorcism is still needed *and* performed in this century as it has been in every century before it. Though the exact number is probably the best kept secret in the world, I can tell you that well over six hundred major exorcisms have had to be performed between 1970 and 1980 in North America alone."

Ultimately, people are not supposed to be possessed by any other spirit than their own—least of all by inhuman demonic spirits. Therefore, positive supernatural power is required to undo the spiritual catastrophe of possession. The devil "respects no man," therefore this disruption of the natural order can be rectified only by a properly ordained clergyman who functions as a direct representative of God. This singularly difficult task requires an especially pious individual who alone would be able to confront the decidedly vile entities that engage in the possession of human beings. "In most non-Christian religions, the ritual tends to be conducted by specialist clergy," says Ed. "In other words, the exorcist has a specialized function the other clergy of his religion do not have. This is especially true with Oriental religions. In the Jewish faith, exorcism is conducted by an exorcist reading from the Holy Torah while customarily being assisted by a minyan of ten pious men from the temple. In the Christian denominations there are specialist clergy too; although every ordained Christian clergyman is a *potential* exorcist, because Christ was an exorcist.

In fact, Jesus Christ was the greatest exorcist who ever lived. He not only exorcised the possessed, he brought the dead back to life!" Moreover, Scriptures indicate Jesus passed on this power to exorcise the demonic from the body of man to the Disciples, using these words recorded in Chapter 10 of the gospel of Saint Luke:

> *He who hears you, hears me; and he who rejects you, rejects me; and he who rejects me, rejects Him who sent me. . . . Behold, I have given you power to tread upon serpents and scorpions and over all the might of the enemy; and nothing shall hurt you. But do not rejoice in this, that the spirits are subject to you; rejoice rather in this, that your names are written in heaven.*

Though one might expect the higher clergy to be the ones called upon to actually conduct a major exorcism, this is rarely the case. "I've worked with exorcists from almost every major religion," says Ed Warren. "I've found them to be older men, usually between forty and eighty. They tend to be very saintly, humble men who care deeply about people and their welfare. Usually they have no other title than monk, priest, rabbi, minister, or yogi, but they all seem to embody a combination of wisdom, kindness, and compassion that you don't see in ordinary people."

But piety, wisdom, devotion, and humility are not enough. As a person, the exorcist must embody the virtues of goodness and morality that represent the very best aspects of man. And no less important, the exorcist must be strong enough to withstand the mental and physical torments that frequently occur in the struggle to win back a human soul from the clutches of the demonic. "At some time in his life, without exception, the demonic attacks the exorcist for being the good man that he is. The exorcist's task is the most thankless job on earth. Although he may be a man of enormous personal stature," Ed asserts, "he is often chastised and ridiculed by those too ignorant to recognize his worth."

When a major exorcism is to be conducted, the date, time, and location of the ritual is usually fixed beforehand, whenever, possible. "Preference is given to holy days or the feast days of saints," Ed notes. "The ritual is normally scheduled for the morning hours to avoid the assaults the devil—the Prince of Darkness—is capable of launching during the psychic hours of night. The exorcism may take place in the home of the possessed individual, but more likely it will be conducted in some religious dwelling. Potentially violent exorcisms involving extremely vicious or powerful entities are usually carried out in a religiously-affiliated hospital where doctors and life-support equipment are on hand."

Meanwhile, in the days preceding a major exorcism, the exorcist will subject himself to rigorous preparation. He will abstain from food and take blessed water only as necessary. This is called the Black Fast. Spiritually, the exorcist will cloister himself in prayer for a minimum of three days in order to be emboldened with the three Theological Virtues of faith, hope, and charity: faith in what he is doing; hope that he will be successful; and charity in giving freely of himself in the interest of another. Finally, having put himself in a state of grace, the exorcist will implore Divine assistance, insofar as man has no inherent power over these negative angels of perdition.

On the day of the exorcism, assistants who have also prepared themselves for the ritual by prayer and fasting will assemble. If the potential for violence exists during the exorcism, the possessed will be laid out on a bed in loose-fitting clothing. "Anything that can move, burn, or be thrown will be removed from the room," Ed reveals. "If you give the demonic a club, it'll beat you with it. This is why the only thing that will remain in the room is a table where candles, holy oils, and the Sacrament are placed. All other furniture and objects will have to be taken away for the safety of the exorcist and his assistants."

With that, the incredible ordeal begins.

"Exorcism," noted Father John Nicola in his book *Diabolical Possession and Exorcism,* "is not a battle, but a war." This war is won only when the demonic abandons the possession of the individual because it can no longer endure exposure to all that is opposite to itself, the Holy. Therefore, the exorcist reads:

> I cast thee out, thou unclean spirit, along with the least encroachment of the wicked enemy, and every phantom and diabolical legion. In the name of our Lord Jesus Christ, depart and vanish from this creature of God. For it is He Who commands thee. He Who ordered thee cast down from the heights of heaven into the nethermost pit of the earth. . . .Quake and fly afar, as we call upon the name of the Lord, before Whom hell trembles, to Whom the heavenly Virtues and Powers and Dominions are subject, Whom the Cherubim and Seraphim praise with unending voice as they sing: Holy, Holy, Holy, Lord God of Hosts!

Although the *Rituale Romanum* exorcism amounts to no more than an approximately twenty-five-page ceremonial document (of which half the pages are psalms), many times the possessing spirit(s) will depart only after a long, excruciating ordeal—as was the case in the West German exorcism. Without interference, the Roman Ritual exorcism takes about two hours to recite. However, what occurs *during* the reading of the text becomes the ordeal. The phrasing of the document is so strong and challenging to the demonic that the possessing entities' resistance to the statements can hold up the ritual for hours, days, weeks, even months on end.

What transpires during the course of major exorcisms is not

publicly available information: an exorcism is not a performance. As a demonologist, however, Ed Warren works closely with exorcists, and has assisted at some forty-three different exorcisms in both America and England. He has witnessed the bizarre phenomena and he has also been subject to the terrible attacks and persecutions that are frequently part of the ordeal.

"First understand," says Ed, "that my task is always to *assist* the exorcist. I don't march around like some kind of Holy Joe and play priest; I'm there to help. I know the danger signs, so when problems arise, I can lend knowledgeable assistance. The exorcist, on the other hand, is the one who takes on the really dangerous burden of expelling the demonic, and it's against the exorcist that the demonic ultimately focuses its vengeance.

"As for what goes on during an exorcism, let me first say that in approximately six out of ten cases, the spirit obeys the commands of the exorcist and leaves on the first reading of the ritual. It's apparent that the spirits have left the body of the possessed because of the peace and tranquility in the room. Usually in those cases, the possessed himself will say 'It's over,' or 'The possession is finished.' Of course, the exorcist has got to be leery of this. The most effective exorcists have what's called the 'gift of discernment': they know with certainty whether the spirit is still possessing the individual or not.

"But four out of ten times, there is trouble. Phenomena occur in the room, and the possessing entities put up resistance. In such cases, no sooner does the exorcist begin reading the ritual than the spirits reply with a counterassault, designed to stop the exorcism from going on. Usually it's a matter of wild screaming, or hooting, or shouting by the entities in the person. The whinnying of horses, the barking of dogs, the snorting of pigs are typical stuff put out by the demonic to interrupt the ritual. Interruptions, in fact, are the name of the game during a major exorcism. The unworldly howling and baying and caterwauling is liable to go on for hours on end. To the exorcist, though, these bestial sounds are no more than a disturbing nuisance.

"As the exorcism progresses," continues Ed, "the possessing entities usually pour forth vulgar, blasphemous language—crude, filthy, gutter talk. Speaking in a gross, inhuman voice, these things will also challenge the Scriptures being read, and sometimes even 'correct' the exorcist should he happen to omit a phrase or mispronounce some word—Latin or English—in the ritual. These insults and slanderings will later change into a demoralizing personal assault directed against all those present. These spirits, you see, not only know the Scriptures, they also know the life of everyone in the room. They'll try to drive the exorcist and his assistants away by bringing up hurtful incidents in these people's lives, recounting their personal tragedies with perverse delight. They'll reveal personal things that a person may feel terribly guilty about, or dredge up events that provoke great pain and sorrow. When that doesn't work, they'll humiliate each and every person present by reciting all their mortal sins in front of everyone, dwelling on those sins that are likely to be the most embarrassing to a particular person. For Catholics, this latter problem is avoided through confession: strangely enough, the demonic has no knowledge of sins that have been confessed!

"When the personal attacks on the exorcist and his assistants prove to be insufficient to stop the exorcism, then incredible, frightening phenomena are liable to occur in cases where very powerful entities are involved. In these cases, I have seen what *ought not* to be; I have seen what *could not* be. In one exorcism, for instance, the demonic materialized something like six or seven bucketloads of a substance that looked like a combination of spaghetti and hair. And the smell of excrement intermingled with it was so intense it made the stomach retch. But really, the worst phenomena is inflicted on the possessed.

"In at least six cases, I have seen the possessed levitate off the bed. I have seen the victim's hair yanked out of the scalp by invisible hands. I have seen the possessed individual throw up *gallons* of putrid, disgusting substances, usually smelling of excrement. I have seen psychic burns and slashes show up all over the body of the possessed, causing frantic, painful screaming when the individual is not unconscious during the ritual.

"In the case of a thirteen-year-old girl who was possessed by an Incubus, we saw teeth marks appear on the girl's arm. From the best we could determine, they were animal bites with wet saliva surrounding them. The marks broke the flesh and caused bleeding. I have also seen the demonic bloat up the body of the possessed individual to twice its normal size. The head, the torso, the arms, the fingers, the legs, the whole body was so bloated and disfigured that the skin began to split open and ooze blood; we actually thought the individual was going to explode! Yet all these physical burns, marks, and changes to the body disappear immediately when the possessing entities have been exorcised, which is what I meant by 'peace and tranquility' in the room at the end of a successful exorcism.

"These are things I have personally experienced. But let me remind you," Ed goes on, "that this kind of gross phenomena is definitely reported in other exorcisms, ones in which I have had no part. In 1977, for example, about a year before Pope Paul VI died, an unaccountable spate of possessions apparently occurred to a number of Vatican nuns and priests. In those cases, the possessed not only took on grotesque forms, they regurgitated nails, broken glass, bile, and live animals." Ed flips open a book entitled *Begone Satan*. "And here's what happened to the woman in Earling, Iowa, during a twenty-three-day exorcism in 1928."

Countless brats of devils also interrupted the process of exorcism by their disagreeable and almost unbearable interferences. As a result of these disturbances, the woman's face became so distorted that no one could recognize her features. Then, too, her whole body became so horribly disfigured that the regular contour of her body vanished. Her pale, deathlike and emaciated head, often assuming the size of an inverted water pitcher, became as red as glowing embers. Her eyes protruded out of their sockets, her lips swelled up to proportions equalling the size of hands, and her thin emaciated body was bloated to such enormous size that the pastor and some of the Sisters drew back out of fright, thinking the woman would be torn to pieces and burst asunder. At times her abdominal region and extremities became as hard as iron and stone. In such instances the weight of her body pressed into the iron bedstead so that the iron rods of the bed bent to the floor.

"This is what our friend the devil does to people," Ed says in obvious contempt. "Still, no matter how intense and irrational the phenomena might become, it is unthinkable that the exorcist would ever break during the process. Working in the interest of good, the exorcist and those around him must contend with repulsive physical phenomena that would make even the most hardened individual recoil in shock and disgust. But yet the exorcist endures, and keeps on repeating the ritual over and over again, sometimes to the point of near-death, until finally the possessing entities identify themselves and leave in the name of God.

"When the exorcist steps in," Ed concludes, "he confronts the *real thing*. After the whole sorry process is over, the individual is freed from an alien spirit that, by its own admission, seeks to dominate man and bring about his total ruin and destruction. For the exorcist, though, the ordeal really isn't over at all. No exorcist ever comes away from a confrontation with the Awful One unscathed.

He forever remains alone, apart from other men, feeling the sting and biting hate the devil reserves for God. *That* is the true nature of major exorcism!"

What is the worst case Ed and Lorraine ever investigated?

"That is something I never, ever talk about," admits Ed, suddenly turning quite serious. "The case was almost the end of us, that's for sure. We found ourselves taken to a place out of this world that you'd never believe existed, even if I were to describe it. Every minute, every second of those long hours was so unbelievable, so incomprehensibly horrible, that I believe I now know the true meaning of hell, and the value of life on earth."

14

The Enfield Voices

"Anyone alive in that car down there?" the Pennsylvania state trooper wanted to know.

The black Ford LTD had careened off the highway, rolled down a steep embankment, and came to rest some thirty feet below the road surface in a pile of ice and snow.

"Everybody's okay," said the driver,

After the trooper called a tow truck, he flipped open his leather notebook and asked, "What happened?"

A tractor-trailer driver told him: "I was trailing the car about a half mile behind. For no apparent reason, it went out of control. The back end swung from left to right, right to left, until the driver got it back under control. A couple of seconds later, the car went into a full spin. But the spin wasn't normal: it looked to me like the wheels of the car weren't even on the road—that the car was actually spinning in the air! And then, while it was in the air, it seemed to be pushed from the side, before it went off the road, over the ridge, and down the embankment."

"Who's the driver?" the trooper asked next.

"I am," said Ed Warren. "The car went out of control twice. The second time I wasn't able to steer it. . . . "

What *really* happened, though, was a different matter—something few policemen would have understood even after a lengthy explanation.

"Everything was fine," Ed recalls. "It was a clear day. Lorraine and I had been talking about the status of a number of cases we were involved in at the time. Two or three minutes before the accident we got to talking about the Amityville case which as it goes, was no different or more violent than the other cases we'd been going over. Suddenly the car went out of control.

"Now, I drive fifty thousand miles a year, so I can handle my own car. But this was unnatural; it felt like an immense hand belted the car from behind. The first time the rear of the car lifted off the ground. The second time *the whole car went up!* We traded ends once or twice, and the next thing I knew we were flying down an embankment at fifty miles an hour, *backwards*. The only thing that kept us from crashing at the bottom was the snow the car plowed up while it was going down.

"Incredibly, there was no damage, except for some bent car trim. A wrecker towed the car up the hill and we were on our way within an hour. The strange thing is," Ed puts in, "the night after we were in Amityville and the swirling black entity confronted me, it projected a vision of that automobile accident. Ironically, the incident happened in the Poconos, in a place they call the Lord's Valley!"

Next to exorcism, demonology is perhaps the most dangerous business on earth. Therefore, no case is ever routine to the Warrens. Indeed, with each succeeding year, and each additional case, the Warrens live in even greater peril. For after devoting their whole lives to the study of the supernatural, Ed and Lorraine Warren risk their lives each and every time they become involved in a case where more than earthbound human spirits are active. And though they may face down vile, blasphemous forces or help resolve a disturbance so the tenants can live in peace, one way or another the spirits they encounter continue to plague them for years to come. It is an unpleasant, though real, hazard of their work.

An exorcist goes through elaborate preparations before confronting the demonic. Is there anything special the Warrens do to guarantee their own safety?

"Before we go forward with a serious case," answers Lorraine, "we take a number of precautions. First, we thoroughly assess the people we're dealing with. We won't put our lives in jeopardy for someone who's going to turn around again and bring in the same spirits a week later. So we start by looking for sincerity and need on the part of the person or family who's called on us. After that, we examine our own motivations and conscience. Are we the right people to take on this case? Could someone else—perhaps the clergy—do a better job right from the beginning? However, we've never once backed out of a case because it was too difficult or dangerous.

"Now, if we decide to go ahead with an investigation, then we take additional precautions," she goes on. "We're Catholic, and I'll usually spend an afternoon or longer in church, praying for our safety and effectiveness. I use a rosary. Those of us in this work are aware of the very real power of the rosary. If it's a bad case, we'll have a number of priests praying for us, and many times we'll also have a Mass said. Some might think this strange, but from experience we know there is no other way: it takes more than good intentions to be effective in this work. Let's not mince words. We're not dealing with an idea, or a concept, or an illusion. *We're dealing with the real, physical manifestation of the devil* in one of his many powerful forms.

"As for what protects us," Lorraine concludes, "that's something else entirely. When we finally do go into a home where these negative spirits are at work, we wear special, blessed holy medals, and we carry a relic of a saint. Against demonic forces, these spiritually positive items carry a lot of metaphysical weight. But we never really go in a home alone: many others go in with us in spirit. Beyond that, we find we do have the help of *positive* spirits in particularly difficult cases. As a clairvoyant I am also able to communicate with spirit guides who give us both protection and guidance. Ultimately, Ed owes his safety to Saint Michael, whose presence is sometimes shown to us in positive symbolic signs.

"In short, you don't get to do this work and stay alive all at the same time without help from above; and I mean sometimes *physical* help from above. There are occasions where total mayhem is occurring inside a house when Ed is about to go in. Then an impenetrable force will either surround the house, or two strong 'hands' will push Ed back, to prevent him from going in. We know the presence is of a positive—perhaps even angelic—nature because the smell of perfume or fresh flowers is projected at the very same time. So, you see, we don't just stroll into some hell-house and challenge the devil or his legion. Instead, if we're successful in our work, it's based on our knowledge of the supernatural, along with the prayers, concern, and guidance of all those who support us. If we didn't take these precautions, or approached our work only out of curiosity, then there's no two ways about it: we'd be dead by now!"

With that, Ed picks up the discussion. He's just returned from England the day before. His trip to the United Kingdom was to visit a family in whose home inhuman spirit phenomena have been occurring with increasing regularity over the past three years. It was Ed's third visit to Enfield in the last year alone. This time, the purpose of his visit was to gather evidence of the phenomena occurring in the house which could be used as proof for the need to exorcise the premises.

"This Enfield case makes Amityville look like a playhouse," says Ed. "I mean that truly. The Lutzes were able to move out after twenty-eight *days* of terror; this is a case where the people can't move out for economic reasons, and have had to put up with the disturbance for three *years*. Those who are being victimized, as the London press has exhaustively reported, are a divorced fifty-year-old woman and her three children who live together in a government-supported council house in the north London suburb of Enfield. In the family there are two girls, aged fifteen and twelve at this time, and a boy of eight. Though phenomena first erupted in August 1977, the case began in 1976, when the two girls drew inhuman entities into the house after playing with—you guessed it!—a Ouija board. The girls had no sinister purposes in using it: they simply had nothing else to do, and were playing with the board as a game. Unfortunately for them, London is a spiritually active place. As a result, the girls made contact with a demonic spirit that did its thing, and wrangled permission out of the girls to enter the house. A few weeks later, this spirit infested their home, but it didn't come alone: it brought six buddies along! Those six spirits are present in the home right now as I am speaking.

"When the spirits were first drawn in, the usual run of infestation phenomena erupted: knockings, rappings, scratchings, poundings, and so forth. As time went on, the phenomena upgraded. Objects materialized, people levitated—especially the girls—and a number of black forms manifested and floated around the house at night. After the mother reported the problem to the local police constabulary, the police investigated the complaint, but to no avail. In no time at all, however, the press got wind of the case and reporters and psychic researchers descended on this brick rowhouse, and between 1977 and 1978 they not only put the family in the public eye, they thoroughly documented the reality of the phenomena occurring there. Then they went away, without anyone once telling these people how they could get rid of the disturbance. In fact, it seems no one even *knew* what was happening. The case had been dubbed a so-called 'poltergeist attack,' and was left at that.

When I was in England in the summer of 1978, the case was brought to my attention, and I visited the family.

"At that time," Ed goes on, "I spent a week in Enfield. I thoroughly interviewed all the members of the family, separately and together, while witnessing the phenomena go on around me in the house. As a demonologist, I was able to see that these individuals were being systematically oppressed, and sometimes even possessed, by inhuman spirits. For example, the girls would levitate off the floor, *crisscross* in the air, and then be set back down again in a display of inhuman power. Every week, in fact, it seemed one or the other of these two girls would be subject to levitation, often in the company of witnesses. The mother told me she has walked into the girls' bedroom and found her younger daughter sound asleep, levitating in midair. On other occasions, she has witnessed her daughters rise up and down on the bed, 'like a yo-yo' as she says, with none of them able to control the activity. The children also spoke about a black mass that manifests itself in their bedrooms at night and terrorizes them with its presence.

"Even as I talked with the family, things would rise up in the air and float around the room. One evening a wooden chair lifted up in the air, stayed still for a moment, then exploded. On another occasion, a big, hefty rock the size of a softball manifested out of thin air in the middle of the living room and slammed to the floor with a thud! I later took that rock to a geologist at the University of London, without telling him where I got it. I simply asked the professor to tell me where the rock could have come from. 'The stone is indigenous to only one place in the British Isles,' he told me. 'That place is the Isle of Wight.' The Isle of Wight is of course located in the English Channel, some seventy-five miles southwest of London, as the crow flies.

"More serious than the outward phenomena," Ed continues, "is what's happening to the children in this home. The girls, in particular, are coming under episodes of possession where they take on the features of an 'old dead woman,' according to the mother, 'and have the strength of an Amazon.' The most dangerous feature of the possession episodes is that one of the daughters is often caused to attack her mother and attempts to kill her with her bare hands—and a number of times she's almost succeeded. A few weeks before I arrived, one of the girls came under possession. After the possessing entity stalked around the house, it put the girl in a state of agitated frenzy. The mother was forced to bring the daughter to a local hospital, where doctors worked for six or seven hours trying to bring her out of it. The incident suddenly stopped after the spirit withdrew from her body, at which time she got up and simply walked out of the casualty ward.

"By far, though, the most compelling aspect to this case is the physicalized voice manifestations that occur in the house. The voices of six different spirits talk out loud *in the room*. It's as though there were six invisible people present. It's incredible: you can't believe it even when you're there!

"Even while the family is eating in the kitchen, the voices are speaking in another room! The British Society for Psychical Research—who worked on the case before I came in—went over the house with a fine-tooth comb, and determined that in no way were the voices being projected by loudspeakers or by any other electronic means.

"The voices themselves speak with a distinct cockney accent. The demonic spirit is a mimic, so here it speaks in cockney because the family can understand it although one of the spirits does lapse off into German when it prefers. And these voices are not a matter of some occasional phrase or sentence they talk *all the time*. These spirits not only talk out loud to the people in the room, when no one is addressing them, they talk to each other! They talk more than the people do.

"The British Society for Psychical Research have their own recordings of these spirit voices, but because their organization is private, the evidence has so far not been made available to the general public. I went there for the express purpose of getting these voices on tape which could be used to document the need for exorcism."

Did Ed get a recording of the voices?

"You better believe it," he replies, tapping a pair of cassettes before him on the table. "Although it'll take some time before the content of these tapes can be analyzed, the evidence is right here. And in my estimation, it represents some of the most important evidence yet on the existence of the inhuman spirit I'll play them now. . . ."

The tapes run for well over three hours; what comes across on them is something truly incredible. The recordings were made while Ed and his two assistants, Paul Bartz and John Kenyhercz, interviewed the mother and her three children in the Enfield home. While the three men were questioning the family, other voices—those of spirits—can be heard speaking out loud in the room at the same time: "Let's put the lights out"; "Go pull the wallpaper down"; "Throw the table"; "Stop him from going into that room" were among the many comments the voices made when not being addressed by human beings in the house. Once every so often, a bizarre parrot-like voice interjected itself saying only, "Hello." Sometimes the other spirits joined the parrot voice in a round of hello's. Not all the sounds produced by the spirits were in the form of language, though. Fully ten percent of the recording is taken up with grunts, moans, "yeccchs," and the imitation of animal sounds, of which the most often repeated is that of a barking dog.

As for communicating with these spirits, there was no evident problem. Sometimes the spirits addressed the people in the room; sometimes the people in the room addressed the spirits. The quality of the voices is extremely raspy, and guttural. The elocution is definitely cockney—in fact, *so* cockney it's quite hard for the American ear to sort out. The quality of the spirits' statements would place them low on a scale of human intelligence, though they're far from ignorant. Most every question put to the spirits was answered.

Although the inhuman voices usually supplied straight, rational replies, much of what they said was also nonsensical and capricious. There is a predominating voice in the crowd, and on this occasion, the spirit took on the identity of "Fred." It was to Fred that Ed Warren addressed most of his questions. What follows is an extract of that interrogation.

Ed: Hello?

Voice: Hello.

Ed: Do you know who I am?

V: Yeah.

Ed: Who am I?

V: Ed.

Ed: That's right, Ed. Who are you?

V: Fred-die.

Ed: You're Freddie, huh? What's your real name?

V: Yecccccch . . . *(noise)*

Ed: When are you going to leave here, Fred?

V: Five hundred years.

Ed: That's a long time. Can you move something to show us you're here?

V: No.

Ed: Why not?

V: Tommy pulled my arm out.

Ed: Oh, there's two of you? Put Tommy on.

V: *(A new voice, though still gruff and gutteral)* Yah. I'm Tommy.

Ed: Tommy, how do you think we could get rid of all the problems that are happening in this house?

V: Kill the ghosties!

Ed: Kill the ghosties? Aren't you a ghostie?

V: No!

Ed: Tell me, how did you get into this house?

V: Came up from under the floorboards.

Ed: How many of you are there all together?

V: *(Counting slowly and deliberately)* Ah . . . uh . . . one . . . two . . . three . . . four . . . five . . . six. Six are here— no, five.

Ed: What are their names?

V: Fred-die, Tom-mie, Billy, uh . . . Charlie, and Dick. John's not here.

Ed: Where's John?

V: Don't know.

Ed: Who's the leader? Are you the leader?

V: Nobody. Nobody's the leader. I'm a liar.

Ed: Who else is here? Is there anyone else here?

V: Yeah.

Ed: Who?

V: Gutter-Man's here.

Ed: Put Gutter-Man on. Let him speak. Are you there, Gutter-Man?

V: Yeah *(a different gutteral voice, this one a bit clearer).*

Ed: Gutter-Man, what do you have to say?

V: *(Yelping noises)* This house is haunted. Kill the ghosties!

Ed: Gutter-Man, were you ever alive?

V: Yeah.

Ed: Where?

V: In soldiers. I'm a soldier.

Ed: In whose army are you a soldier?

V: All armies. I'm a soldier.

Ed: Who else is here, Gutter-Man?

V: Ah . . . uh . . . Zachary's here.

Ed: Put him on, Gutter-Man. Let Zachary speak.

V: *(Suddenly there is incredible moaning and groaning. The voice is utterly bizarre. The wailing ends up in a long cry of "Help" that takes ten seconds to come out.)*

Ed: Holy cow. What was that? Put Zachary back on.

V: *(Woeful moaning recurs.)*

Ed: Who else is here, Fred?

V: I ain't Fred, I'm Tommy!

Ed: Put Fred on. . . . Fred, are you there?

V: Yeah, Fred's here. *(Voice change indicates "Fred" is speaking)*

Ed: Fred, put Zachary back on.

V: Won't come. *(Pause)* I'll tell you someone else who's here. Teddy's here. Teddy-Man's here.

Ed: Put Teddy-Man on, Fred.

V: Yecccch... *(Noise. Then silence, broken every few seconds by a parrot-like voice saying, "Hello." A second voice then picks up and says "hello," to which the parrot-voice responds with two hello's. A third voice joins in the hello's, then a fourth voice chimes in with its "hello"; then a fifth and a sixth voice join informing a chorus of parrot-like voices all saying "hello," which build finally into loud, wild shrieks. The additional voices then fall away, leaving the original parrot-voice repeating its singular hello."*

(Ed addresses the spirits again after the outburst, but there is no feedback.)

"All the while I was talking to these spirits," Ed notes during the lull in the tape, "things were flying around the room. That's what those crashing and bumping sounds are in the background. Chairs and tables were lifting and dropping. Small, little objects would whiz across the room and bounce off the wall. In the dining room, the wallpaper was peeling away from the walls as we watched. A butcher knife materialized in the lap of my assistant, Paul. A nail was also produced out of thin air. And, as has come to be expected in the house, the spirits left a pile of excrement on the mother's bedroom carpet upstairs at three in the afternoon."

When the spirits on the recording weren't going through a it of random insanity, they seemed to amuse themselves by filling the room with grunts, quacks, barks, shrieks, and a variety of other animal sounds—the most annoying being that of a shrill, screeching cat. One particular spirit put out a tortuous, unworldly howl which brought on another interchange.

Ed: You guys sound like something right out of hell. Do you know where hell is, Fred?

V: Yeah.

Ed: Where is hell, Fred?

V: Yeccch... *(noise)*

Ed: How old are you, Fred?

V: Sixteen.

Ed: Are you a ghost, Fred?

V: No . . . uh . . . yes. I'm a ghost

Ed: Who?

V: Batman. I'm Batman.

Ed: Batman isn't a ghost.

V: *(Spirits lapse into an array of animal sounds, the most predominant being that of a barking dog.)*

Ed: You want to be animals? Imitate some animals. Imitate a pig.

V: *(The snorting of a pig.)*

Ed: How about a dog?

V: *(Barking.)*

Ed: How about a cat?

V: *(Loud, screeching meow.)*

Ed: How about a turkey?

V: *(Gobbling.)*

Ed: How old are you, Fred?

V: Seventy-eight. I'm a liar. Tommy's a liar.

Ed: I know.

V: Can I sing a song?

Ed: Sure, Fred, go ahead and sing.

V: La-de-da-de-da . . . *(gruffly)* Jack and Jill went up the hill to fetch a pail of *holy* water . . . ha . . . ha . . . ha . . .

Ed: Are you a Christian, Fred?

V: Yick. A soldier. I'm a soldier!

Ed: When did you die, Fred, as a soldier?

V: I'm *always* dead.

Ed: Were you ever married, Fred? Did you ever have a wife?

V: Yeah.

Ed: What was her name?

V: I don't know.

Ed: How old are you now?

V: Thirty. I'm thirty.

Ed: Do you know what day it is?

V: Yeah. The uh . . . seventh.

Ed: Right. Do you know what month it is?

V: Au-goos. Awwguss. August. August seventh!

Ed: Where did you get those names: Fred and Tommy and Billy and so on?

V: The graves.

Ed: Do you go over to the old graveyard near here?

V: Yeah.

Ed: Why?

V: To read the graves.

Ed: Do you like the graveyard, Fred? Why do you like the graveyard?

V: Death! *(grunts)*.

Ed: What do you think of us Americans?

V: I hate you, I hate you, I hate you. . . .

Ed: Do you know where America is, Fred?

V: I don't know. Can I come?

Ed: No, Fred. I've got enough to do without you.

V: Ed. Ed . . . Ed . . .

Ed: What do you want, Fred?

V: Smash the recorder.

Ed: You'd like that, wouldn't you?

V: Yeah. *(Spirits pull original tape out of recorder during session.)*

Ed: *(Resuming)* Do you know what I'm going to do with these tapes, Fred? I'm going to play them to some scientists I know in America. They're going to be very interested in you, Fred!

V: I'm gonna smash it in the night! *(A quarrel then develops between two spirits as to who is going to "smash" the tape recorder. As the voices rise from the level of argument into one-against-one "yikes" and "howls," Ed sends Paul out to the car to get a bottle of holy water drawn from Walsingham Shrine, north of London. Paul returns to report the bottle of holy water is missing.)*

Ed: Where's the holy water, Fred?

V: I slung it!

Ed: You slung it? If you don't bring that holy water back, we're going to perform exorcism *on you!*

V: Ha, ha, ha.

Ed: Do you want me to bring a priest in here?

V: Yeah, all right. Bring 'im in. I'll kick 'im in the backside.

Ed: What would you say if the Blessed Mother told you to leave, Fred?

V: Yecccch. Ugh.

Ed: Do you know what this is Fred? What do you see?

V: Uh . . . a cross.

Ed: That's right, a cross. That cross means your days are numbered here.

V: I'm gonna chop somebody's head off.

Ed: The next time I come back here, Fred, you'd better be gone. Because the next time I come I'm bringing a very powerful exorcist with me, someone you won't want to mess with.

V: *(There is a long lull)* Ed. Ed. Ed . . . Ed . . . Ed-ward

Ed: What is it, Fred?

V: Let's play exorcist. Go get the holy water. . . .

Having played the recording, Lorraine suddenly jumps up from the couch and strides purposefully to the bedroom door. She then calls to Ed. Upon checking, the room reeks of alcohol; and on Lorraine's dresser, an ornamental crucifix set in a grotto is turned upside down!

Prudently, discussion about the Enfield case ceased. Yet in a way, it seemed to be only the tip of the iceberg in terms of demoniacal phenomena these days. Newspapers periodically report gruesome mass murders carried out by people who, afterwards, boldly assert they were instructed to kill "by the Devil" or by some malevolent "figure in black."

At least once or twice every decade, a major case of diabolical possession occurs, wherein the possessed harbors entities that identify themselves as being devils *and* demons, some even proclaiming their names for all to hear.

In 1978, over nine hundred people died in tropical Guyana in an unprecedented case of mass suicide that could possibly have been due, in some respect, to demoniacal oppression. Although Billy Graham went a step further, telling a National Press Club audience in Washington that he believed the Reverend Jim Jones was under "possession," and that "he used the church for his own demonic ends."

Why is so much negative supernatural activity happening right now?

"Inhuman spirits have roamed the earth since the beginning of time," Lorraine responds, "so there's nothing new about that. What is new is the situation we witness in the twentieth century. In line with that, I'd say there are two basic reasons why excessive negative activity is taking place these days. One reason has to do with numbers. There are more people in the world now than ever before in history. A great many of these people are dissatisfied with life, alienated from religion, or seeking after extraordinary knowledge. Concurrently, never in history has so much profane, negative information been available to everyone. In the past, this information was secret knowledge, used by some of the most wicked people who ever lived. Today, much of it is printed in books and sold like candy. This information is the real thing, and a gullible person who decides to use it for personal ends is quite capable of bringing about infestation, oppression, or possession by inhuman spirits. So essentially, we have a very large, literate population with twenty-four-hour-a-day access to really horrendous information. All that's needed is the desire, the wrong motivation, to use it. From there it's a very short step to bringing on the demonic.

"The other reason we're getting so much negative spirit activity," Lorraine continues, "has to do with people's *lack* of mystical knowledge. You see, spontaneous assaults initiated by the demonic are extremely rare. In the nineteenth and twentieth centuries, the clear majority of demoniacal activity has been instigated by people. It boils down to the fact that demoniacal phenomena is a 'people problem.' It's people who open doors to the underworld through their own free will.

"As we say many times, the demonic realm isn't something a person automatically finds out about. One learns by accident, or by voluntarily *doing* something to cause the phenomena to occur. Most of the time, the demonic is brought on deliberately, through someone's formal choice to do so. This is the heart of the matter because man can *choose* between good and evil. Therefore, every time an individual calls up one of these inhuman spirits, he goes through the whole Adam-and-Eve trip all over again. That is, long ago man was warned about the devil, but he was also given freedom to choose whether or not to accept its influence. How ever, nowadays, people *don't even know* they have a formal choice until it's too late—until *after* they've tapped into the demonic realm. The basic problem is that this century has seen a major breakdown in religion, which means a major breakdown in the teaching of mystical knowledge; so that, once again, people are having to learn by mistake. 'Those who don't learn from the past are doomed to repeat it,' as the saying goes. When Ed and I lecture, we remind people that there are mystical aspects to the world, both positive and negative, and demonic spirits should be left to stew where they belong. When it comes to this subject, knowledge is a weapon. Incidents of demoniacal phenomena would drop *drastically* if people knew what a bum trip the negative occult can be. And they'd drop even further still if the wherewithal for conjuring wasn't so readily available on store shelves."

While millions of people are playing with fire by dabbling in the occult, other quasi-religious cults operate in America, some of which invoke negative spirits to assist them as "guides" through life. Toward the even blacker extreme, other groups are actively engaged in ritual black witchcraft—not to mention the Satanists, who avowedly "prefer the ass of Satan to the face of Jesus." But just how prevalent is black witchcraft today?

"There are probably more people practicing black witchcraft now than in any other period in history," Lorraine explains. "Of course, these people don't walk around wearing black hats. Instead, the Satanists and black witches we've had to deal with in our work come off as very contemporary, with-it types—or else act strange and kooky to encourage the thought they're simply eccentrics. The black arts are practiced far more than people think or know. In fact, let me cite something I just saw in the paper this morning," says Lorraine, opening up the *Hartford Courant*:

> The city dog warden has found the corpses of 15 domestic animals believed to have been mutilated in a ritual-like process and then dumped or hung in trees. The warden has been investigating several recent incidents in which piles of dead goats, sheep, rabbits, and chickens have been found, some apparently within hours after they were slain. Two weeks ago, dogs and cats also were found hanging from branches. Some of the animals were bloodless. Police sources say a possible link between the apparent slayings and an occult religious group is being probed.

"Little do the police know," Lorraine resumes, "that this ghastly destruction of life—and the drawing of blood for later use in conjuring rituals—is a fairly routine practice by black witchcraft groups. But with macabre things like this going on regularly around the country, the public is slowly coming to learn that the practice of negative witchcraft is far more common than they previously supposed. But let me utter a warning here. The last time there was awareness of black witchcraft was during the Inquisition, a hideous period. At that time, between the sixteenth and eighteenth centuries, some 200,000 people were tortured and murdered in England, Europe, and America under the most fiendish conditions. Back then, the real crime was not done by those accused of witchcraft, but by the religious fanatics who cruelly and systematically slaughtered all those tens of thousands. So although black witchcraft is being practiced today, and it does represent a very serious, very dangerous problem, it should nevertheless be attacked through education or proper religious training—*not* through finger-pointing, torture, and murder. As the psychologist Carl Jung once said, 'If our civilization were to perish, it would be due more to stupidity than to evil.'"

No doubt the single greatest storehouse of information on the demonic is the Vatican in Rome. But those records, which go back some two thousand years, are completely inaccessible; indeed, the Catholic Church will not allow even its own priests to examine the data, except on a strict need-to-know basis. Evidently the negative aspect to the world is a story that is not meant to be told. But why? If the religious establishment knows all this "iniquitous" activity is going on, why don't they give more information about what Ed and Lorraine call the "black facts of life"?

Ed Warren's straightforward answer: "The basic reason why the religious establishment, Christian or otherwise, will not reveal information about the subject is that the demonic spirit is considered to be the physical manifestation of the Devil.

"More information *should* be made known," he goes on, "but if the church came forward and made an across-the-board admission that possession and exorcism are everyday realities, then suddenly everybody and their brother would be calling up churchmen, priests, ministers, rabbis, complaining of oppression or possession by 'evil spirits.' Every lonely person who hears a door slam shut by the wind in the middle of the night will want an exorcism. So going fully public with this information would turn into an absolute debacle. As it works now, legitimate cases do come to the attention of proper religious authorities, and things *do* get done about them—although they get done far too slowly.

"Not that something shouldn't be said about the subject, though," continues Ed. "Religious authorities *should* release more details about cases of possession and exorcism. They *should* let people know these negative spirits are real, not some throwaway superstition from the past. Otherwise, *how* are people going to find out that using the Ouija board and holding séances have the potential to draw spirits that can ruin one's life? You know, when Lorraine and I lecture at a college or municipal auditorium, word gets around town days before. When we do speak, every seat in the house is usually filled, leaving the overflow either standing or sitting in the aisles, while a couple of hundred have to be turned away at the door. Why? Because in the midst of this data-fact society, people are craving for *subjective* information about life, and where man fits in the universe. We're all in this together, you know! And if people are so vitally interested in the subject, then the religious establishment ought to pick up on it and calmly explain these metaphysical things to their congregation on Saturdays or Sundays when they meet. Again, if the needed information is withheld, how else are people going to make an accurate evaluation of life and death and the world around them? So the answer is yes, an argument can be made for the release of *some* information about spirit phenomena. But it's also got to be done in an intelligent, credible way."

In addition to their work as investigators, counselors, and lecturers, the Warrens also teach an undergraduate course once a year on Demonology and Paranormal Phenomena at Southern Connecticut State College.

"This is where we really get into the material," explains Ed, one sunny day after class. "Here there's time to examine the whole panorama of the problem in an academic setting. The first step is to acquaint the student with paranormal phenomena—events that are strange or unusual, but which have a natural explanation. Then we move on to spirit activity. We cover what spirits can and can't do. We go into the philosophy, psychology, physics, and metaphysics of the subject as much as possible. But more than just talk, we lay the evidence out on the table. We show the students *real* physical objects that were materialized or teleported from the other side. We show them the actual conjuring instruments that were used to summon particular spirit entities. We discuss cases in detail, and examine the tactics, strategy, and meaning of the phenomena that resulted. We show the students pictures and slides of spirit activity in progress, although in the future, I'd also like to use films and videotapes taken while disturbances are going on. The visuals allow the student to see spirits in manifest form. They can also see levitations while they're occurring, as well as see what people look like under demoniacal oppression and possession.

"We also get into what's called *psychic photographs*—where images show up on film that weren't visible at the time the photograph was taken. Many times, photographs taken in a haunted house or psychically active area show a living person looking just like an apparition-—that is, he's half invisible. You can see right *through* him! It kind of shows man for being the spirit he really is! Other times, psychic photos will show bioluminescent forms, ghosts, apparitions, demon faces, objects that weren't present when the picture was snapped, and so forth.

"Finally, we wrap up the course with tape recordings of spirit voices, both human and inhuman. This allows the students to hear for themselves the messages and statements these entities put out. They hear earthbound spirits giving accurate facts about themselves and their long-dead relatives.

"We also have them listen to voice recordings of some inhuman spirits, spitting out their blasphemies and threats and maledictions and predictions and boastings about the Other Kingdom, along with references by name to the ancient diabolical entities they serve. It's strong stuff, I grant you. But do you know that Satanists form one of the fastest growing groups on college campuses these days? And many unsuspecting students are being drawn into that web because no one has ever given them any information to the contrary. The material we teach is factual and objective, and I guarantee you that none of our kids will ever become future victims of the negative. In fact, when it's all said and done, they come up and say 'Thank you for telling us. We would never have known otherwise.'"

15

One More Question, Please

It is no exaggeration to say that Ed and Lorraine Warren live very full lives. For one thing, they are rarely at home. Their lecturing and field work keep them "out in the world," as Lorraine puts it, ten out of twelve months a year. One weekend a month, though, Ed and Lorraine manage to return to Connecticut and check in with home base.

On those weekends when the Warrens are at home, their house is a beehive of activity. Friends, relatives, and professional colleagues come and go like members of one big extended family. When there are no visitors, it seems the phone is perpetually ringing, with calls coming in from all over America. And every call is urgent—or so it seems to those who do the calling.

"Pardon me," says Lorraine, reaching over to answer the porch phone for the tenth time that hour. By chance, the telephone has been set on "broadcast" so the Warrens can both hear the call.

"Are you Lureen Wern, or Warn, or whatever?" asks a none-too-articulate woman, almost challenging Lorraine.

"I'm Lorraine *War*-ren," she replies, emphasizing the syllables. "May I ask your name, please?"

"Sure," says the woman.

"What is it?" Lorraine is forced to ask.

"This is Celia Hayden."

"Celia, is there something I can help you with?"

"Yeah, that's why I'm callin', Lureen. Ain't you the uh . . . clair*boyalist* that was on the radio last night in New Haven? You was talkin' about knowin' a ghost, and yer husband is a demonism or somethin'?"

"That's close," Lorraine replies patiently. "Is there something I can help you with, Celia?"

"Yup."

"Then what is it?"

"Well, Lureen, I tell ya, this is serious! I mean I got a real mysterious problem here! Are you *sure* you're the same one that was on the radio, and the cops ask you if you'll go find them a murderer and then the cops go and arrest the guy at his house, right?"

"Right," Lorraine answers, smiling. "Please tell me what your mysterious problem is, Celia. I've got work to do."

"Okay, I just hope you got time for my *case* . . . "

"Go ahead so we can find out," Lorraine coaxes her.

"Okay. Well, I put 'em right here on the stove, Lureen. I always warm 'em up before eatin'. And now they're gone. They disappeared!"

"What disappeared?" asks Lorraine, now almost laughing.

"*My false teeth!* I always put 'em on the stove, and now some ghost or dee-mon took 'em. I can't find them teeth no place. And I looked."

Lorraine breaks into laughter. "That's terrible," she manages to say.

"What's so funny, Lureen?" the irritated woman asks. "*How am I gonna eat?*"

"Celia," Lorraine manages to answer, "I bet I can tell you where your false teeth are!"

"Where?" the woman asks eagerly,

"Take your right index finger and hold it up in the air in front of you. Got that, Celia?"

"What one?"

"Your right index finger—the finger on your right hand next to your thumb. Okay?"

"Okay," the woman replies obediently.

"Now, put that finger in your mouth, and bite down easy. See, your teeth have been there all along."

There is a long pause. "Jesus Christ, you're right!" says the astonished woman. "You're *really good,* Lureen. Wait'll I tell Ernie about this. . . ."

Click.

Lorraine, bemused by the incident, hangs up the phone, and then jokes, "What can I say? When you're good, you're good. . . . "

Considering that no one in his right mind wants to wake up in the middle of the night to be confronted by a terrifying spirit at the foot of his bed, the question arises how can one prevent this phenomena from happening to him? That is, how can we be spared unpleasant confrontations with the supernatural?

When the Warrens lecture on demonology, they never fail to stress the fact that "doors must be opened before spirits can enter." Customarily, these doors are opened through either the Law of Invitation or Attraction, as Lorraine reminds us.

"The Law of Invitation applies when people invite spirits into their life by performing some occult ritual or by deliberately trying to communicate with the spirit world through séances, rituals, and the like. Although inviting spirit contact often produces some ersatz communication from the other side, what isn't commonly recognized is that the communicating entity isn't always human— though it may profess to be—and it doesn't always go away when the conjuring exercise is over.

"The Law of Attraction," she goes on, "comes into play when an individual or family is *drawn* for some psychic reason to a *particular* place where infestation by negative spirits has already occurred. Conversely, obsessive negative thinking can also attract negative spirits, because the will is displayed as being open and vulnerable. But, be it the Law of Invitation or the Law of Attraction, some way or other the individual has left the door to his free will unlocked, either by not properly caring about life, or by seeking beyond himself for powers that are not man's. The point is, *the demonic spirit is a spiritual beast with the wisdom of the ages and the power of angels.* Your best bet is to avoid it, but you don't do that by denying the fact that the phenomenon exists. Instead, you avoid it by knowing it's there—so you can stay out of its way!"

Why is so much spirit activity centered around houses?

"Earthbound spirits prefer emotionally familiar places," says Ed, joining the conversation on the front porch. "Therefore, they inhabit the same dwellings that were familiar to them during their physical lifetime. However, inhuman spirits exist to plague people, so they infest homes because that's where people tend to be the most vulnerable to influence. There's also another reason: buildings and dark places help contain spirit vibrations. Open spaces and bright light weaken spirit forces."

Are old homes more apt to be haunted or infested than new ones?

"In general," Lorraine replies, "older homes have a greater *potential* for being haunted because more living has gone on in them. But more important than the age of the house is its history. If there's been a murder, a suicide, or some other form of tragic death in the house, then the chances of encountering earthbound spirit activity are enhanced. If a former owner has practiced black magic, sorcery, or witchcraft, then there's a strong possibility that inhuman forces have been drawn into the home—and unless that home has been exorcised, negative spirits will remain to infest the dwelling.

As for what you can do about avoiding a haunted or infested house, be suspicious when house-hunting. Be leery of houses that have remained vacant for long periods of time. Often houses remain empty because they really are unlivable. Talk to the neighbors about the house, or check around town and try to find out some scuttlebutt on it. Another thing: when you're checking out a house, old or new, be aware of physical signs of a spirit presence. You might notice odd smells that are detectable but have no obvious source; or strange cold spots in rooms or areas where there would be no reason for a change in temperature. If you want to go a step further, ask a psychic friend to walk through the house with you."

If you buy a house you're not sure about, what can you do to minimize the chances of arousing a dormant spirit?

"Well, I'll tell you a few tricks," says Ed. "If there are a lot of bushes or evergreens outside the house blocking the windows, chop 'em down. Let the sun in! Inside, paint the walls white, yellow, or light blue. These colors interfere with spirit vibrations. Get rid of pictures and mementos of previous owners found in the attic or basement or garage. You might also consider selling mirrors and pieces of old furniture that came with the property, and it would also be a good idea to have the house blessed. *But most of all, a happy family, a happy home is the best protection against evil.* Negative emotions usually trigger spirit activity, so along with everything else, create an emotional atmosphere in the home where no problems *can* occur. Of course, it goes without saying that trouble shouldn't be encouraged, so throw away any and all occult paraphernalia. This way a person can't be encouraged, either through curiosity or oppression, to use it."

If a person suspects he has a *ghost* in his house and wants no part of it, what would be the procedure to take?

"Make the physical environment bright, light, and cheery," Lorraine answers. "Many times, just rearranging the furniture will turn off an active spirit. If that doesn't work, consult a clergyman and have the house blessed. After these steps have been taken, if the problem persists, then go back to your clergyman and have *him* help solve the problem. Or, if you're not religious, get in touch with a reputable psychic research organization who can put a clairvoyant on the case and send the spirit on its way. But under no circumstances should you speak to an unknown entity, no matter how pleasing a form it may take. And especially don't hold a séance: that's like using a CB radio. You may *think* you're communicating with the haunting spirit, but in reality, a dozen, ten dozen different spirits may respond to the recognition you're offering."

If there *is* a spirit in one's home, what are the telltale signs that distinguish an earthbound spirit from an inhuman one?

"A ghost *may* scare you," Ed replies. "A demonic spirit *will* scare you—and eventually threaten your life. In the early stages, the phenomena associated with both human and inhuman spirits may be the same. Both types of spirit will seek to make their presence known by manipulating the physical environment. The difference is the nature of the activity associated with each. As a rule, ghosts will do things to the house, while demonic spirits will do things to people. One tries to scare you out of the house. The other tries to scare you out of your mind—truly. Ghosts will do weird, spooky, scary, or strange things, but only infrequently terrifying. A ghost will switch lights on and off, move small objects from room to room, or even project the sound of footsteps, shrieks, and cries. On occasion, a ghost will manifest itself, but that's about it. Earthbound-spirit activity tends to occur *occasionally*. Strange things may happen, but it won't be a wild fury. In short, the ghost cares about itself, not about you, so it will do things that may give you goose bumps, but not much more.

"If there's an inhuman spirit in the house, on the other hand, that means the dwelling is now the realm of the demonic. Rarely if ever will an inhuman spirit manifest at the beginning. Instead, what should be looked for is truly sinister activity. The demonic is a negative spirit, so it eventually brings about unmistakably negative phenomena. At first, you're liable to hear knocks, raps, poundings, and scratching noises that are designed to try your patience—and sanity. Foul smells or unaccountable feelings of terror may also be experienced at this stage. Also pay attention to the behavior of children and animals. Children are clairvoyant up to about the age of twelve; all animals are naturally clairvoyant. If children or animals have a bad reaction to the house, that's a good sign of a spirit presence. Nevertheless, if the house is infested, then over the course of time the external phenomena will upgrade into openly noticeable activity that's not just strange or scary, but downright terrifying. If allowed to do so, this negative activity will go on and increase in frequency, power, and negativity until it develops into nothing less than perpetual, all-out pandemonium. Naturally, the point is to be suspicious right from the beginning. If you notice strange or unnatural phenomena going on and do nothing about it, the infesting spirit will take it as permission to continue.

"As for internal oppression brought about by inhuman spirits, that will be noticed in terms of changes in thinking, habits, behavior, or personality. If the person lives alone, the best recommendation here is to 'Know thyself.' If the oppression is happening to only one member of the family, others should look for negative changes in the person: depression, morbid interests, reclusiveness—or excesses, like wild fits of anger, falling-down drunkenness, or bursts of destructive violence."

If a person has reason to believe that an inhuman spirit actually is infesting his home, what should he do?

"Get out immediately," says Ed. "Then go directly to a clergyman. Explain the problem in as much detail as possible, and then ask for his help. But under no circumstances should an individual act like an amateur demonologist or exorcist and parade around the house with blessed objects. That would only provoke a diabolical attack."

Finally, given the odd chance that an individual must deal with a friend or relative who has actually come under possession, what would one do?

"It's doubtful anyone would need to know this," Ed answers, "but if the entity that comes through isn't especially violent, but more accusatory or blasphemous, then call a clergyman. If the possessing entity is threatening and violent, leave the house and call the police. *Then* get hold of a clergyman. In either case, get help immediately. But don't stay in the company of the possessed person alone."

"As I tell the young priests I work with, that which is speaking is not the person but a diabolical entity. Therefore, refuse to give it recognition. Do not speak to it. Concentrate on surrounding yourself with what we call a Christ-light, and then attempt to extricate yourself from the premises until someone like myself or an exorcist can go in and confront the entity."

What would you say is the *ultimate* danger in dealing with the demonic?

"On the transitory level," Ed replies, "the life you live would not be your own, but instead one directed by another. Throwing your will open to the demonic is to allow yourself to be its stooge. The ultimate danger, though, would be to allow your human spirit to absorb the reprehensible, blasphemous characteristics of the demonic—the enemy of being. For when this happens, the individual runs the potential risk of sharing the fate of these spirits of darkness: separation from the source of being. That would be the sobering danger of allowing yourself to be taken over by these negative spirits of perdition. You see, theologically, holy angels are the supreme ratification of life; but moving to the negative side, the demonic spirit is a *corruption* of nature—a spirit of perdition that, rather than affirming life, exists to destroy it. As a human being, therefore, you can choose to either be part of the problem—or part of the solution."

In the end, then, what chance does man stand against such incredible forces of doom?

"In my opinion," answers Ed, "man's best protection is his inherently positive self. As we've said before, the demonic spirit is something that is going the other way. But on its way down it's determined to take as many of us with it as it possibly can. Our task as people, on the other hand, is to live properly, and to ratify the positive. Cosmic law tells us, 'good begets better, bad begets worse.' By taking our positive nature, and putting it to work in a basically positive universe, we can build a good life—and taking it further, a good world. But you don't just kneel down and pray for this to happen. You have to go out and *do* it every day because—through practice—you know and believe the principle is true."

"Conversely," Lorraine notes, "the demonic spirit recoils when confronted with the positive. It absolutely thrives on the negative, or what religion calls 'sin.' And what I mean by sin is not the violation of arbitrary rules, but the deliberate transgression of the good. That is, sin is something that has a *detrimental* effect on life itself. Sin, ultimately, is spiritual immaturity, and those who are foolish enough to underestimate the value and purpose of life, actually draw the demonic to them. They do so because, like it or not, by performing negative actions that take away from life, they are actually assisting these spirits in their cosmic role. Asserting the positive generates a power of its own. Therefore, *being* positive is your best protection against that which is called 'evil.'"

"You see," Ed affirms, "what is not properly understood is that there is a mystical negative *and* a mystical positive. As above: so below. So much attention has been given to the negative that people have forgotten there are also powerful *positive* forces in the world—real forces that can be understood and used for practical benefit. However, in this century, we've been on sabbatical from the ongoing problem of good and evil, so these positive forces have been relegated to the trash heap as so much superstitious bunk. But it doesn't change the fact that by stressing the positive, you set in motion a chain of events that ratify life and being; while accenting the negative brings forth tragedy, chaos, and death.

"The whole trip of life," Ed sums up, "is to work with, and emphasize the positive—that's the real mother lode. People are looking for solutions in this world, and the answer isn't with the occult. It's to go *with* the positive flow of nature, because it is good and it insures life, rather than death."

Few people ever learn, even in the course of a whole lifetime, the deeper nature of the world we live in. But the Warrens' research and experience convincingly suggest there is a whole other realm of being out there: a realm of being called spirits—nonphysical entities that exist separate and independent from man.

Ed and Lorraine Warren's findings do nothing to support the point of view that man is simply a physical creature that lives and dies and is no more. Rather, their research ineluctably points to the conclusion that man is a far more vital and dynamic creature than our restrictive perceptions and philosophies have hitherto led us to believe. For this reason, the Warrens contend that an open understanding of the spiritual dimension of life can, rather than being a threat or detriment, "enhance our understanding of the world, so that we may be free to live life to its fullest."

A light wind rustles through the leaves, breaking the spell of silence that summer afternoon on the Warrens' front porch. Looking up, Lorraine sees that Ed's attention is fixed intently in the garden.

"Is something the matter, Ed?" she asks.

"There's a snake around here," he declares, gazing into the flowers. "I know it. I feel it. I can tell the thing's here."

No snake, however, is visible. Not, at least, until a moment later. Then, sure enough—out from under the porch there crawls a long, black snake. It lingers just long enough to be seen, then slithers off into the ivy.

"Ed," Lorraine assures me, "always knows when there's a snake in the garden."

GERALD BRITTLE is a nonfiction writer with advanced degrees in literature and psychology specializing in mystical theology.

ED and LORRAINE WARREN both had supernatural experiences when they were growing up in Connecticut. They became high school sweethearts, and on his seventeenth birthday, Ed enlisted with the US Navy to serve in World War II. A few months later his ship sank in the North Atlantic, and he was one of only a few survivors. Soon after, Ed and Lorraine were married and had a daughter.

In 1952 Ed and Lorraine formed the New England Society for Psychic Research, the oldest ghost hunting group in New England. From Amityville to Tokyo, they have been involved with thousands of investigations and Church sanctioned exorcisms all over the world. They have dedicated their lives and extraordinary talents to help educate others and fight against demoniacal forces whenever they are called.

Ed and Lorraine Warren also wrote many bestselling books based on some of their most famous and terrifying real-life cases. Their titles include *Graveyard, Ghost Hunters, The Haunted, In a Dark Place, Werewolf,* and *Satan's Harvest.*

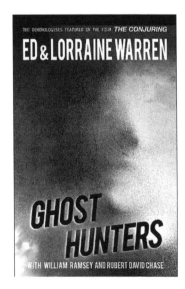

Printed in Great Britain
by Amazon